unemployment, the regions and labour markets: reactions to recession

London Papers in Regional Science

1. **Studies in regional science**
   edited by Allen J Scott
2. **Urban and regional planning**
   edited by A G Wilson
3. **Patterns and processes in urban and regional systems**
   edited by A G Wilson
4. **Space-time concepts in urban and regional models**
   edited by E L Cripps
5. **Regional science—new concepts and old problems**
   edited by E L Cripps
6. **Theory and practice in regional science**
   edited by I Masser
7. **Alternative frameworks for analysis**
   edited by Doreen Massey, P W J Batey
8. **Theory and method in urban and regional analysis**
   edited by P W J Batey
9. **Analysis and decision in regional policy**
   edited by I G Cullen
10. **Developments in urban and regional analysis**
    edited by M J Breheny
11. **Regional planning in Europe**
    edited by R Hudson, J R Lewis
12. **Technological change and regional development**
    edited by A Gillespie
13. **Planning and analysis in health care systems**
    edited by M Clarke
14. **Discrete choice models in regional science**
    edited by D E Pitfield
15. **Integrated analysis of regional systems**
    edited by P W J Batey, M Madden
16. **Spatial pricing and differentiated markets**
    edited by G Norman

Pion Limited, 207 Brondesbury Park, London NW2 5JN

edited by I. Gordon · London papers in regional science 17 · a pion publication

unemployment, the regions and labour markets: reactions to recession

Pion Limited, 207 Brondesbury Park, London NW2 5JN

ISBN 0 85086 128 4

Printed in Great Britain by Page Bros (Norwich) Limited

Contributors

D Blanchflower	*Department of Economics, University of Surrey, Guildford, Surrey GU2 5XH, England*
L Curry	*Department of Geography, University of Toronto, Toronto, Ontario M55 1A1, Canada*
P Elias	*Institute for Employment Research, University of Warwick, Coventry CV4 7AL, England*
M M Fischer	*Department of Geography, University of Vienna 1010 Vienna, Austria*
I R Gordon	*Urban and Regional Studies Unit, University of Kent at Canterbury, Canterbury, Kent CT2 7NF, England*
F R Harrigan	*The Fraser of Allander Institute, University of Strathclyde, Glasgow G4 0LN, Scotland*
D R Holden	*Department of Economics, University of Strathclyde, Glasgow G1 1XQ, Scotland*
I Jenkins	*The Fraser of Allander Institute, University of Strathclyde, Glasgow G4 0LN, Scotland*
J S Kowalski	*Institut für Wirtschaftspolitik und Wirtschaftsforschung, Universität Karlsruhe, Postfach 6380, 7500 Karlsruhe 1, FRG*
J G Lambooy	*Institute of Economic Geography, University of Amsterdam, 1011 NH Amsterdam, The Netherlands*
P G McGregor	*The Fraser of Allander Institute, University of Strathclyde, Glasgow G4 0LN* and *Department of Economics, University of Strathclyde, Glasgow G1 1XQ, Scotland*
I J Molho	*Department of Economics, University of Newcastle upon Tyne, Newcastle upon Tyne NE1 7RU, England*
P Nijkamp	*Department of Economics, Free University of Amsterdam, 1007 MC Amsterdam, The Netherlands*

P H Renooy — *Institute of Economic Geography, University of Amsterdam, 1011 NH Amsterdam, The Netherlands*

L Worrall — *District of the Wrekin Council, PO Box 213, Malinslee House, Telford, Shropshire TF3 4LD, England*
and
Department of Civic Design, University of Liverpool, Liverpool L69 3BX, England

Contents

Introduction: Space, Segmentation, and Labour-market Processes

I R GORDON
University of Kent at Canterbury

1 Recession and spatial labour-market studies

Since the late 1970s, recession in the industrialised countries has widened regional disparities in unemployment and renewed interest in the spatial dimensions of labour-market behaviour. In a number of countries there has been a strong ideological charge to the consequent debates as orthodox Keynesian approaches have been confronted by contrasting neoclassical and structuralist perspectives. Few of the protagonists would claim that current regional unemployment stemmed principally from regional causes. But there are widespread doubts about how readily it would be reversed when national and international economies recover. In part this is because the 'sunrise' industries of the 1980s appear to have different locational preferences from those which have suffered most in the previous decade. As important, however, are questions about the adequacy of labour mobility—substantially curtailed during the recession—and wage flexibility, together with the issue of how the long-term unemployed can bring their skills back into productive employment. Or, failing this, how particular economies and communities can adapt to cope with a continuing shortfall in formal employment opportunities.

Although concern over problems of employment and unemployment has been the motive for much work on urban and regional economies, regional scientists have until recently not given much serious attention to the functioning of labour markets (compare Isard, 1960; 1975). Commonly, regional economic models, whether neoclassical, Keynesian, or Leontief in style, have treated the explanation of output changes, or at best demands for labour services, as close enough in the causal chain to serve as an explanation for employment fluctuations and for the incidence of unemployment. Indeed, the more readily available data on these labour variables have often been regarded as in effect second-best indicators of output variations. When attention has been explicitly on employment issues, the tools of analysis, whether neoclassical or Keynesian in orientation, have been drawn from traditional aspatial economics, treating cities and regions as analogous either to single firms or to national economies. What is lost then is any real sense of the heterogeneity which is inherent in spatial relationships. In effect, spatial units are seen as corresponding *either* to the whole *or* to a small part of an essentially homogeneous labour market: in the first case the local or regional labour market is assumed to be entirely closed, in the second case it is assumed to be perfectly open with respect to the rest of the nation. Similarly on the occupational dimension *either* complete fluidity *or* complete rigidity in skill structures and requirements are in effect assumed, although this assumption (and its geographical counterpart) may be camouflaged in the adoption of a convenient classificational schema. What has commonly been lacking is a recognition of the normal tendency for mobility to be attenuated by spatial, occupational, or institutional separation, without ever becoming negligible, *and* a theoretical interest in understanding how these uneven market processes operate.

Correspondingly, labour economics has lacked a spatial perspective, to its cost, since spatial disaggregation brings into focus a number of factors and elements of heterogeneity which are of general significance to the operation of labour markets, but lost in a more abstract view of their functioning. A classic case is that of inner-city unemployment where the central issue is of how whole communities come to be at a disadvantage in the competition for available employment and why this disadvantage assumes the form of a greater propensity to unemployment, rather than simply lower wages. Even when, as in the case of search theory, labour economics adopts an essentially spatial metaphor, it is striking that the key question has been seen to be not *how* individuals search, but the more abstract issue of what rule they would employ to *accept or reject* opportunities which they are presumed to have found. In a spatial context, however, it seems clear that the outcome and duration of search will depend at least as fundamentally on the modes of search available to, and chosen by, particular groups of individuals, the specific sets of opportunities to which these give access, and (in relation to both of these) the recruitment strategies pursued by various sets of employers. The relevance of these factors is not limited to their influence on spatial (or social) variations in employment prospects but, since everybody occupies a particular spatial (and social) position, they will also affect the operation of national labour-market aggregates. The regional perspective, however, does serve particularly to highlight the concrete situations within which employers and managers operate.

But there is much also in the labour economics literature, both in terms of microfoundations and the recognition of institutional factors, which regional analysts neglect to their cost. Examples would include hysteresis effects of past unemployment on the 'natural rate of unemployment' (Phelps, 1972), stock-flow models of vacancies (Holt, 1970), employment discrimination (Sloane, 1985) and job competition theory (Thurow, 1983), together with the bargaining models discussed by Harrigan and colleagues in this volume. All of these have clear applications in urban and regional labour markets, although they need to be adapted to the case of open labour markets, and related to the varying structures which these display. Similarly there is much that needs to be drawn from recent sociological analyses of labour-market operations and the labour process (Roberts et al, 1985) if regional analyses are to advance beyond the classificatory stage.

Against this background, the newer work on urban and regional labour-market issues has given more explicit attention to three aspects, the role of *space*, *segmentation* of labour markets, and the actual *processes* involved as distinct from the patterns of outcomes. The issues involved in each will be briefly discussed here in relation to the contents of this volume before the individual papers are reviewed.

2 Space

Spatial factors condition labour-market behaviour in crucial ways, not simply because of the choices which workers face about whether or not to incur commuting or movement costs to jobs which are unevenly distributed over space, but also because information about available opportunities is disseminated along specific channels to which workers do not have simultaneous or equally costless access. Taking space more seriously involves, on the one hand, a focus on how distance and spatial structures modify the potentially equilibriating flows of information and labour supply between areas *and*, on the other, a recognition of the distinctive patterns of labour-market development which spatial separation permits in different areas.

The first of these is given particular emphasis in the papers in this volume by Gordon, Curry, and Molho for whom the significance of location lies in the pattern of spatial interrelationships to which it gives rise, in terms particularly of commuting and migrational flows. The approach in each case is relatively static, but a central concern is with how existing flow patterns would be affected by changing circumstances, and with what that would imply for labour-market outcomes in particular areas. The analyses demonstrate clearly the extent to which labour-market states in particular areas are contingent on developments in their hinterlands, and even the meaninglessness of concepts such as demand deficiency when attached to regions treated in isolation.

The second line of approach to the spatial dimension, most directly associated with the work of Massey (1983), focuses on the ways in which the labour-market structures of particular places embody the specific economic histories of each and their evolving role in the spatial division of labour. Much of the emphasis here has been on how specific industrial histories are reflected in levels of unionisation and the perception of a work force in an area as particularly militant, conservative, or amenable. Also of importance, however, is the question, addressed by Elias and Blanchflower, and Gordon in this volume, of how a history of unemployment in an area affects employment stability, occupational attainment, and the competitiveness of indigenous workers. Even outside the formal economy, Lambooy and Renooy suggest that the scope for the development of alternative forms of work and sources of income is likely to be heavily conditioned by the human capital and opportunity structures of particular areas.

3 Segmentation

Occupational aspects of the labour market may also be treated 'spatially', with occupations being seen as separated from each other by distances across a series of dimensions, and with the possibility of movement over this distance being induced by the shifting pattern of opportunities and incentives. In this case the Markovian assumption, that access to opportunities is governed solely by the present (or last) location, is perhaps less justified than in the case of movement over geographical space, but it is at least preferable to the crude assumptions either that access is equal, or that individuals' occupational locations are fixed. A more fundamental limitation of this perspective, however, is its apparent implication that interoccupational 'distances' are in some sense natural, or exogenous to the labour market, simply reflecting the skill requirements and typical human capital endowments associated with particular occupational positions. Increasingly it has been recognised that this is not the case and that segmentation of the labour market is the outcome of a series of decisions, principally taken by employers.

Labour is a peculiar, heterogeneous, and somewhat recalcitrant commodity presenting its purchaser with real problems both in evaluating its productivity ex ante and securing it ex post (compare Thurow, 1983). Employers respond to this problem variously, according to their market situation, available technologies, competition for labour, etc, by designing sets of jobs with distinctive skill requirements, opportunities for training and advancement, modes of discipline or motivation, channels and criteria for recruitment, and, crucially, different expectations about the rates of turnover or stability of workers. Segmentation is the outcome of these strategic decisions, together with such consequential successes as groups of workers achieve in effecting closure over a set of jobs. Given this pattern of structuring of labour markets, it is of little relevance to take a fictional set of markets in homogeneous labour as a point of departure and to proceed to analyse 'imperfections' in the real world. Signalling, heuristic screening criteria (or prejudice), and alternative modes of recruitment exist for both good and bad reasons, but they are quite fundamental to the ways in which specific urban and regional labour markets operate and interact with each other.

Kowalski's paper in this volume describes an extreme situation where, in a centrally planned economy with competition for resources rather than markets, all industrial jobs appear to be filled through internal labour markets and where, in consequence, unemployment is concentrated within enterprises, concealed as labour hoarding, rather than appearing in an open form. Fischer and Nijkamp's paper, however, underlines the trend in most market economies for such primary labour markets to be cut back during the recession period with employers increasingly relying on a periphery of workers on temporary and/or part-time contracts. The papers by Elias and Blanchflower, and Gordon suggest that in areas of high unemployment, whether or not there are a higher proportion of secondary *jobs*, a higher proportion of *workers* are liable to be restricted to this part of the labour market. Alternatively, they may be steered towards work entirely outside the formal economy. However, Lambooy and Renooy's paper indicates that the importance of the informal sector of employment is not simply a function of rising levels of unemployment in the formal economy.

In several respects the work on labour-market segmentation remains less than conclusive owing to the lack of relevant data categorised on this basis. Worrall's paper offers one solution to this data deficiency, using a combination of employer size, industry, and occupation to classify groups of workers in terms of three main labour-market segments.

4 Process

The renewed concern with process in labour-market studies has three main roots. One of these is theoretical: feminists, labour sociologists, and radical geographers have each shown, in different contexts, just how problematic and contingent are some of the most conventionally taken-for-granted concepts and variables in the field. A clear case in point is that of 'skill', assessments of which turn out to be highly discriminatory condensations of a series of judgments about workers' competences, dispositions, *and* power. To understand the significance of 'skill', either for the role of an area in the changing division of labour or for the employment prospects of individuals, we clearly need to look both at the operational uses of this concept by employers and at how particular groups of workers gain or lose the title 'skilled'.

The second root is empirical: with the recession, large-scale restructuring of employment and the weakening of unions' legal status, much that could once commonsensically be treated simply as a set of initial conditions has proved subject to change. Most notably, unemployment, particularly long-term unemployment, is well beyond the bounds of postwar experience, and predictions about labour-market behaviour now have to take account of the ways in which adjustment processes, such as migration, are likely to be influenced by a much riskier environment and lower rates of job turnover (compare Clark et al, 1986). The balance between processes which have always coexisted may also shift in ways which require a clearer distinction to be made between them. In the case of labour mobility, for example, the shrinkage of worker-initiated moves has focused attention for the first time on the significance of intrafirm moves initiated by employers (Flowerdew, 1982).

The third root is policy oriented: unemployment is unacceptably high, but, to say the least, there is no consensus amongst policymakers that it could be lowered simply by a general reflation. Hence, there is a strong interest, among Keynesians and monetarists alike, in microeconomic interventions which might effect a reduction in the overall level, or the more socially threatening concentrations, of unemployment, as well as in those which might enable reflation to proceed without accelerating inflation. The design of such interventions depends critically, however, on an understanding of *how* groups of workers get channelled into or out of employment, of which are the binding constraints on labour mobility, of why part-time employment is growing, and of how the unemployed affect wage bargaining.

In this collection of papers, Harrigan and his colleagues are concerned with whether wage bargains at the regional level are linked institutionally *or* by market forces; Gordon seeks to relate structural unemployment to processes of competition between workers in the light of their work histories; and Molho's model simulates the interactions between employment change, commuting, construction, and various forms of housebuilding in a metropolitan region. The emphasis on process, and its variation across labour markets, is at its clearest in the path model of occupational attainment developed by Elias and Blanchflower which starts to identify the critical points in early work experience, on which labour-market interventions could usefully focus.

5 The papers

This set of papers is based on a group of sessions on Urban and Regional Labour Market Analysis at the Bristol conference of the British Section of the Regional Science Association in September 1986, although a number of papers have been added subsequently to reflect other important strands of current research. Neither the authors nor the approaches are exclusively British and the questions which they address are of general relevance to developed countries in the grip of protracted recession.

The papers have been roughly grouped on the basis of their spatial level of analysis, into those which are primarily 'regional' or 'urban' in focus. This distinction has some practical relevance because policymakers (in the broadest sense) have a differential interest in the two levels and because the problems and appropriate solutions are both perceived as being rather different. The policy issues raised by the first group of papers are closer to those of national economic policy, focusing on the causes of unemployment and its relationship with demand pressure or with wage levels, whereas in the second group the central issues are more clearly ones of inequality in the social outcomes of labour-market processes. Analytically, however, it is clear that no sharp division between urban and regional issues can be accepted—for example, seeing regional unemployment in demand-side, and urban unemployment in supply-side, terms—and that the treatment of the two needs to be integrated. And it will be evident that the key emphases, on space, segmentation, and process, recur in both halves of this volume.

The first paper, by Fischer and Nijkamp, provides a broad review of regional labour-market trends in fifteen developed countries since the early 1970s. They show that absolute differences in regional unemployment have tended to widen as the general level has increased, but that there were rather different responses to the two oil-price crises, with the more developed regions being less protected in the second recession after 1979/80. Other important structural shifts in the composition of employment have greatly reduced the importance of full-time male employment in manufacturing jobs and led to an increasing polarisation of employment opportunities particularly in the larger conurbations. Yet they observe that in a range of countries labour-market policies in the 1980s have reverted to an emphasis on securing efficiency improvements at the national level with a trickle-down approach to regional and urban problems.

A theoretical basis for this shift of emphasis in the British case may be found in the contention of Conservative ministers that regional unemployment is largely the consequence of the rigidity and lack of spatial variability in wages. A more formal version of this argument is developed by Minford (1985) who attributes regional wage rigidity to the combination of a state benefit 'floor' with union pressure and explains regional unemployment as the result of this inflexibility plus constraints on mobility for those in regulated housing tenures. The evidence for the contention that regional unemployment is attributable to excessive wage levels is problematic, however, and the actual processes of adjustment to recession have been more complex and varied than Minford's model allows. It must, for example, be significant that in the southern regions employment contractions have largely been achieved through natural wastage, whereas in the northern regions higher rates of redundancy have been required (Jones and Martin, 1986) which are more damaging to reemployment prospects. As far as wage flexibility is concerned, rather more support for the Minford position can be derived from Harrigan, Holden, Jenkins, and McGregor's analysis of the wage-determination process in Scotland. They develop a set of bargaining models for a regional economy, which encompass neoclassical and real wage resistance variants and allow for varying degrees of interdependence between the Scottish and external labour markets. The evidence is by no means clear-cut, except in rejecting the assumption of complete independence. Nevertheless, no clear role could be found for market forces in Scotland and the process appeared to be one in which target earnings were determined by those in the rest of the United Kingdom.

However, it is far from clear that wages are a crucial factor in allocating or misallocating the supply of labour. Migrational studies have suggested that quantity signals, in the form of job availability and unemployment rates, can be sufficient to produce rapid and full adjustments in the face of demand shifts. Competition for jobs too appears to be governed more by workers' perceived qualities than by their reservation wages. Gordon focuses on the persistent character of regional unemployment differentials within Great Britain, contending that, although the level and variance of unemployment rates at any time reflect the national pressure of demand for labour, regional differentials must be largely structural in character. With an open-market version of the conventional classification of unemployment he shows that non-demand-deficient unemployment has been substantially higher in the peripheral regions, but that this cannot be accounted for simply in terms of 'mismatch'. Rather, he argues, it is a consequence of the relatively weak competitive position of workers in these regions, which itself reflects an experience of above-average unemployment leading to deskilling.

The very different labour-market processes operating in the centrally planned 'shortage economies' of Eastern Europe are discussed by Kowalski, who seeks to show that (in Poland at least) these too produce substantial regional differentials in unemployment. In this case, however, the surplus labour supply remains within the enterprise and there is minimal open unemployment. High levels of hidden unemployment reflect not a shortfall in demand but failure to obtain other complementary inputs. Direct estimates of unemployment within enterprises are lacking, but the author derives a series of comparative indicators for the Polish regions by relating levels of output with those of productive potential. These regional variations appear to reflect the differing political capacities of the regions and their ability to secure requisite supplies of industrial inputs. Some parallels with the unequal ability of regions in market economies to secure investment in new plants to complement their stocks of employable labour may perhaps be drawn.

In the second half of the volume, focusing on urban labour-market questions, Curry addresses most directly the conceptual issues of labour-market analysis in a world where spatial friction produces a whole series of overlapping labour-market areas *and* where the heterogeneity of labour endows different groups of workers and employers with variable amounts of monopoly power in different locations. He examines a system of many small areas open to commuting, and bargaining relationships dependent on the degree of competition which employers and workers face in particular locations and occupations. The properties of such a spatial labour-market system in terms of labour returns, income variance, and commuting distances are investigated in the context of a random landscape and a general model of opportunity–agent interaction is derived.

Molho similarly focuses on the implication of interactions between sublabour-market areas but with a numerical approach applied to data for a specific regional context, the districts of the London metropolitan region. He outlines a simulation model, calibrated on cross-sectional data, and encompassing housing as well as labour-market interactions and several sets of interarea migrational flows. Having solved the model for the base period he uses it to investigate the potential effects of a series of policy instruments on inner–outer differentials in unemployment. In most cases, including conventional job-creation schemes, policy effects appear too easily diffused to be helpful, the only exception being measures to reduce the concentration of the unskilled in Inner London.

Worrall too uses a particular urban setting, Telford New Town, to demonstrate the potential of a methodological innovation for practical planning situations. He contends that existing labour-market data are inadequate for the purposes of urban social planning, which requires an accounts-based information system linking stocks and flows related to an appropriate theoretical model. The Telford information system links together population, employment, and unemployment records in a form which permits analysis of distributional issues, using a system of classifications derived from segmented labour-market theory. Two particular applications of this database, to the analysis of changing employment structure and of influences on unemployment duration, start to show the kind of understanding of labour-market processes which would be required for effective local employment policies or social policy responses properly sensitive to the local situation.

Whether the development of such a system with its extensive survey requirements is feasible or cost-effective for the average local authority must be questionable. Arguably it is more appropriate to concentrate resources on the development of national databases which allow comparison of labour-market processes across a range of areas. The power of a properly designed longitudinal survey to cast light both on key processes in the labour market and the way in which these are mediated by local labour-market conditions is well illustrated in Elias and Blanchflower's paper. They make use of a linked data set from the various sweeps of the National Child Development Survey (NCDS) to develop a path model of individual and areal influences on occupational attainment at age 23. Local labour-market conditions are found to be very significant, although the effect appears not to be a positive one, with growing areas offering superior 'ladders of opportunity' (compare Donnison, 1980), but a negative one, with high unemployment disrupting normal career progression. The key finding, consistent with several sociological studies, is that in labour markets with high unemployment young people are substantially more likely to have unstable work histories and that this in turn is a significant source of labour-market disadvantage. Clearly there are links here with Gordon's hypothesis about the conversion over the course of time of what was initially demand-deficient unemployment into a form of structural unemployment in the depressed regions. Processes of the type identified by Elias and Blanchflower among the NCDS cohort of young workers may be halted if and when the creation of secure employment opportunities is resumed, but are unlikely to be reversed unless employment regeneration is accompanied by active manpower policies to modify existing recruitment practices.

Observers who take a more pessimistic or jaundiced view of labour-market trends suggest that the only answer is a greater development of the informal economy to fill the gaps left by attrition of the formal sector; more cynical new classical economists even believe that the 'unemployed' have in fact chosen to work in the informal economy, the wage costs of which are being unfairly subsidised through the medium of state benefits. Lambooy and Renooy present a more complex picture of the various forms of product, enterprise, and rewards which can be embraced by the 'informal' label, and suggest that it may not be a simple substitute for lost employment opportunities. Drawing both on their own studies in the Netherlands and on international comparisons, they suggest that a combination of factors, beyond the simple availability of unemployed labour, condition the scale and character of the informal economy. Many of these factors are regionally variable and likely to favour conurbation areas with a cosmopolitan population, a differentiated economy, and a stock of old buildings, rather than the most depressed regions. Their conclusions are somewhat speculative since there has been little comparative regional study, but the picture seems to be one in which inequalities in the informal labour market reinforce rather than complement those experienced in the formal economy.

In sum, these papers suggest no simple remedies, at least within the parameters of current macroeconomic policies, to either the problems of regional unemployment or those of urban inequality. What they do show, however, is that these problems cannot be seen simply in terms of the logic of production but need to be analysed, and tackled, in relation to the structure and performance of spatial labour markets. These have now become one of the central concerns for regional scientists, and recent research in this field marks a substantial advance in understanding from which policy analyses can now be developed, if the political will exists to engage seriously with these problems.

References

Clark G L, Gertler M S, Whiteman J, 1986 *Regional Dynamics: Studies in Adjustment Theory* (Allen and Unwin, Hemel Hempstead, Herts)

Donnison D, 1980 *The Good City* (Heinemann Educational Books, London)

Flowerdew R, 1982, "Institutional effects on internal migration", in *Institutions and Geographical Patterns* Ed. R Flowerdew (Croom Helm, Beckenham, Kent) pp 209-228

Holt C C, 1970, "How can the Phillips curve be moved to reduce both inflation and unemployment", in *Microeconomic Foundations of Employment and Inflation Theory* Eds E S Phelps, and others (W W Norton, New York) pp 224-256
Isard W I, 1960 *Methods of Regional Analysis* (MIT Press, Cambridge, MA)
Isard W I, 1975 *Introduction to Regional Science* (Prentice-Hall, Englewood Cliffs, NJ)
Jones D R, Martin R L, 1986, "Voluntary and involuntary turnover in the labour force" *Scottish Journal of Political Economy* **33** 124-144
Massey D, 1983, "Industrial restructuring as class restructuring: production decentralization and local uniqueness" *Regional Studies* **17** 73-90
Minford P, 1985 *Unemployment: Cause and Cure* 2nd edition (Basil Blackwell, Oxford)
Phelps E S, 1972 *Inflation Policy and Unemployment Theory* (Macmillan, London)
Roberts B, Finnegan R, Gallie D (Eds), 1985 *New Approaches to Economic Life: Economic Restructuring, Unemployment and the Social Division of Labour* (Manchester University Press, Manchester)
Sloane P J, 1985, "Discrimination in the labour market", in *Labour Economics* Eds D Carline, C A Pissarides, W S Siebert, P J Sloane (Longman, Harlow, Essex) pp 78-158
Thurow L C, 1983 *Dangerous Currents: The State of Economics* (Random House, New York)

Part 1

Regional Unemployment, Wages, and Labour-market Policy

Current Trends in Regional Labour Markets

M M FISCHER
University of Vienna
P NIJKAMP
Free University Amsterdam

1 Introduction

Since the beginning of the 1970s various drastic shifts have taken place in the labour market. After a period of rapid economic growth until early 1974, the economies of industrialised countries were hit by the recession of 1974–75 induced by the first oil-price shock and the destruction of the international monetary system with the replacement of fixed by generally fluctuating exchange rates. The recovery phase, 1976 until spring 1980, was followed by a second downswing, consequent on the second steep rise in oil prices in 1979. The dynamics in the Western world were clearly reflected both in national and in regional labour markets.

In the present paper we focus attention on current trends in regional labour markets and consider the results of a cross-national comparative study on regional and urban labour markets in various industrialised countries. This study is based on a systematically designed survey questionnaire to guarantee a meaningful review of developments, problems, and policy issues from different countries. The countries included in the comparison were selected on the basis of four criteria. The aim was to have a representation of small and large countries, of planned and free-market economies, of countries with favourable and unfavourable employment situations, and of stagnating and growing economies. This has led to the selection of the following countries: Australia, Austria, Canada, France, the Federal Republic of Germany, Great Britain, Greece, Hungary, Italy, the Netherlands, Poland, Sweden, Switzerland, USA, and Yugoslavia (for more details, see Evers-Koelman et al, 1987).

In a cross-national comparison two major problems exist for an adequate statistical description of regional labour markets: the definition of the regional labour market and the definition of (un)employment. The demarcation of regional labour markets is fraught with problems. In many countries (for example, Canada, the FRG, Greece, Hungary, Italy, the Netherlands, Poland, Sweden, the USA, and Yugoslavia), the delimitation is based on administrative or institutional principles rather than on functional or economic criteria. Consequently, in some countries information on regional labour markets is gathered on the basis of provinces or other administrative units, whereas in other countries economic planning regions or commuting areas constitute the definitional basis for information gathering (see appendix). Needless to say, such divergent ways of data collection hamper an unambiguous comparison of labour markets in different countries.

The definition of employment also varies between countries. Sometimes only the number of full-time jobs is counted, whereas in other countries employment data also include persons with part-time jobs and self-employed persons. Unemployment is of course the complement of employment and unemployment figures are also hard to compare. In some countries, such as Austria, France, the FRG, Great Britain, Switzerland, and Yugoslavia, unemployment data refer to persons who register officially as unemployed. In most of these countries there is a tendency either to include only the recipients of unemployment benefits, as in Great Britain, or to exclude certain marginal groups (for example, persons looking for part-time or temporary jobs, students in search of a job, employed persons who fall ill, or the older unemployed, even if they receive unemployment benefits). In other countries, such as Australia, Canada, Italy, and the USA, unemployed persons are those who were out of work during a certain survey week, were actively looking for (paid) work, and were available for work at least during the reference week. Thus (un)employment data in different countries are hard to compare, and the notion of unambiguous comparative research in this field is illusory. Numerical data in such a cross-national context can only be seen as indicative of major trends and the rank ordering of countries, not as cardinal representations of their labour-market situations.

In the paper we discuss some important aspects of labour-market change in the countries mentioned above. First, we look at the recent evolution of unemployment. Second, we consider recent shifts in patterns of employment. Third, the nature of labour-market segmentation is examined. Last, the most important labour-market problems and policies are briefly discussed.

2 Recent trends in unemployment

In the recent past the dynamics of labour-market processes have received increasing attention for at least two reasons. First, most advanced economies have been experiencing very high rates of unemployment because of a combination of global recession in demand for goods and services, a lack of international competitiveness, problems of adjustment to structural change, and shifts in labour supply. Second, these countries have displayed sharp spatial variations in unemployment. On the one hand, those regional economies specialising in depressed sectors such as shipbuilding, coal, steel, textiles, and with older manufacturing cities have faced severe adjustment difficulties in the face of deindustrialisation, with consequent high levels of unemployment. On the other hand, some of the more diversified cities and their metropolitan regions have enjoyed a substantial expansion of new jobs mainly in service industries, but also in manufacturing. Regional fluctuations in unemployment, however, reflect not only spatial variations in rates of job creation and job redundancy, but also changes in the occupational structure of labour demand and supply, as well as in commuting and migration patterns (see Gleave, 1987).

A widely discussed question is whether regional unemployment rates tend to converge or diverge in times of recession (see Steinle, 1983; Lever, 1987). This issue is better studied at the national than at the international level, simply because national frontiers offer linguistic and fiscal or financial barriers to the movement of labour, even if there are no legal barriers (Lever, 1987). The survey allows us to compare trends across a range of countries, although for practical reasons data on unemployment were only gathered for the minimum, the maximum, and the average level in each country.

The development of (minimum, maximum, and average) regional unemployment rates in four successive time intervals between 1970 and 1985 is displayed in figure 1. In the centrally planned economies of Poland and Hungary, there is officially no unemployment. In fact, there is a form of hidden unemployment within enterprises resulting from tendencies to hoard labour in these shortage economies. But it is very difficult to measure this form of unemployment. Thus, no figures can be provided for these two countries. Data for France and Germany are missing for the period 1970–73, and for Greece for the periods 1975–78 and 1983–85.

In the first period (1970–73), as indicated in figure 1(a), regional unemployment was generally highest in Canada and the USA, although the regional dispersion of unemployment in the USA was much greater than in Canada. As the other extreme the very low unemployment rate for Switzerland was notable. Relatively low levels were also found in Australia, Great Britain, and the Netherlands. As well as the USA, Italy and Austria showed considerable interregional disparities in unemployment. In the Italian case this reflected particularly high unemployment rates in the southern regional labour markets of Basilicata and Calabria.

Following the energy crisis of 1974, unemployment increased significantly in most of the countries except Switzerland and Sweden, although Italy and Austria also performed rather well. In particular, high increases occurred in the Netherlands, Australia, and Great Britain. The recovery of the world economy from the 1974–75 recession did not, however, lead to a rapid fall in unemployment as had been the rule in all the previous postwar recoveries. On the contrary, unemployment remained high by postwar standards, as indicated in figure 1(b) which shows minimum, maximum, and average regional unemployment rates in the period 1975–78.

The picture for 1980–82 outlined in figure 1(c) shows quite clearly that the oil-price-induced world recession of 1979–80 increased the

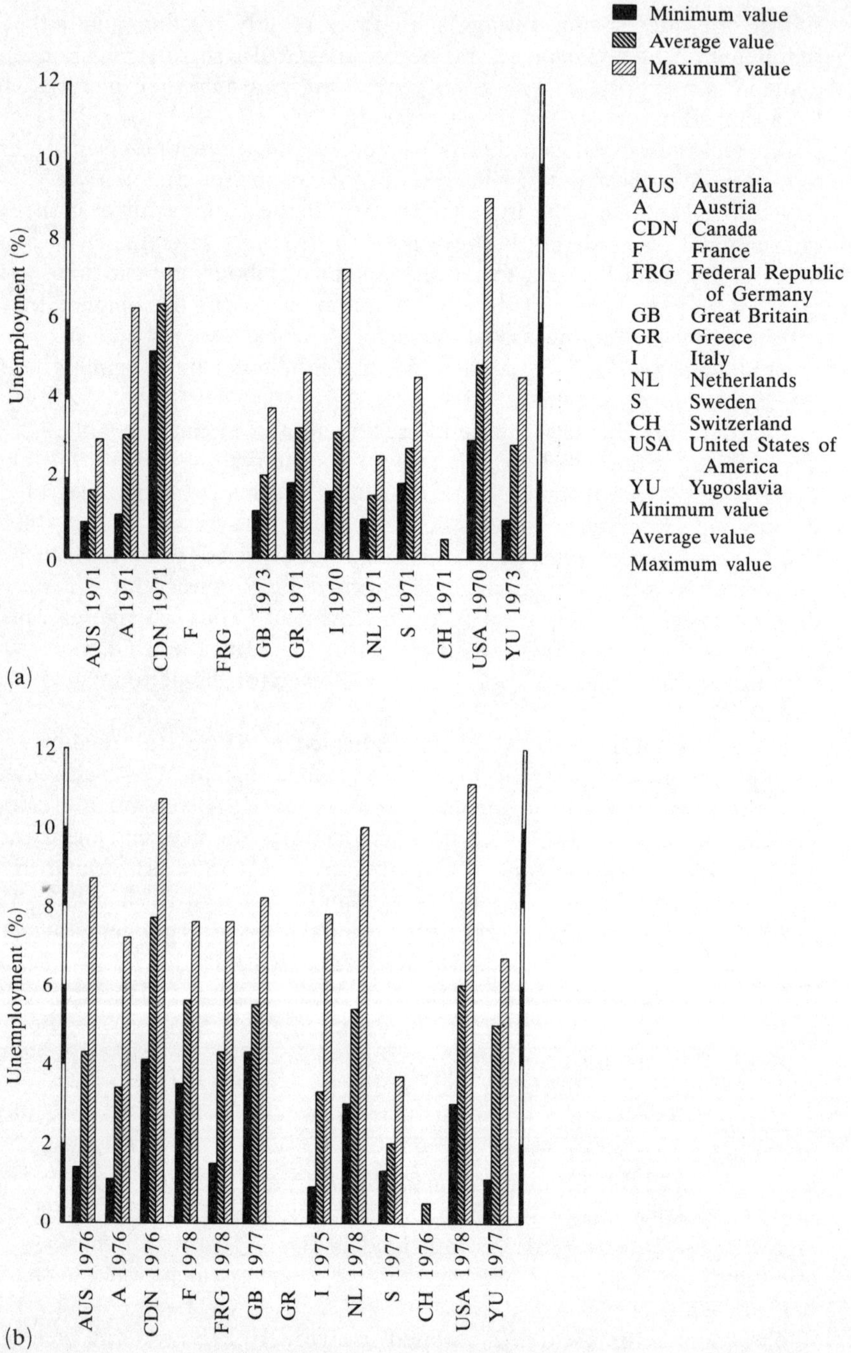

Figure 1. Percentage unemployment in regional labour markets: (a) 1970–73, (b) 1975–78, (c) 1980–82, (d) 1983–85.

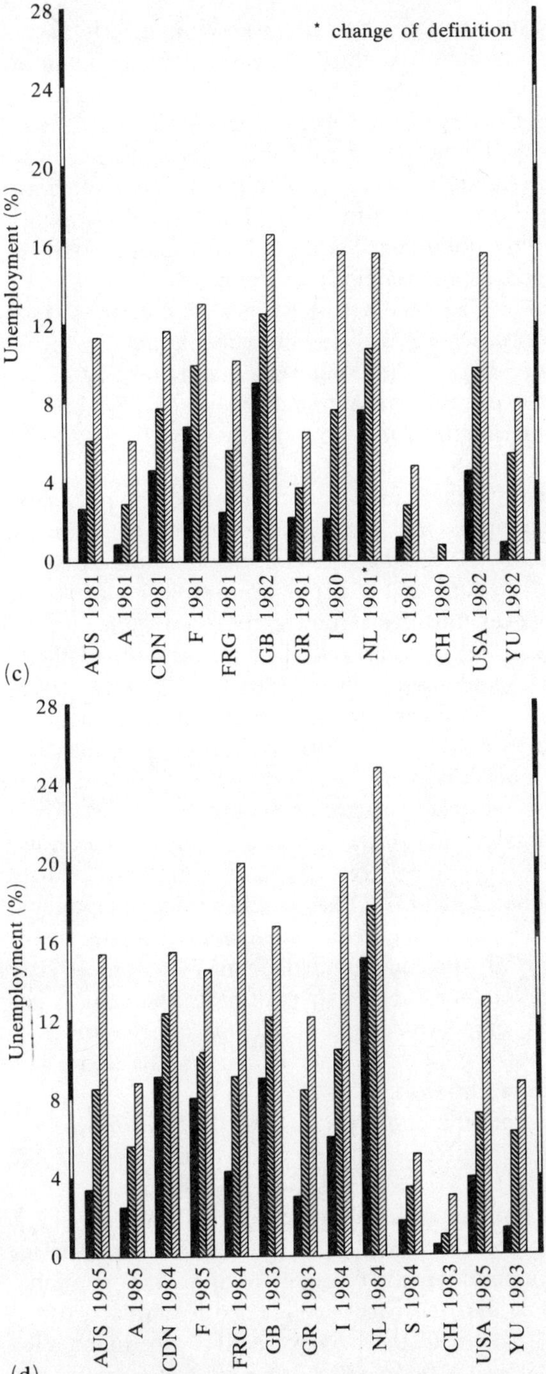

Figure 1 (continued).

level of regional unemployment more or less markedly in nearly all countries. Only Austria exhibited a slight decrease in the minimum and maximum regional unemployment rates. However, with only slight increases, Switzerland and Sweden also performed very well. Great Britain had the highest rise and led in the ranking of unemployment, followed by the Netherlands, the USA, and Italy. [A redefinition of unemployment in the Netherlands induced an increase in the regional unemployment rate of 1.6 percentage points (minimum value), 1.7 percentage points (average value), and 3.0 percentage points (maximum value)].

With the exception of the USA and Great Britain all countries showed a substantial increase in regional unemployment rates in the period 1983-85 [see figure 1(d)]. The Netherlands and the FRG exhibited the highest increases. With a minimum value of 15.0 and a maximum value of 24.6, the Netherlands now became the leader in the ranking league.

The figures clearly illustrate that some countries were generally more successful in mastering unemployment during the international economic crises of the 1970s and early 1980s than others. Sweden and Austria (together with Switzerland) are inevitably listed among the countries with the greatest success. However, the two countries pursued quite different policy priorities and used different measures. Sweden developed three main responses to the new challenges of the 1970s (see Scharpf, 1983). First, active labour-market policy was expanded from an instrument of facilitating (spatial) labour mobility to an instrument providing jobs in traditional regions of high unemployment. Regional employment subsidies and publicly financed labour-market programmes both became major policy measures. It is estimated that in the absence of these programmes open unemployment in deficit regions would have increased by a further four percentage points (Scharpf, 1983). The second important policy response was an increase in public-sector employment, especially at the local level, raising its share of total employment from 20.6% in 1970 to 29.8% in 1979. Third, Sweden increased its share of part-time employment. The expansion of part-time employment—to about one quarter of all wage earners—enabled a much greater number of persons to share a slightly shrinking total volume of work.

Quite in contrast to Sweden, the employment effects of Austrian labour-market policy were negligible, at around 0.3% of the labour force in the 1970s (see Scharpf, 1983). Whereas Sweden was able to maintain low levels of national and regional unemployment by managing to translate a modest growth into very large gains in employment, Austria attempted to avoid mass unemployment through traditional Keynesian demand management and a hard-currency policy, both aimed at maintaining or stimulating growth in the private sector. No doubt, the Austrian labour market of the 1970s profited from several favourable circumstances, including the emigration of guest workers after 1974 (their share in total employment decreased from 8.7% in 1973 to 5.1% in 1985 through a more restrictive foreign worker policy). In the 1980s fiscal constraints have operated and Austria too has had increases in national and regional unemployment in the more recent periods [see figure 1(d)].

An analysis of the question of convergence or divergence in regional unemployment depends critically on the regional framework chosen. In general, larger regions (such as, for example, those chosen for Sweden) will tend to exhibit smaller differences in unemployment rates than smaller ones. Small area disequilibria in employment are often the effect of very specialised economic structures whereas larger spatial units tend to contain a wider variety of activities. However, despite the large difference in the design of the spatial framework between countries in the cross-national study, it seems useful to consider the convergence-divergence issue.

For this purpose a simple measure of the interregional distribution of unemployment within a country is used, the min-max ratio, r, which is defined as the minimal divided by the maximal regional unemployment rate. This measure may be regarded as an indicator of regional inequality and may be used to reveal regional convergences or divergences in unemployment within countries. It should be noted that the ratio is not likely to be independent of the level of unemployment, but because of mobility responses it tends generally to fall as unemployment rises (although not as markedly as the alternative absolute differential measure tends to increase) (compare Gordon, 1985). Moreover, the ratio has the following properties. If $r = 1$, unemployment is entirely equally distributed over all regions. If r approaches 0, a maximum inequality exists. Even if the unemployment figures used are not particularly reliable, especially because unemployment is measured differently in different countries (in particular with respect to the treatment of married women, school-leavers, males aged between 60 and 65 years, part-time workers, self-employed, etc), it is possible to reveal some interesting national and international trends in the evolution of regional unemployment.

Figure 2 shows the min-max ratio values of unemployment in regional labour markets per country in five selected years in the period 1970-85. The unemployment figures were selected by the country coordinators of the project on the basis of data availability. The figure reveals quite clearly that in France interregional equality has increased since 1970. In other words, there is evidence of regional convergence in unemployment. Yugoslavia and Sweden until the later 1970s exhibit a declining pattern of interregional equality. Other countries such as Canada, Italy, and the Netherlands show a more or less clear U-shaped curve which suggests that—after a period of regional divergence in the mid-1970s—a new trend of regional convergence is emerging in the early 1980s.

An examination of the evolution of the min-max ratio values with due consideration to the overall cyclical movements since 1970 produces the following results. There is no evidence that regional rates of unemployment converge, ceteris paribus, as national rates increase. Rather, figure 2 illustrates that the pattern reflects different reactions to the two periods of recession ushered in by the two oil-price shocks of 1973-74 and 1979-80. In the first recession period, general rises in regional unemployment accompanied by restructuring processes disfavouring the periphery and coupled with the mobility-reducing effects of recession have produced a more or less substantial widening of the gap in regional unemployment (except in France), implying a fall in the min-max values. In the more recent period, however, restructuring worked not only to the disadvantage of the traditional regions of high unemployment (mostly peripheral and rural), but also affected the previously successful regions, more strongly than in the first recession. The depressed regions seem to have caught up relative to the more developed regions. Consequently, a more or less substantial tendency

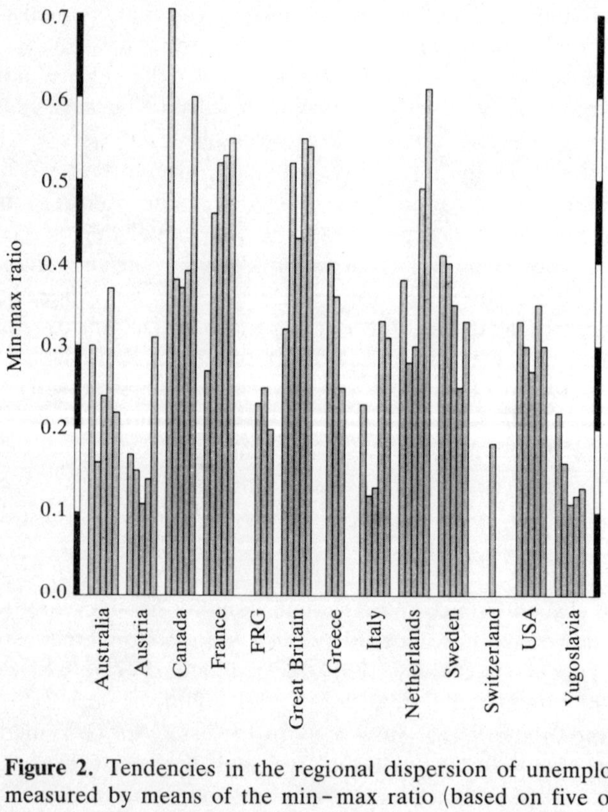

Figure 2. Tendencies in the regional dispersion of unemployment since 1970: measured by means of the min-max ratio (based on five observations).

towards regional convergence (measured in terms of the min–max ratio) occurred in all countries except Sweden. Nevertheless, it should be emphasised that the reduced significance of regional disparities does not mean that regional problems have lessened. The traditional regions of high unemployment have incurred steep increases in unemployment over the whole period of 1970–85. The unemployment crises in these regions are particularly severe for the young and the long-term unemployed.

3 Recent shifts in patterns of employment

Over recent decades a number of marked intersectoral shifts in labour have taken place in industrialised countries, and a number of common trends are clearly discernible (see figure 3). In almost all countries (except Poland and Hungary) there has been a steady decline in employment in the primary sector (agriculture and mining). The decline in agricultural employment has been generally accompanied by a considerable increase in agricultural output. A pattern of jobless growth of output has been established. Nevertheless, in several countries, for example in Australia, agriculture remains one of the most important sources of employment in many of the nonmetropolitan regional labour markets, as it is in regional labour markets of South Italy (Campania, Abruzzi, Mohise, Puglia, Basilicata, Calabria, Sicilia, Sardegna).

During these last decades the role of industry also has been weakened in the national and regional economies of advanced countries in North America, Australia, and Western Europe, and—to a lesser extent—also in Hungary and Poland. But the pattern of employment change in manufacturing is not so clear-cut as in the primary sector. There are significant variations between countries and peculiarities in the direction of change of employment growth over time. Sweden, Great Britain, and the USA experienced considerable deindustrialisation in terms of employment from the early 1960s, whereas Italy (in particular the Mezzogiorno) and, to a lesser extent, the FRG showed considerable industrialisation up to the late 1960s.

There is clear evidence that the recessions since 1973 affected manufacturing employment in the countries concerned at different rates and with varying time lags. The USA, Canada (the Atlantic region), and Great Britain were hit rapidly and severely, and in these countries the cyclical recovery of manufacturing following each successive recession has become smaller and smaller. Italy, however, seems to have escaped the worst of the employment cutbacks, at least at the national level. Job reductions in the northeast were largely offset by increases in the south, at least in the 1970s. Austria and France were cushioned from the 1974–75 recession because of government policies, but both countries have experienced rapid industrial decline in the post-1979 recession.

Characteristics	AUS	A	CDN	F	FRG	GB	GR	H	I	NL	PL	S	CH	USA	YU
Sectoral shifts															
Decrease of employment in the primary sector	■ agriculture	■ agriculture and forestry	■ natural resources	■	■	■	■		■ central/ south	■		■ agriculture and forestry		■	■ north, northwest
Decline in industrial employment	■	■	■ especially in the Atlantic Region	■	■ especially Ruhr area, Bremen	■ North, Northwest, West–Midlands		■ only in Budapest	■ northwest	■	■ recently	■	■ slow decline	■ Mid-Atlantic and Midwest	
Decline in Employment in Construction Sector	■			■	■		■	■ recently		■	■ recently		■		
Growth in Jobs in the Service Sector (especially in large cities)	■	■	■	■	■ especially south	■ especially on the London–Bristol–axis	■		■ northwest and northeast	■	■ recently	■	■	■	■ especially in north and northeast
Spatial trends															
Regional specialisation in high-tech sector			■ especially Ontario Region	■	■ especially south			■ Budapest	■ northwest		■ esp. in the largest urban labour markets	■ especially Stockholm region		■ esp. New-England and California	■ north and northeast
Relative decentralisation of manufacturing towards nonmetropolitan regions	■			■	■	■	■	■	■	■		■	■		■ Bosnia–Hercegowina
No change in the unfavourable position of regions in the periphery		■			■				■	■		■			

■ Denotes the existence of the characteristic concerned

AUS Australia, A Austria, CDN Canada, F France, FRG Federal Republic of Germany, GB Great Britain, GR Greece, H Hungary, I Italy, NL the Netherlands, PL Poland, S Sweden, CH Switzerland, USA United States of America, YU Yugoslavia

Figure 3. Nature of the most important changes in regional labour-market conditions since 1970.

In the USA deindustrialisation occurred on a rather massive scale. The larger corporations, especially in the car, steel, and tyre industries, have shut down capacity in older plants and closed plants in the industrial heartland in order to move to new industrial zones in the New South and overseas. Small businesses confronting bankruptcy, closed down or were bought up. Bluestone and Harrison (1982) estimate that at least 32–38 million manufacturing jobs were eliminated in the US economy during the 1970s. Nor was the process of deindustrialisation limited to the old industrial 'Frostbelt'. Plant closures could be observed in many regions of the country, including the 'Sunbelt' states. But in these states jobs created through new business formation usually exceeded job losses resulting from shutdowns, quite in contrast to the northeast. Characteristically, however, the firms that opened tended to be located in different places, to be in different industries (in services rather than manufacturing), to require different skills, to pay lower wages, to offer unstable or only part-time jobs, and quite often to practise race and sex discrimination in hiring and wage policies.

In Europe the problem of industrial decline is most visible in Great Britain where about 1.2 million manufacturing jobs were lost in the period of 1973–81 (Wabe, 1986). Only two sectors, electrical and electronic engineering, have shown signs of net job growth. In the post-1979 recession industrial output fell by 17% (compared with a fall of only 11% during the economic crisis of 1929–32) and gross investment in manufacturing fell by a third in the period 1979–81. Firms have cut operations and shed workers onto the labour market more markedly than in the 1975 recession (Martin, 1982), causing the high increases in unemployment rates outlined in figure 1(c).

The contraction of manufacturing employment—in Great Britain intensified by the pursuit of tight monetary policies and restrictive public spending since 1979—has reflected fundamental changes in the economy which have taken place in the last fifteen years (see Rothwell, 1982; Hamilton, 1987):

(1) the reduction of domestic real disposable incomes caused by rapidly increasing real energy costs (especially the oil shock of 1974 and 1979) and the oil-price-related inflationary pressures;

(2) the declining demand for many old-established products;

(3) severe pressures to improve labour productivity in all sectors in the face of increasing national and international competition, not at least from Japan and the developing new industrialising countries;

(4) the adoption of new technology applications (for example, computerised numerical control machines) as process innovations by the existing industries.

In order to adjust to the changing internal and external pressures, multinational and multiregional corporations were stimulated to reduce costs and the power of labour (especially in the USA) by moving production to less developed (that is low-wage, nonunion) sites in the periphery. The drift of the shoe and textile industries away from New England and of apparel manufacturing from New York to the Carolinas are well-known examples and illustrate the spatial implications of intrafirm restructuring processes resulting in an increasing international and interregional division of labour between skilled production and routine assembly operations. At the international scale, restructuring changes caused a substantial contraction, if not disappearance, of inefficient labour-intensive sections of production chains (for example, in textiles and shoes) in the more advanced economies, leaving only specialised and high-quality product lines. At the interregional scale the metropolitan labour markets experienced a greater specialisation in knowledge and skill-intensive activities on the one side and were thinned of manufacturing jobs (especially in the inner cities) on the other.

A feature common to all advanced economies has been the steady postwar growth in service employment. For many countries, the service sector now employs more than the primary and secondary sectors combined. In Great Britain, for example, the service sector employed approximately 62% of the work force in 1981. Similar values hold for North America. The marked shift of employment to the service sector is not so much a result of changes in final consumer demand (see Miles, 1986), but is strongly related to

(a) an increase in demand for nonmarket services (such as administration, education, medical, welfare, and cultural services) in the early 1970s supplied by the state as a consequence of political decisions;
(b) an increase in producer-related services including jobs within the factory and elsewhere in the public or private sectors which are oriented to the production of goods (such as planning, design, financing, legal, insurance, marketing, retail distribution, commercial and technical consultancy activities);
(c) an increase for marketed consumer services including a range of functions (for example, blue-collar activities such as building maintenance, equipment service and repair, hotels and catering, as well as domestic and personal services) oriented to servicing manufactured goods at the place of use.

After a period of relative expansion, the nonmarket services in most countries are experiencing recent declines even in countries with socialist governments such as Sweden and Austria, mainly because of efficiency-directed changes in policy in the 1980s. In the early 1980s the growth of the service sector was largely made up by producer-related and market consumer-services. The growing 'tertiarisation' of manufacturing and the increasing involvement of service firms, both closely related to organisational and technical changes, are important shifts in the division of labour. Jobs are being reallocated between increasingly interrelated manufacturing and service activities (Wood, 1986).

It is widely agreed that not only increased consumer and government spending on service needs, but also low productivity growth in the service sector—in comparison with manufacturing—played a major role in the relative and absolute increase in service employment. Pressures for increases in labour productivity are greater in the corporate segment, especially in delivery and in routine clerical functions (see Wood, 1986). Up to now, however, there is only limited evidence of process innovations reducing labour demand in the service sector, mainly because of the increased demand for information-related services which has more or less offset labour-saving.

The importance of service-sector employment varies substantially between countries and regional labour markets. Relatively high levels of service employment can be found in Great Britain (especially in the southeast) and France, with relatively low levels in, for example, the FRG. At the regional level, service employment is generally concentrated in the larger agglomerations. In several countries, however, service employment has increased more rapidly in rural and particularly tourist regions in the past decade; in the FRG, for example, at more than twice the national rate.

Embedded in these broad sectoral changes there have been other important changes in the composition of the workforce. In particular, there has been a shift from full-time employment, both towards self-employment, especially in market consumer-services, and towards an increasing proportion of part-time jobs, particularly for females (for example, see Townsend, 1986, for the British case). In the service sector in particular, the growing proportion of part-time jobs has drawn large numbers of married women into the labour force, despite relatively low pay and poor career prospects. As a consequence the proportion of workers in part-time employment rose in Italy, for example, from 2.6% in 1979 to 4.8% in 1983, in the FRG from 9.4% to 14.4%, and especially dramatically in Great Britain from 15.4% to 22.8%. About 85% of all British part-time work involves females, and almost all of this is in the service sector (Lever, 1987). In regional labour markets with declining industrial employment for males, there has been a particular tendency for females to enter the labour market and take up semiskilled manufacturing jobs and new jobs in the service sector to maintain family incomes and welfare.

4 The evolution and nature of labour-market segmentation

In periods of slack in the labour market, increasing interest has focused on theories suggesting duality or multiple segmentation in national and regional labour markets. Various types of segmentation with differing levels of detail have been suggested. In the simplest theory, the dual labour-market version, the labour market is viewed as a two-segment system with a primary sector characterised by a high degree of job security, good working conditions, high earnings, career and promotional opportunities; and a secondary sector characterised by job uncertainty, poor working conditions, low wages, little on-the-job training, and poor promotion prospects. Secondary jobs are filled mainly by minority or guest workers, women, and youths (for a discussion of the dual and multisegment labour market theories see Fischer and Nijkamp, 1987c).

One particular subset of the secondary labour market is the informal sector, characterised by very low entry requirements, high turnover rates, informal work patterns, and especially by unstable employer-employee relations. This informal part of the labour market has several important functions. Through its greater flexibility it serves to reduce friction in regional labour markets. It can provide temporary and part-time jobs on an ad hoc basis without bureaucratic regulations. And it may act as a breeding ground for innovative behaviour. Gershuny (1983) explains the emergence of the informal sector as a consequence of the productivity gap between the industrial and the service sectors. Wage rates in both sectors have gone up in the past decade to almost the same extent, whereas the productivity rise in the industrial sector has been much greater, so that real wage costs in the service sector have increased. This has led to a decline in the demand for products from the formal service sector and has induced the emergence of informal circuits in this sector, with employees recruited from the low-paid or from reserves of unemployed labour.

The nature and size of the informal sector is a source of much uncertainty, because of the lack of an operational definition and consequently of reliable statistical data. This is especially true at the regional level. In some countries the informal sector is regarded as a residual, comprising all activities outside the official market system. In other countries, this sector includes both the black or underground market and the household economy (sometimes also the communal economy). All countries in the cross-national study indicate that little is known about the size of the informal sector, particularly at the regional level. But nevertheless there are good reasons to believe that the importance of the informal economy has increased in recent years. In the US economy, there is some evidence in the largest cities of daily labour markets (with labour paid very low wages for hourly work without day-to-day contracts) employing illegal aliens and other minorities outside the normal wage sectors. In the USA, and elsewhere there also seems to be a significant informal sector at the top end of the wage distribution, in this case principally to avoid taxes.

The time of full employment throughout most of the 1960s brought a number of problems for employers. It fostered competition for labour, increasing labour turnover and upward wage pressures. As a consequence, employers became increasingly concerned to create internal labour markets at least for their upper primary workers. So-called enterprise-centred labour-market segmentation (Sengenberger, 1981)—which is characterised by a division in the labour-market structure between firms with strongly developed internal markets and other firms where internal markets are only weakly developed or even absent—manifests itself strongly in those regional labour markets dominated by a single large firm or industry, especially in old industrial areas with a high degree of unionisation such as, for example, Upper Styria in Austria.

Given the changes in the industrial and service structure of the economy in the recent past there are good reasons to suppose that some of the primary job categories have become secondary, whereas the primary sector has changed to include, for example, more research and development and computer-related jobs. There seems to be agreement that the size of the secondary sector has increased in several countries and that the size of the external sector has expanded. Lever (1987), for example, presents empirical evidence for this increase of the secondary labour market in Great Britain. Using data on vulnerability to unemployment, wage rises, and labour turnover to identify secondary workers, he is able to show that the percentage of the total work force, in work, in the secondary labour market rose from 18.4% (4.1 million) in 1977 to 24.9% (5.7 million) in 1983. At the same time there was a massive increase in unemployment from 1.6 million to 3.2 million. The vast majority of this group should probably be added to the total of secondary workers. Valkenburg and Vissers (1978) also present some empirical results on segmentation tendencies in the Dutch labour market, and Osterman (1975) has shown some similar results for the US labour market.

During and after the recession of 1974–75 the boundaries between primary and secondary workers became more clearly visible. The reduction of the recruitment flows from the secondary to the primary labour force made the gap between the two segments more obvious (Sengenberger, 1981). After 1974, employers in most countries (but especially in Italy, France, and the FRG) followed a strategy of gaining flexibility both in the internal and in the external markets to improve the quality of the work force, to reduce job security for primary workers, to improve work discipline, and to reduce pressures for enhanced wages and working conditions (see Sengenberger, 1981). Despite considerable resistance from labour, especially in large and highly unionised companies (in particular in the northwestern Italian regions and in France), this strategy has led to an increasing marginalisation of part of the labour force, above all in France.

Even if it is difficult to indicate the nature of segmentation in regional labour markets with precision because the theory of segmented labour markets is based on terms and conditions of employment and career-development opportunities, which do not map neatly into sectoral and occupational classifications of employment, there are several types of segmentation tendencies which may be observed in most of the countries.

The most evident element of segmentation is sex segregation. In most regional labour markets men and women tend to be employed in different occupations. The dominant employment for women continues to be in office and service work. Wages in the female segment are usually lower than in comparable male jobs, despite the introduction of 'equal pay' legislation for women in several countries. Labour-market segmentation along sex lines is manifest especially in Australia, Canada, France, Great Britain, the Netherlands, and Sweden.

Another important source of segmentation is nation of origin. Most of the temporary guest workers (in the FRG, Austria, Switzerland, France, and the Netherlands) and the permanent immigrants (in Great Britain, France, and the Netherlands) are concentrated in large urban labour markets, primarily in the conurbations. They tend to be employed in secondary jobs with few skill requirements, to suffer discrimination, and to receive lower pay. In the FRG and France, there is a 30% differential between the wages of indigenous and foreign workers (Lever, 1987). Moreover, foreign workers experience a higher incidence of unemployment during periods of recession than do their counterparts in the host community. Racial discrimination seems to have little visible effect on regional variations in unemployment, particularly because ethnic minorities and guest workers were attracted to regions of relatively low unemployment, but it is certainly a major factor in the high level of 'inner-city' unemployment in several cities, such as London and Birmingham.

In Great Britain, the Commonwealth is the major source of immigration. The two largest immigrant groups are Asians from India, Pakistan, and Bangladesh, and blacks originating primarily from the West Indies. The majority of nonwhite foreign-born workers are located in the South East region (two thirds of blacks, half of Asians), mainly in London. There are also high concentrations of blacks in the West Midlands and of Asians in Yorkshire and Humberside and in the East Midlands. Many Asians are employed in retail trading, textiles and clothing manufacture. Blacks are employed in most sectors, but mainly in unskilled and semiskilled occupations. There is a disproportionately high incidence of unemployment among blacks, particularly young blacks, because of racial discrimination, location in disadvantaged local labour markets, and low educational attainment. Asians with relatively good educational attainments experience average unemployment though still suffering discrimination.

Foreign workers form also a very important segment of the US economy. Many of these workers are illegal aliens. Official figures put the number of illegal aliens somewhere between 5 and 15 million persons. Most (illegal and legal) aliens come from Central America (especially Mexico).

Regionally, aliens are located in the southwest, Florida, California, and New York. Most large US cities also have a significant number of aliens. For states such as Texas and Florida aliens are a very important part of the regional economy. In Texas, aliens work at the low end of the wage distribution in factories which specialise in employing such workers. In Florida, on the other hand, the Hispanic population is more broadly spread through the wage and salary distribution. In fact, it is the resident black population in Florida which seems to have the lowest jobs. In the largest urban labour markets in Texas, the Hispanic population has also become important in the service and trade sectors.

By 1974, when the recession was already beginning to have an impact, several countries, especially the guest-worker countries, attempted to stem the flow of immigrant workers and to stimulate and force reemigration and, thus, to export some of the increase in unemployment. In Austria, for example, a more restrictive foreign worker policy slowed down the inflow, increased the outflow, and, thus, decreased the share of guest workers in total employment from 8.7% in 1973, to 7.2% in 1975, to 5.1% in 1985. In Switzerland—the country with the highest share of guest workers (27.9% in 1973 and 24.8% in 1984)—the authorities have established a classification scheme of foreign workers which allows them to impose strong restrictions on immigration and to select among applicants for work permits only those who most closely meet the requirements of the economy or other noneconomic criteria. The regulations, however, are not oriented towards regional policy issues, but towards a balanced relationship between the native and the foreign population. In France an immigration stop was introduced in 1974, and an attempt was made to suppress illegal immigration by means of increased controls, making family reunion more difficult, and stimulating return migration by providing financial assistance.

There is a serious polarisation of employment opportunity in several countries, in terms of both quality and quantity of jobs on offer. Very many newly created jobs in services are low skill and part-time and these are usually filled by women. The polarisation is most severe in larger conurbations. Even in regional labour markets without this problem, there is still a pronounced contrast between labour markets for professional workers and those for unskilled workers (for example, in tourism and leisure).

In the USA a spatial polarisation of skill, education, and training is now apparent. The New England region, like Silicon Valley in California, is very dependent upon skilled younger workers and on technological innovations in advanced electronics (capital goods) and in related technology-based commodities (computers). Universities and technical institutes have become a crucial source for innovation and training in advanced electronics (Hall and Markusen, 1985). At the same time, in the smaller towns and cities of New England, assembly work is being 'manned' by women workers with very little formal training. Education in this setting is in the routine of production, not the technology of innovation. In these kinds of industries, there is a spatial and functional segmentation of labour (Clark et al, 1986). It has been also observed that there is an increasing segmentation of professional tasks between US cities. That is, it is supposed that regional cities have claimed increasing shares of professional tasks. The result is a concentration of high-price service functions in larger cities and the peripheralisation of those professional services for which there is less demand or for which there is an oversupply of labour (Stanback and Noyelle, 1982).

5 Labour-market problems and policies

Clearly, the structural changes in the past fifteen years have triggered off a wide variety of problems for the efficient functioning of regional labour markets. The most significant ones appear to be the persistence of spatial mismatches of labour (especially the lack of job opportunities for young workers and females in rural and peripheral labour markets), a relatively low labour mobility in several countries, high levels of unemployment in regions suffering most from deindustrialisation, a marginalisation of certain categories of the labour force, and failures in (regional) labour-market policy (see figure 4).

For all countries included in the cross-national study (except Poland) spatial mismatch of labour is a major and pressing regional labour-market problem. In Australia, for example, a spatial mismatch of labour was caused by the rapid spread of suburbs around the capital cities during the period 1947–71, increasing the concentration of population in these regions. The suburbanisation of jobs and residents produced small self-contained labour markets in the middle and outer suburban areas for a specialised labour demand largely in manufacturing and transport warehouse activities. The process left behind a blue-collar work force tied to state welfare housing, but unable to reach jobs at their skill level in outer suburban locations. A short-run consequence is higher inner-area unemployment, especially among youth, as the population who suburbanised seek jobs in what is a very narrow labour market.

In most countries it is rural and peripheral areas as well as those regions where a dominant industry is undergoing stress (such as the old iron and steel based industrial areas) which suffer worst. Unemployment is a severe and chronic problem in those regions which have lost their main employment sectors and have been unable to attract new ones. The USA has widespread unemployment in those manufacturing cities which have lost their employment base (Lall, 1985). In Youngstown, OH, for example, unemployment is estimated to be in the range of 25% to 30%. Similar levels of unemployment may be found in the USA in southwestern communities including Houston and Dallas. In these cities

Problems	AUS	A	CDN	F	FRG	GB	GR	H	I	NL	PL	S	CH	USA	YU
Spatial mismatches	■	■	■	■	■	■	■	■	■	■		■	■	■	■
Low labour mobility		■			■	■			■			■	■		■
Lack of effectiveness of governmental policy for regional labour markets	■	■		■	■	■	■	■	■	■				■	■
Marginalisation of certain categories of the labour force	■			■	■		■		■					■	
Low investment on human capital by private firms							■		■						
Inner-city decline						■								■	

■ Denotes existence of the problem concerned

Figure 4. The most important regional labour-market problems (1970–85).

not only unemployment itself is a problem, but also the nature of employment opportunities. The jobs available are in the service sector, paying between $400 and $1200 per month as opposed to around $2200 per month for unionised manufacturing jobs. Thus, real incomes have drastically declined for many manufacturing workers who have been laid off. Households have reacted with increased labour-force participation, but even so, poverty became a real problem for a significant segment of people who would have otherwise been part of the lower middle class. These cities and regions urgently need a concerted intervention by government to revitalise their economic and employment base.

If vacancies and labour supply coexist in space, low labour mobility (both occupational and geographical) is a major problem. This was the case in Great Britain in the early 1970s, especially with respect to those groups of workers who were most susceptible to unemployment. A principal constraint affecting geographic mobility in Great Britain is the housing tenure structure of residents. About 30% of the residents live in public-sector rented accommodation. The 'entry-requirements' into this housing segment effectively prevent interregional migration for most residents in this sector. At a time of demand deficiency in all regions this problem obviously becomes less important. But even in a generally mobile society like Australia—where information on job opportunities is available nationally—there exist rigidities brought about by distance and home-ownership which constrain mobility and produce spatially uneven labour-market performance. In Swiss regions, too, where new industry has developed in recent years, labour-market problems are caused by the low degree of mobility in some qualification groups. Craftsmen have been found to be unsufficiently mobile, and employers complain about a chronic shortage, one reason being that small and medium sized companies cannot recruit from the labour markets of other, particularly nonperipheral, regions.

Discrimination in employment is a fundamental problem facing blacks and other minorities in the USA and Great Britain as well as guest workers in continental European cities, especially in times of recession when employers have more applicants to choose between, and probably need to make more use of mechanical criteria in sifting among them. Problems of racism and access to employment appear especially important in US cities like Chicago and Boston. Blacks are particularly hard hit because they are increasingly concentrated within central cities and in those regions where plant closures and economic dislocation have been most pronounced. There is, of course, a debate over the relative contribution of racial discrimination and locational isolation as factors in the extremely poor employment prospects for blacks. And, there is some debate over the relative standing of blacks in relation to other minorities. Nevertheless, these two problems are so severe that whole neighbourhoods of large metropolitan areas in the USA have no working adults, let alone working youths.

Last, shortcomings in governmental regional policies of different kinds are a major problem. In most countries there is no regional labour-market policy at the national level. Regional labour-market policy is rather carried out in the framework of sectoral policies and regional development policies. In practice, sectoral policies aimed, for example, at propping up declining industries such as coal, steel, and shipbuilding have had a strong spatial impact on a limited number of local labour markets, areas located primarily in the regions of high unemployment. They have generally brought temporary relief to problems of unemployment in the short run, but in the long run there is little evidence that the industries affected have restructured into a competitive position. Thus, in general, decline has only slowed down.

If regional (development) policies are to be judged in terms of equalising and reducing regional rates of unemployment, then they have failed in most countries. However, they could alternatively be examined against a scenario of what would have occurred if such policies had not been in operation. In this respect, there is some evidence that mobile jobs have been directed to less favoured regions. The promotion of inward public investment to generate employment, however, has had only limited success in changing regional disparities in unemployment substantially. And in Great Britain, for example, it has been to the cost of the West Midlands region which has plummeted from being a healthy region to a disadvantaged one over a period of just ten years. There are very few cases where this type of policy has been really effective. However, Scotland, which has some autonomy on regional employment-support policies, higher public expenditure, and an effective institutional arrangement—the Scottish Development Authority—has shown that such policies can influence the spatial balance of unemployment. Scotland is the only traditional manufacturing region which managed to improve its relative unemployment ranking in Great Britain during the recession, although this was at least partly because of the employment effects of North Sea oil.

Since the 1970s (regional) labour-market and related policies have played an important role in relation to the structural changes affecting the Western economies. Most labour-market policies appear to be based on a blend of efficiency and equity considerations. However, it is interesting to observe that in various countries (for example, Austria, the FRG, Sweden, Great Britain, the Netherlands) the beginning of the 1970s was marked mainly by an interest in efficiency strategies, followed by a strong emphasis on (economic, social, and political) equity aspects from the mid-1970s, whereas since the beginning of the 1980s an efficiency orientation has again come to the fore.

This wave-like pattern, which is of course closely related both to the changes in economic structure and to intellectual or political swings of fashion between Keynesian and classical approaches to unemployment, may be briefly illustrated for the British case. In Great Britain three major policy phases may be distinguished: the period 1970–74 (mainly efficiency oriented), the period 1974–79 (mainly equity oriented), and the period 1979–85 (strongly efficiency oriented). In the first phase the main policy aimed at ameliorating the regional problem was an expansionary macroeconomic dash for growth. This increased employment, but led to high inflation. Regional policy per se was pursued with moderate enthusiasm. When the Labour Party came to power after the first oil-price shock it attempted to pursue a negotiated form of incomes policy in the form of a social contract which would commit the unions to voluntary wage restraint in return for government commitments to full employment and an active industrial policy. Although regional policy was pursued with more vigour, the effects of austerity measures were to increase aggregate unemployment and regional divergence of unemployment rates. In the later years of the second phase there was some expansion and regional unemployment rates began to converge, but inflation again became rampant—mainly for cost-push reasons, and wage moderation broke down in 1979. Restrictive public spending, tight monetary policy to control inflation, and strengthen international competitiveness (without an incomes policy)—the policies pursued from 1979 onwards, when the Conservative government came into office—have hampered the pace of recovery in many sections of industry in the depressed regions, primarily through their destabilising impact on the exchange rate and on interest rates (Martin, 1986). Explicit regional policies have been run down, and implicit regional policies, particularly defence expenditure, have assisted the already favoured regions.

Labour-market measures fall into two main groups, supply-oriented and demand-oriented ones. The most important policy instruments used in the countries of the cross-national study are summarised in figure 5. Typical examples of supply-oriented instruments are measures stimulating spatial mobility and training or retraining programmes to reduce spatial and occupational mismatches from the supply side, as well as early retirement schemes, interregional migration control (Poland), restrictions to immigration, and assistance to return migration of guest workers, to reduce labour supply.

Demand-oriented policies are aimed at reducing job loss and promoting job creation, usually through sectoral and regional development policies. Important direct instruments are the relocation or establishment of government activities or of state-owned companies, investment allowances, and provision of work by regionally differentiated employment programmes. Indirect instruments include financial incentives to companies, subsidies on labour, and protectionist measures. In recent years policymakers have looked to high-technology industries as the primary source of new jobs. Efforts to attract 'high-tech' employment have resulted in a variety

Policy measures	AUS	A	CDN	F	FRG	GB	GR	H	I	NL	PL	S	CH	USA	YU
Supply-oriented policy measures															
Measures stimulating spatial mobility	■	■	■		■	■	■			■	■	■		■	
Measures stimulating professional (re)training	■	■	■	■	■	■	■	■	■	■	■	■	■	■	
Interregional migration control											■ ●				
Stimulation of remigration of guestworkers		■		■	■					■			■		
A more restrictive foreign worker policy	■	■		■	■					■			■	■	
Early retirement schemes		■		■	■	■		■	■		■	■	■		
Demand-oriented policy measures															
The relocation or establishment of government activities or of state-owned companies							■	■	■	■	■				
Investment allowances				■	■	■	■	■	■	■			■	■	
Provision of work by regionally differentiated employment programmes		■					■		■	■		■	■		
Slowing down measures						■		■	■		■			■	
Investments in economic infrastructure	■	■		■	■			■		■			■	■	
Financial incentives to companies		■	■	■	■		■	■	■	■		■			
Subsidies on investments		■			■	■	■		■	■					■
Subsidies on labour		■		■	■	■	■		■			■			
Subsidies on moving expenses								■		■		■			
Subsidies on energy use		■			■		■		■	■					
General financial support to companies	■	■			■	■		■	■	■		■			
Tax facilities		■	■		■	■	■		■	■			■	■	
Innovation policies		■	■	■	■		■		■	■		■	■		■
Protectionist measures			■				■								

■ Denotes existence of the policy measure concerned

● In the 1960s only

Figure 5. The most important regional labour-market and related policy measures (1970–85).

of creative strategies undertaken by all levels of government in many countries. Innovation-oriented regional policy emphasising the importance of small firms and new high-technology industry is also receiving a higher priority in several countries.

Australia and Great Britain may serve to illustrate the policy measures used in more detail. In Australia regionally focused labour-market policies have emerged on an ad hoc basis for severe spatial mismatches of labour. Two examples may underline this point. The first refers to resource regions which experienced a very rapid growth in demand and severe skill shortages during the 1970s. Here local and state initiatives to ameliorate the regional labour-market conditions were undertaken, including attention to housing-market shortages to facilitate in-migration and special short-term training and retraining of labour. These efforts were carried out in the context of regional development policy associated with the overall expansion of the resource regions. The second type of initiative emerged from the regionally severe effect of a shift in national policy in 1972, namely a cut in import duty which had a major impact on employment, especially in the clothing and textile industry. Much of this industry is spatially concentrated in inner areas of metropolitan regions or small nonmetropolitan regions. The Structural Adjustment Assistance Programme provided relocation assistance and income maintenance for six months and assistance to firms to compensate for closure. The scheme operated for three years on a small budget and the main emphasis of its expenditure was on income maintenance rather than relocations. Experience with this programme has been carried forward into policies to assist industries to cope with structural adjustment. Recently, policies for the steel industry and the car industry have been put in place, and work is proceeding on the meat-processing and black coal industries. Under the scheme of Labour Adjustment Training Arrangement, workers are assisted to broaden their skill base through vocationally oriented training and, thus, facilitate their adjustment into alternative employments. Indeed, the major focus of Australian labour-market policy is skill retraining to facilitate reemployment. There is no nationally coordinated effort directed at increasing the demand for labour in depressed labour markets, though some areas do attract financial assistance for community and social development which could lead to local economic development.

In Great Britain, since the 1960s policy has been directed at reducing spatial disparities in unemployment. The most direct measures influencing the workings of regional labour markets were the Regional Employment Premium which provided a labour subsidy to the disadvantaged regions and the assisted mobility scheme which provided subsidies for migration from these regions. The first, however, was abolished in 1976. Other measures have included selective assistance such as capital grants and fiscal allowances, provision of advance factories, etc. Negative tools have included the need to obtain industrial development permits in the advantaged regions although this system too has been ended. Sectoral policies aimed at propping up declining industries such as coal, shipbuilding, and motor vehicles have had a strong spatial impact on areas located primarily in the regions of high unemployment. There is no clear attempt, however, to focus attention on regions suffering the worst impacts of recession and economic restructuring. Only the efforts of the Scottish Development Agency, and to some extent the Welsh Development Agency, to coordinate current development grants and policies and to provide additional grants and facilities appear to be really effective from a regional labour-market point of view.

The cross-national study clearly reveals differences in the way that unemployment problems in regional labour markets are tackled. The general tendency in the 1980s is, however, for governments to pay less attention to regional differences in unemployment and to focus on the national level, aiming at improving efficiency. In doing so, it is hoped that regional unemployment will decline as well. Yet the worsening unemployment situation—in some countries (for example, the United Kingdom and the USA) intensified by a rigid pursuance of monetarist policies to fight against inflation—emphasises rather than diminishes the need for further research on the regional dimensions of the unemployment problem.

References

• References not specifically quoted in the text but of particular relevance to this chapter.

• Bade F-J, 1986, "The de-industrialisation of the Federal Republic of Germany and its spatial implications", in *Technological Change, Employment and Spatial Dynamics* Ed. P Nijkamp (Springer, Berlin) pp 196–220

Baumann J, Fischer M M, Schubert U, 1983, "A multiregional labour supply model for Austria: the effects of different regionalisations in multiregional modelling" *Papers of the Regional Science Association* **52** 53–83

• Blackaby F (Ed.), 1979 *De-industrialisation* (Heinemann Educational Books, London)

Bluestone B, Harrison B, 1982 *The Deindustrialization of America* (Basic Books, New York)

• Castells M, 1984, "Technological change, economic restructuring and the spatial division of labor", paper presented at the Symposium on Regional Development Processes/Policies and the Changing International Division of Labour, Vienna, August 1984, copy obtainable from the Interdisciplinary Institute for Urban and Regional Studies, University of Economics, Vienna

• Cheshire P C, 1981, "Labour-market theory and spatial unemployment: the role of demand reconsidered", in *Regional Wage Inflation and Unemployment* Ed. R L Martin (Pion, London) pp 189–207

• Christopherson S, 1983, "The household and class formation: determinants of residential location in Ciudad Juárez" *Environment and Planning D: Society and Space* **1** 323–338

• Clark G L, 1983 *Interregional Migration, National Policy and Social Justice* (Rowman and Allanheld, Totowa, NJ)

• Clark G L, Gertler M S, 1983, "Local labor markets: theories and policies in the United States during the 1970s" *The Professional Geographer* **35** 274-285

Clark G L, Gertler M, Whiteman J, 1986 *Regional Dynamics: Studies in Adjustment Theory* (Allen and Unwin, Hemel Hempstead, Herts)

Evers-Koelman I, Fischer M M, Nijkamp P, 1987, "Cross-national comparisons of regional labour markets in 15 countries", in *Regional Labour Markets: Analytical Contributions and Cross-national Comparisons* Eds M M Fischer, P Nijkamp (North-Holland, Amsterdam) in press

• Fischer M M, Nijkamp P (Eds), 1987a *Regional Labour Markets: Analytical Contributions and Cross-national Comparisons* (North-Holland, Amsterdam) in press

• Fischer M M, Nijkamp P, 1987b, "Spatial labour market analysis: relevance and scope", in *Regional Labour Markets: Analytical Contributions and Cross-national Comparisons* Eds M M Fischer, P Nijkamp (North-Holland, Amsterdam) in press

Fischer M M, Nijkamp P, 1987c, "Labour market theories: perspectives, problems and policy implications" in *Regional Labour Markets: Analytical Contributions and Cross-national Comparisons* Eds M M Fischer, P Nijkamp (North-Holland, Amsterdam) in press

• Fischer M M, Nijkamp P, 1987d, "The structure of regional labour markets: problems and perspectives", in *Society-Economy-Space* Eds M M Fischer, M Sauberer (AMR Info, Vienna) in press

• Fothergill S, Gudgin G, 1982 *Unequal Growth: Urban and Regional Employment Change in the UK* (Heinemann Educational Books, London)

• Frost M E, Spence N A, 1983, "Unemployment change", in *The Urban and Regional Transformation of Britain* Eds J B Goddard, A G Champion (Methuen, Andover, Hants) pp 239-258

Gershuny J I, 1983 *Social Innovation and the Division of Labour* (Oxford University Press, Oxford)

Gleave D, 1987, "Dynamics in spatial variations in unemployment", in *Regional Labour Markets: Analytical Contributions and Cross-national Comparisons* Eds M M Fischer, P Nijkamp (North-Holland, Amsterdam) in press

Gordon I, 1985, "The cyclical sensitivity of regional employment and unemployment differentials" *Regional Studies* **19** 95-110

Hall P, Markusen A (Eds), 1985 *Silicon Landscapes* (Allen and Unwin, Hemel Hempstead, Herts)

Hamilton F E I, 1987, "Industrial organization and regional labour markets", in *Regional Lbour Markets: Analytical Contributions and Cross-national Comparisons* Eds M M Fischer, P Nijkamp (North-Holland, Amsterdam) in press

• Hamilton F E I, Linge G J R (Eds), 1983 *Regional Economies and Industrial Systems* (John Wiley, Chichester, Sussex)

• Healey M, Clark D, 1984, "Industrial decline and government response in the West Midlands: the case of Coventry" *Regional Studies* **18** 303-318

• Keeble D, Wever E (Eds), 1986 *New Firms and Regional Development in Europe* (Croom Helm, Beckenham, Kent)

Lall B (Ed.), 1985 *Economic Dislocation and Job Loss* New York State School of Industrial and Labor Relations, Ithaca, NY

• Lawrence R Z, 1984 *Can America Compete?* (Brookings Institution, Washington, DC)

Lever B, 1987, "New trends in the supply and demand patterns of labour in Western economies", in *Regional Labour Markets: Analytical Contributions and Cross-national Comparisons* Eds M M Fischer, P Nijkamp (North-Holland, Amsterdam) in press

Martin R L, 1982, "Britain's slump: the regional anatomy of job loss" *Area* **14** 257-264

Martin R L, 1986, "Thatcherism and Britain's industrial landscape", in *The Geography of the De-industrialisation* Eds R L Martin, R E Rowthorn (Methuen, Andover, Hants) pp 238-290

Miles I, 1986, "Information technology and service activities: two scenarios" paper presented at the IIASA International Conference on 'Technology Alternatives and Employment Policy Options to the Year 2000', Laxenburg, March, 1986; copy obtainable from International Institute for Applied Systems Analysis, Laxenburg, Austria

• Norton R D, Rees J, 1979, "The product cycle and the spatial decentralisation of American manufacturing" *Regional Studies* **13** 141-151

• Office of Technology Assessment, 1984, "Technology innovation and regional economic development" OTA-STI-238 (US Government Printing Office, Washington, DC)

Osterman P, 1975, "An empirical study of labor market segmentation" *Industrial and Labour Relations Review* **28** 508-528

• Owen D W, Gillespie A E, Coombes M G, 1984, "'Job shortfalls' in British local labour market areas: a classification of labour supply and demand trends, 1971-1981" *Regional Studies* **18** 469-488

Rothwell R, 1982, "The role of technology in industrial change: implications for regional policy" *Regional Studies* **16** 361-369

Scharpf F W, 1983, "Economic and institutional constraints of full-employment strategies: Sweden, Austria and West Germany (1973-1982)" DP-20, Labour Market Policy, International Institute of Management, Berlin

Sengenberger W, 1981, "Labour market segmentation and the business cycle", in *The Dynamics of the Labour Market Segmentation* Ed. F Wilkinson (Academic Press, London) pp 243-259

• Soete L, 1986, "Employment policies with regard to new technologies: the case for technology policies", paper presented at the IIASA-Conferencc on 'Technology Alternatives and Employment Policy Options to the Year 2000', Laxenburg, March, 1986, copy obtainable from International Institute for Applied Systems Analysis, Laxenburg, Austria

Stanback T, Noyelle T, 1982 *Cities in Transition* (Rowman and Allanheld, Totowa, NJ)

Steinle W J, 1983, "Regional labour markets: trends, structure and relevance from an European perspective" *Papers of the Regional Science Association* **52** 3-21

• Sternlieb G, Hughes J (Eds), 1978 *Revitalizing the Northeast* Center for Urban Policy Research, Rutgers University, New Brunswick, NJ

• Townroe P M, 1986, "Technological change in the service sector: urban and regional implications", in *Technological Change, Employment and Spatial Dynamics* Ed. P Nijkamp (Springer, Berlin) pp 76-90

Townsend A R, 1986, "Spatial aspects of the growth of part-time employment in Britain" *Regional Studies* **20** 313-330

Valkenburg F C, Vissers A M C, 1978 *Theorie van de Dubbele Arbeidsmarkt* (IVA, Tilburg)

Wabe J S, 1986, "The regional impact of de-industrialization in the European Community" *Regional Studies* **20** 23-36

Wood P A, 1986, "The anatomy of job loss and job creation: some speculations on the role of the 'producer service' sector" *Regional Studies* **20** 37-46

APPENDIX

Criteria used for defining regional labour markets

For *Australia* a regional labour market (RLM) is an area within which 75% of labour employed in a centre live, or alternatively the area where at least 75% of the population both live and work. The key criterion for the definition of the 117 regional labour markets is, thus, journey to work. (Country coordinators: Kevin O'Connor and Moira Gordon.)

The definition of *Austrian* RLMs is based on the journey-to-work criterion. RLMs have been identified by using the three-stage functional regionalisation procedure MFPT/WARD-REG/HC-Z1-REG suggested by Baumann et al (1983). (Country coordinators: Ewald Brunner and Uwe Schubert.)

For *Canada* five so-called Canadian Economic Development Regions (mainly defined according to administrative and policy purposes) are used. (Country coordinator: Mieke Kesik.)

The definition of the *French* RLMs is based on a two-stage approach. First, 365 spatial units have been defined on the basis of criteria such as journey to work. Then these spatial units have been grouped in view of the application of regional economic and social development plans and physical planning, to form twenty-one regional labour markets. (Country coordinator: Michel Micheau.)

The seventy-five RLMs in the *Federal Republic of Germany* are defined on the basis of the official standard regional classification provided by the Federal Institute of Regional Planning. (Country coordinator: Wolfgang Steinle.)

The RLMs for *Great Britain* are the standard regions (excluding Northern Ireland) which are based on economic planning criteria and modified to take account of changes in local authority boundaries. They are the only regions for which reliable time-series data on labour-market variables are available (ten regions). (Country coordinator: David Gleave.)

The definition of the ten *Greek* RLMs is based on the official regional economic subdivision that is adopted by the Bureau of Statistical Services of Greece. (Country coordinators: Evangelia Dokopoulou and Maria Giaoutzi.)

In *Hungary* nineteen provinces and the capital city of Budapest form the set of regional labour markets. (Country coordinator: Peter Klekner.)

For *Italy* twenty administrative units have been used. (Country coordinators: Riccardo Cappellin and Rodolfo Jannacone Pazzi.)

In the case of *the Netherlands* the eleven provinces have been used. (Country coordinators: Jouke van Dijk and Henk Folmer.)

For *Poland* the forty-nine RLMs correspond to the upper-level administrative units (the so-called vovoidships). (Country coordinator: Piotr Korcelli.)

The definition of the *Swedish* labour-market regions was mainly based on journey-to-work and migration patterns. But data availability was also a major criterion (eight regions). (Country coordinator: Anders Harkman.)

The definition of the *Swiss* RLMs is based on a two-stage approach. First, the country is divided into 106 MS (*mobilité spatial*) areas based on size, and political or institutional attributes. These spatial units have been aggregated mainly on the basis of interregional commuting flows to form 16 RLMs. (Country coordinator: Beat Hotz-Hart.)

The RLM definition of the *USA* employs the fifty standard state labour markets and is, thus, mainly based on administrative or institutional criteria. (Country coordinator: Gordon L Clark.)

The eight *Yugoslavian* RLMs are standard regions and are the only regions for which reliable time-series data are available. (Country coordinator: Vlasta Dugonjić.)

Bargaining Models of Regional Earnings Determination: Theory and Scottish Evidence

F HARRIGAN*, D R HOLDEN**, I JENKINS*, P G McGREGOR* **
* Fraser of Allander Institute, Glasgow
** University of Strathclyde, Glasgow

1 Introduction

The macroeconomic debate on the nature of earnings determination ranges over a whole spectrum of visions of labour-market processes. At one end of this spectrum, monetarist advocates of the rational expectations hypothesis regard the price of labour as continuously clearing the labour market, ensuring full-employment equilibrium (on average) and the efficient allocation of human resources(1). At the other extreme, Keynesian institutionalists regard the price of labour as being determined largely, if not entirely, independently of market forces. Intermediate theories include conventional statements of the natural rate hypothesis, the simple Phillips curve, and various theories of unions' and firms' wage-bargaining behaviour.

At the regional level the likely spatial interaction of labour markets adds an additional dimension, and thus layer of complexity, to the debate. Within any given perspective on the efficacy of the labour-market mechanism, a range of views is possible as to the degree of spatial integration of labour markets. At one, admittedly almost inconceivable, end of the range would be an 'insular' view of labour markets in which regions were effectively spatially segmented. At the other end of the 'spatial spectrum' would be a perfect-spatial-integration vision of the regional market under which a 'law of one (labour) price' would prevail.

A comprehensive investigation of regional earnings determination would consequently necessitate consideration of a matrix of possible combinations of market efficacy and degree of (labour-market) spatial integration.

In the present paper, however, we are much more modest in our objectives. First, possible mechanisms through which space may impinge on the wage-determination process are examined in the context of a sample of 'bargaining' theories of wage determination which embody often radically different views of the importance of market forces. Although bargaining models have recently found extensive application at the aggregate UK level (for example, Nickell and Andrews, 1983; Layard and Nickell, 1985; 1986; Newell and Symons, 1985; 1986) there have, as yet, been no systematic attempts to investigate the approach in a spatially disaggregated

(1) Admittedly, various mechanisms in 'new classical' macroeconomic models, such as transactions costs and stockbuilding, can result in nonpersistent expectational errors causing prolonged deviations from full-employment.

context (although, as will shortly become clear, intuitive notions of a bargaining process often underlay applied econometric work in this area). Advocates of the approach claim (for example, Layard and Nickell, 1986) that it encompasses alternative approaches, including that predicated upon continuous market clearing under competitive conditions, in the sense that it implies more general specifications of empirical wage equations. In the present paper we do not, however, investigate spatially disaggregated market-clearing models explicitly.

Our second main objective is to conduct an exploratory econometric analysis of the wage functions implied by these alternative views of how market forces and space impact upon the bargaining process. We do this using Scottish time-series data, although it must be conceded at the outset that data constraints preclude the estimation of the most general forms of the bargaining models developed in the theoretical analysis. The investigation is also limited in being confined to a single-equation analysis of data relating to a single region, and we regard further, less restrictive, econometric analysis as a priority. Furthermore, the nature of regional data cannot, in the foreseeable future, permit the full general equilibrium econometric analysis of the labour market which we regard as ultimately desirable(2). Nevertheless, the econometric methodology adopted is designed to minimise the risk of inappropriate inference.

The remainder of the paper is structured as follows. After a brief account of past work on regional earnings determination (section 2), various bargaining theories are augmented, in section 3, to accommodate the spatial dimension. The econometric analysis is then presented and discussed in section 4. Section 5 contains our concluding remarks.

2 Background

Books by Martin (1981), and Blackaby and Manning (1987) contain useful accounts of past work on regional earnings determination and obviate the need for a review. Nevertheless, it is useful at this stage to make a few observations on past work in the area.

Virtually all of the work on regional earnings determination has focused on applied work involving the estimation of equations of the expectations-augmented-Phillips curve (APC) type, extended to incorporate at least one wage 'spillover' term, reflecting wage changes in another region. Such equations are generally of the form (for example, see Cowling and Metcalf, 1967; Thirlwall, 1970; Metcalf, 1971; Thomas and Stoney, 1971; Hart and MacKay, 1977):

$$\dot{E}_{St} = \mathrm{f}(\phi_S) + \alpha_{1S}\dot{P}_S^{\mathrm{e}} + \alpha_{2S}\dot{E}_{R,\,t-k}\,, \qquad (1)$$

(2) General equilibrium linkages could, however, be investigated by means of simulation models (for example, see Harrigan and McGregor, 1987).

where

$\dot{E}$	is the rate of change in earnings,
$\dot{P}^{e}$	is the expected rate of change in prices,
ϕ	is the unemployment rate,
R, S	are regions,
t	is the time period,
α_1, α_2	are parameters.

Often, at least in principle, a full matrix of spillover coefficients is postulated (for example, see Brechling, 1973; Hart and Mackay, 1977; Hart, 1981; Martin, 1981).

Since equation (1) has, to our knowledge, never been derived explicitly from a structural model of the labour market, its ability to shed light on the issues raised by the wider debate on the nature of labour markets appears limited. Of course, if $\alpha_{2S} = 0$, then wage determination appears 'insular' in the limited sense that earnings depend only on price expectations and local labour-market conditions[3], and, if $\alpha_{2S} > 0$, then wage change in region S depends directly on that in the other region, R. Furthermore, $0 \leqslant \alpha_{1S} < 1$ yields a conventional Phillips curve whereas $\alpha_{1S} = 1$ yields a natural rate hypothesis. This information is, of course, useful, but this appears to be as far as equation (1) can take us.

Naturally, economists have expressed a number of views as to how the spillover term in equation (1) ought to be interpreted. The majority who have investigated such equations regard spillover as reflecting some form of institutional mechanism for the direct transmission of wage changes (for example, Hart, 1981; Martin, 1981). A variety of such mechanisms have been suggested [for example, see Burton and Addison (1977) for a review of general 'spillover' analyses], but a common feature is emphasis on elements of imperfect competition in labour markets. On this perspective the collective bargaining process is not a 'veil' which merely acts as a channel for communicating market forces.

Some economists have, on the other hand, offered a 'market-forces' interpretation of spillover, lending particular emphasis to the role of actual and potential migration in limiting spatial wage differentials (Brechling, 1973; Hart and MacKay, 1977; Martin, 1981). Most judge that the apparent insensitivity of migration flows to wage differentials render the 'market' account less convincing than the institutionalist view (for example, Hart and MacKay, 1977), but in fact evidence on this is mixed, and it may be argued that the issue has not generally been properly investigated[4]. The appropriate interpretation of equations such as equation (1) consequently remains unclear.

(3) In a full structural model, however, local labour-market conditions may depend indirectly on those in other labour markets.

(4) For example, Harrigan et al (1986) who find that real earnings have been a major determinant of net migration flows between Scotland and the rest of the United Kingdom.

We should perhaps concede at the outset that our own econometric analysis investigates specifications which are often not radically different in appearance from equation (1). However, the issues of interest identified in the introduction to this paper lead us to examine the theoretical foundations of such equations through explicit consideration of the role of *space* in the associated 'structural forms' of the various bargaining models. This, in our view, considerably enhances the potential rewards from econometric analysis even if, as here, attention is confined to wage equations which constitute reduced forms of selected special cases of general bargaining models.

3 Bargaining theories of regional earnings determination

In this section of the paper we derive a number of 'bargaining' models of wage determination, and discuss their relationship to equation (1). In general, it transpires that previous models of regional earnings determination can be derived as special cases of these bargaining theories.

'Neoclassical' (utility-maximising) models of the union can take essentially three different forms. In the most traditional, the union acts as a monopoly wage-setter, and employment is determined unilaterally by firms. In this model, the union maximises its utility, an increasing function of both the real wage and the employment of its membership, subject to a negatively sloped (in real wage – employment space) demand curve for labour (for example, see Oswald, 1982).

Recently Nickell (1982) and Nickell and Andrews (1983) have developed and implemented a model in which the union and firm actually bargain over the real wage, but once this is determined the firm continues to exercise sole control over the level of employment. *Wage* bargaining is permitted in this model, but firms retain the 'right to manage'—that is, the right to select whatever level of employment they consider to be appropriate in the prevailing circumstances. This model is regarded by its developers as capturing what they consider to be a key 'stylised fact' of the real world: that unions bargain over wages, but not, in general, over employment. [The model has also been applied, inter alia by Newell and Symons (1985; 1986)].

It has long been recognised that the outcomes of both these model types are Pareto-inefficient: unions and firms both could be better off through simultaneous bargaining over both employment and the real wage (Leontief, 1946; McDonald and Solow, 1981). We regard the choice among alternative neoclassical models as an open empirical question. However, since, as Nickell (1982) has shown, the implications of the 'right-to-manage' and simultaneous wage – employment-bargaining models for wage determination are very similar, this is not a question which we address in the present study.

The analysis begins with a consideration of the 'right-to-manage' wage-bargaining model since it accommodates the wage-setter model as a special case. Throughout, the exposition follows Nickell (1982) and Nickell and Andrews (1983) quite closely, but focuses explicitly on how spatial influences may impact on the wage bargain. In effect, we are assuming a two-stage bargaining procedure. In the first stage, which is exogenous to our model, national unions bargain over a 'minimum' wage rate. In the second stage, local unions bargain over local earnings. Relaxation of the two-stage assumption would necessitate consideration of possible multiregional comparisons which could ultimately generate models of the 'multidirectional' spillover type.

3.1 *Space in a 'right-to-manage' wage-bargaining model*
Following Nickell and Andrews (1983) we consider a simple one-period bargaining model, but regard its outcome as perhaps reflecting a longer-term, desired position. The firm sets employment, n, to that level which maximises profits, $n^{\star}(w)$, given the real wage (w). Notwithstanding its well-known limitations (such as the required 'independence of irrelevant alternatives'), convenience leads us to consider a Nash bargaining problem and solution. The 'bargained' wage level solves the problem:

$$\underset{w}{\text{maximise}} \, \langle U\{\pi[w, n^{\star}(w)]\} - U(\bar{\pi})\rangle^{\beta}\{u[w, n^{\star}(w)] - \bar{u}\} \, , \tag{2}$$

where β is a weight. The Nash solution therefore maximises the weighted product of the excess of firm (U) and union (u) utility over their respective 'fallback' levels $[\bar{U} = U(\bar{\pi})$, and $u = \bar{u}$, respectively], which are achievable in the absence of further cooperation. Firm utility is an increasing function of profits, π, which in turn depend both on wages and on employment. Union utility is an increasing function of w and n.

Real profits in the Nickell–Andrews model are given by

$$\pi_t = p_t A_t \mathrm{h}(n_t) - w_t(1+\tau_{1,t})n_t - C_t \, , \tag{3}$$

where

$$p_t = \frac{P^{\mathrm{e}}_{\mathrm{p},t}}{P^{\mathrm{e}}_{\mathrm{c},t}} \, , \qquad w_t = \frac{W_t}{P^{\mathrm{e}}_{\mathrm{c},t}} \, ,$$

W_t is a nominal wage,
$P^{\mathrm{e}}_{\mathrm{p},t}$, $P^{\mathrm{e}}_{\mathrm{c},t}$ are expected producer and consumer prices respectively,
τ_1 is the employment tax rate,
C_t are fixed costs,
$A_t\mathrm{h}(n_t)$ is the production function, where A_t is a given productivity factor.

The profit-maximising level of labour input, $n^{\star}(.)$, is consequently obtained from

$$p_t A_t \frac{\mathrm{dh}(n_t)}{\mathrm{d}t} - w_t(1+\tau_{1,t}) = 0 \, . \tag{4}$$

The union is 'concerned' (to a greater or less degree) about a fixed pool of 'l' workers. The utility of each of the n_t workers employed next period is v_t:

$$v_t = v[w_{S,t}(1-\tau_{2,t})-\bar{w}_t] , \tag{5}$$

where τ_2 is the employees' tax rate. Employees' utility thus depends on the excess of net of tax (expected) hourly real earnings over the 'fallback' wage rate. Herein lies the first possible mechanism through which space can enter. If the first stage of the bargain establishes a 'minimum' wage rate in the United Kingdom as a whole, then $\bar{w} = \bar{w}_{\mathrm{UK}}$. The 'local' union representatives bargain taking this as the fallback position achievable in the absence of any further cooperation with employers at the local level.

The union's concern with 'l' workers implies that its utility is also dependent on the utility of those who fail to find employment in the union sector. In a regional context, those who do not find employment within the union sector will either seek work elsewhere in the region, or migrate. A typical nonmigrant will have utility v_S:

$$v_S = \omega_S v\left(\frac{B}{P_{\mathrm{c}}^{\mathrm{e}}} - \bar{w}_{UK}\right) + (1-\omega_S)v\left[\frac{W_S'}{P_{\mathrm{c}}^{\mathrm{e}}}(1-\tau_2)-\bar{w}_{\mathrm{UK}}\right], \tag{6}$$

where

ω_S is the proportion of the next period which nonmigrants spend in unemployment,

B is the nominal value of unemployment benefits,

W_S' represents nominal hourly earnings attainable elsewhere in region S.

Like Nickell and Andrews (1983, page 187) we treat the replacement ratio, $R_t = \mathrm{B}_t / W_{S,t}'(1-\tau_2)$ as exogenous and follow Jackman and Layard (1981) in assuming

$$\frac{W_S'}{P_c^{\mathrm{e}}} = w_{S,t-1}(1+g_{S,t}) , \tag{7}$$

where

$$w_{S,t-1} = \frac{W_{S,t-1}'}{P_{\mathrm{c},t-1}} ,$$

$w_{S,t-1}$ is the lagged real wage rate in region S, available in the nonunion sector,

$g_{S,t}$ is the expected growth rate of real wages in region S.

Thus v_S can be written as

$$v_S = \omega_S v[R_t w_{S,t-1}(1-\tau_{2,t})(1+g_{S,t})-\bar{w}_{\mathrm{UK}}]$$
$$+(1-\omega_S)v[w_{S,t-1}(1-\tau_{2,t})(1+g_{S,t})-\bar{w}_{\mathrm{UK}}] . \tag{8}$$

A typical migrant who also fails to find employment in the union sector in the rest of the United Kingdom has utility v_R^1

$$v_R^1 = \omega_R v\left(\frac{B}{P_c^e} - \bar{w}_{UK}\right) + (1-\omega_R)v[w_R'(1-\tau_2) - \bar{w}_{UK}], \tag{9}$$

where subscript R refers to 'the' other region[5]. Comparable assumptions to those which yielded equation (8) from equation (6) allow us to write v_R^1 as

$$v_R^1 = \omega_R v[R_t w_{R,t-1}(1-\tau_{2,t})(1+g_{R,t}) - \bar{w}_{UK}] + (1-\omega_R)v[w_{R,t-1}(1-\tau_{2,t})(1+g_{R,t}) - \bar{w}_{UK}]. \tag{10}$$

Those migrants who succeed in gaining employment in the union sector in R enjoy utility v_R^2,

$$v_R^2 = v[w_R^E(1-\tau_2) - \bar{w}_{UK}], \tag{11}$$

where w_R^E represent real hourly earnings in the union sector in region R.

Clearly, equations (6)–(11) introduce a number of additional mechanisms through which space may impinge on the bargained wage. Thus, the pay attainable outside the union includes that in union and nonunion sectors in region R as well as that attainable elsewhere in region S. Outside 'opportunities', of course, also include the returns to unemployment in region S and the rest of the United Kingdom. Furthermore, if, following Nickell and Andrews (1983), we postulate that

$$\omega_i = F(\phi_i, z_i), \qquad i = R, S, \tag{12}$$

where ϕ_i is the unemployment rate in region i, and z_i is a vector of other determinants of ω, spatial labour-market activity indicators now impinge on the wage-determining process where, of course, $\delta\omega_i/\delta\phi_i > 0$.

Notice here that pay in region R exerts an influence via the migration process. In the neoclassical bargaining framework, at least, spatial spillover appears to be rooted predominantly in market forces, reflecting actual or potential migration (and $\bar{w}_{UK}$).

Provided that $n_t > n_{t-1}(1-\delta_1)$, local union utility is given by

$$u_t = n_{t-1}(1-\delta_1)v_t + \alpha[n_t - n_{t-1}(1-\delta_1)]v_t + \alpha(l-n_t)\{(1-\lambda)v_S + \lambda[\gamma v_R^2 + (1-\gamma)v_R^1]\}, \tag{13}$$

where

δ is the separation rate,

α is the weight attached to the utility of those not currently employed in the local union,

[5] For simplicity, benefits, prices, and tax rates are assumed to be the same in regions S and R.

λ is the proportion of those who are not employed within the union next period (but about whom the union is concerned), who migrate,

γ is the proportion of such migrants who find union employment in the other region.

The union 'fallback' level of utility is taken to be that attained if all workers leave the local union:

$$\bar{u}_t = \{n_{t-1}(1-\delta_1)+\alpha[l-n_{t-1}(1-\delta_1)]\}\{(1-\lambda)v_S+\lambda[\gamma v_R^2+(1-\gamma)v_R^1]\}\,, \tag{14}$$

and

$$u_t-\bar{u}_t = [(1-\alpha)(1-\delta)n_{t-1}+\alpha n_t]\langle v_t-\{(1-\lambda)v_S+\lambda[\gamma v_R^2+(1-\gamma)v_R^1]\}\rangle\,. \tag{15}$$

The wage bargain solves the problem

$$\text{maximise } G(w_t) = \beta\ln[U(\pi_t)-\bar{U}_t]+\ln(u_t-\bar{u}_t)\,, \tag{16}$$

where

$$\pi_t = p_tA_t\mathrm{h}[n^*(w_t)]-w_t(1+\tau_{1,t})n^*(w_t)\,, \qquad \bar{U}_t = U(\bar{\pi}_t)\,,$$

and $(u_t-\bar{u}_t)$ is given by equation (15).

The comparative static properties of the system are determined from the first-order condition associated with this problem and the implicit function theorem[(6)]. Table 1 summarises the main qualitative results. If, in the spirit of Nickell and Andrews (1983), λ and δ_1 are treated as parameters of the system, the results are as summarised in the first column of table 1. Consider, first, the impact of the determinants of outside utility (the arguments of v_S, v_R^1, and v_R^2) on the local pay bargain. Increases in $w_{S,t-1}$, $g_{S,t}$, and R_t and decreases in ω_S all improve outside opportunities and so increase union bargaining power and the bargained pay level. The same is true of changes in outside opportunities in the other region, and a 'wage-spillover' effect operating through migration is now apparent. Notice, however, that a labour-market activity rate 'spillover' should also be apparent through ω_R in the present model. The effects of the remaining variables are as given by Nickell and Andrews (1983). An increase in the baseline wage has an ambiguous impact on the pay bargain. This arises through the greater negative influence exerted by an increase in the baseline wage on the utility of the unemployed relative to the employed. This effect acts to offset the otherwise positive influence of an increase in $\bar{w}_{\mathrm{UK}}$. An increase in the tax rate exerts both a 'wage-incentive effect' (through the reduced utility of gross wages) and an 'employment-incentive effect' (through the reduced marginal utility of an increment to real wages) (for example, see Oswald, 1982).

(6) Full details of the derivation are available from the authors on request.

An increase in employment in the last period and a decrease in the separation rate both act to increase the union's bargaining power and so exert a positive influence on the pay bargain. An increase in α, the weight attached to 'outsiders', reduces the pay bargain since it leads to greater emphasis on employment at the margin.

Next consider the employers' side of the model. Here relative producer prices and productivity have an ambiguous effect because of the indeterminacy of the impact of these disturbances on the union's marginal utility of the wage. If $\alpha = o$, both these variables would increase the pay bargain. An additional source of indeterminacy is present in the case of employment taxes, for here the negative impact on the bargained wage coming through the impact of the tax rate on the excess of firm utility over its fallback level tends to be offset by the effect of the tax rate on the firm's marginal utility of profits. Even if $\alpha = 0$ here, the impact of the tax rate is ambiguous.

It seems likely, however, that the separation rate, δ_1, and the migration proportion, λ, should be treated as endogenous variables of the model. If δ_1, for example, is postulated to be an increasing function of the utilities available elsewhere, and a decreasing function of utility within

Table 1. Comparative static properties of the regionally disaggregated version of the Nickell-Andrews model.

	Direction of impact on local pay bargain		
	λ, δ_1 parameters	λ, δ_1 endogenous variables[a]	
		general case	hysteresis and decline
$w_{S,t-1}$	+	?	−
$w_{R,t-1}$	+	?	−
$g_{S,t}$	+	?	−
$g_{R,t}$	+	?	−
R_t	+	?	−
$w^E_{R,t}$	+	?	−
ω_S	−	?	+
ω_R	−	?	+
$\bar{w}_{UK}$	?	?	?
τ_2	?	?	?
n_{t-1}	+		
δ	−		
α	−		
p_t	?		
A_t	?		
$\tau_{1,t}$	?		
π_t	−		

[a] see text for explanation.

the local union, we have

$$\delta_1 = \delta_1(v, v_S, v_R^1, v_R^2), \tag{17}$$

where all but the first of the partial derivatives are positive. In general, this extension of the model introduces considerable further ambiguities since

$$\frac{\delta w}{\delta v_i} = \left(\frac{\delta w}{\delta v_i}\right)_{\lambda,\, \delta\, =\, \text{constant}} + \frac{\delta w}{\delta \delta_1}\frac{\delta \delta_1}{\delta v_i}, \qquad i = R, S, \tag{18}$$

and since

$$\frac{\delta w}{\delta \delta_1} < 0\,; \qquad \frac{\delta \delta_1}{\delta v_i} > 0\,, \qquad i = R, S\,.$$

An increase in the lagged wage in region R, for example, now stimulates the separation rate from the union, reduces union bargaining power, and thus tends to offset the impact apparent when λ and δ_1 are considered to be parameters.

In extremis a predominant separation effect will be associated with 'hysteresis effects'. In such circumstances an increase in the lagged wage in region R will, net, reduce union bargaining power, depress the pay bargain, and further stimulate membership loss. Of course, proper analysis of such effects would require a study of a fully specified dynamic model which is beyond the scope of the present exercise. For the present we simply note the possibility of sign reversals in table 1.

However, it should be recognised that, for hysteresis effects to occur, the union must be in rapid decline. In a dynamic steady state which is associated with constant union membership, the 'separation effects' of any disturbances must be dominated by their 'direct impact' on union utility.

Of course, consideration of δ_1 as a variable does raise questions about the specification of the union utility function. In effect, membership becomes endogenous in the present model and should enter the utility function directly. This would provide a mechanism through which the union's wage bargain would anticipate, and perhaps offset, the δ_1 effect, with obvious consequences for the results reported in table 1. This 'separation-threat' effect represents a generalisation of the 'migration-threat' effect which has sometimes been referred to in the literature.

Although, strictly, the signs on the outside opportunity variables cannot be determined, we would not expect to find evidence of predominant separation and thus hysteresis effects, and indeed there is a presumption that the first column of table 1 is the most relevant.

The bargaining model suggests a general earnings function of the form

$$w_{St}^{\mathrm{E}} = \mathrm{f}(w_{S,t-1}, g_{S,t}, w_{R,t-1}, g_{R,t}, R_t, w_{R,t}^{\mathrm{E}},$$
$$\omega_{S,t}, \omega_{R,t}, \bar{w}_{\mathrm{UK}}, \tau_2, \tau_1, \alpha, p_t, \bar{\pi}_t)\,. \tag{19}$$

If we recall that ω_S and ω_R are functions of the unemployment rates in region S and R, respectively, and note that equation (19) may be reparameterised to yield the same dependent variable as equation (1), it is clear that equation (1) may be derived as a highly restrictive special case of equation (19).

Direct regional 'wage spillover' occurs in this model through the possibility of migration which renders real wages in the union ($w_{R,t}^{\mathrm{E}}$) and the nonunion sectors ($w_{R,t-1}, g_{R,t}$) in region R relevant to the local bargain. Further spillover effects are apparent from the nonunion sector in region S ($w_{S,t-1}, g_{S,t}$). If, at the aggregate level, all wages are, in effect, determined by union bargaining, $w_{R,t}^{\mathrm{E}}$ would reflect the only remaining wage-transmission mechanism. Notice, however, that this model implies that space impacts on the wage bargain through labour-market activity variables as well as through wage spillover, a feature to be contrasted with past work based on equation (1).

If migration were extremely costly, so that λ were approximately zero, (or if the union ignored the utility of migrants and the migration-threat effect) all the labour-market variables relating to region R would be eliminated from equation (19)(7). This model of wage determination would continue to accommodate other insular theories (such as an APC specific to region S) as special cases (since it would, in effect, be the Nickell-Andrews model), but would still allow a role for the nationally negotiated minimum wage rate ($\bar{w}_{\mathrm{UK}}$).

The opposite end of the spatial spectrum may be thought of as a situation in which the local union enjoys no autonomy whatsoever. In this case $w_{S,t}^{\mathrm{E}}$, as well as $\bar{w}_{\mathrm{UK}}$, might be considered to be determined at the national level and would (presumably) be equated to $w_{R,t}^{\mathrm{E}}$ (8). However, this case would amount to arbitrary imposition of a particular bargaining structure which is inconsistent with the present neoclassical formulation. The degree of local union autonomy is, however, likely to be circumscribed by a high degree of labour mobility. The greater the responsiveness of migration flows to utility differentials the greater the tendency towards the equalisation of 'net advantages'.

3.2 *Alternative views of the bargaining process*

What we have termed 'neoclassical' theories of the bargaining process have long been the subject of criticism which has been directed both at the assumed union utility function and at the supposed constraint. Of particular interest in the present context is the view that unions are motivated primarily by notions of 'comparability' (for example, Ross, 1948).

(7) Of course, noninsular commodity markets would imply that labour-market variables in region R could continue to exert an indirect impact on those in region S.

(8) We are assuming that the national union considers only the aggregate constraints it faces. A spatial dimension to the central union's utility function would restore an equation of the form (19).

Institutionalists would undoubtedly object to the notion that regional wage transmission occurs primarily through actual or potential migration, as in the bargaining model developed in the preceding section of the paper. Rather, in effect, interdependence of union utility functions would be emphasised, reflecting ideas of vertical and horizontal equity which are regarded as at least as applicable across space as across industries and occupations. The minimal modification of equation (19) which acceptance of this argument necessitates is recognition that the coefficient of $w_{R,t}^{E}$ will pick up any such comparability impact in addition to the migration influence, and provides a further reason for not expecting hysteresis effects of the type discussed above to be observed.

Separate identification of comparability and migration-induced wage transmission may be very difficult, but clearly the role of cross-location labour-market activity variables and the properties of empirical migration functions promise the possibility of some progress in this respect.

A common further criticism of the neoclassical approach would challenge the supposed importance of 'outsiders' in the wage-determining process. Usually rather more is at stake than setting $\alpha = 0$ in the preceding model, and the implication is that, at least in steady state, the level of unemployment (which impacts on outsiders) becomes irrelevant to the pay bargain determined entirely by 'insiders'. (For example, see Blanchard and Summers, 1987.) More fundamentally, institutionalists often deny the relevance of market forces in the bargaining process, emphasising comparability as an alternative, rather than additional, determinant of pay bargains[9]. In the empirical analysis which follows, we take the Cambridge variant of the 'real wage resistance hypothesis' as representative of more institutionally oriented approaches, although we modify it slightly to accommodate spatial comparability[10].

Figure 1 illustrates the relationships which exist between the various bargaining models. This figure also suggests a strategy for econometrically discriminating among the competing models. Thus starting from the most general model (in terms of parameters)—the generalised Nickell–Andrews model under intermediate spatial integration—the sets of parameter restrictions implied by the alternatives should be subjected to appropriate statistical testing. As noted earlier, however, data limitations preclude rigorous pursuit of this approach since the most general model has more parameters than there are time-series observations. Instead we attempt as far as possible to maintain the spirit of this approach in investigating the properties of the special cases which appear to be of interest from a theoretical perspective.

(9) The inverse real-wage–employment relation could be inapplicable, at least over a range, in the presence of, for example, monopsony, shock effects (perhaps induced through 'collective voice-institutional response'), nonmarket-clearing in the commodity market.

(10) Amongst other restrictions, this approach implies $\beta = 0$ in equation (2).

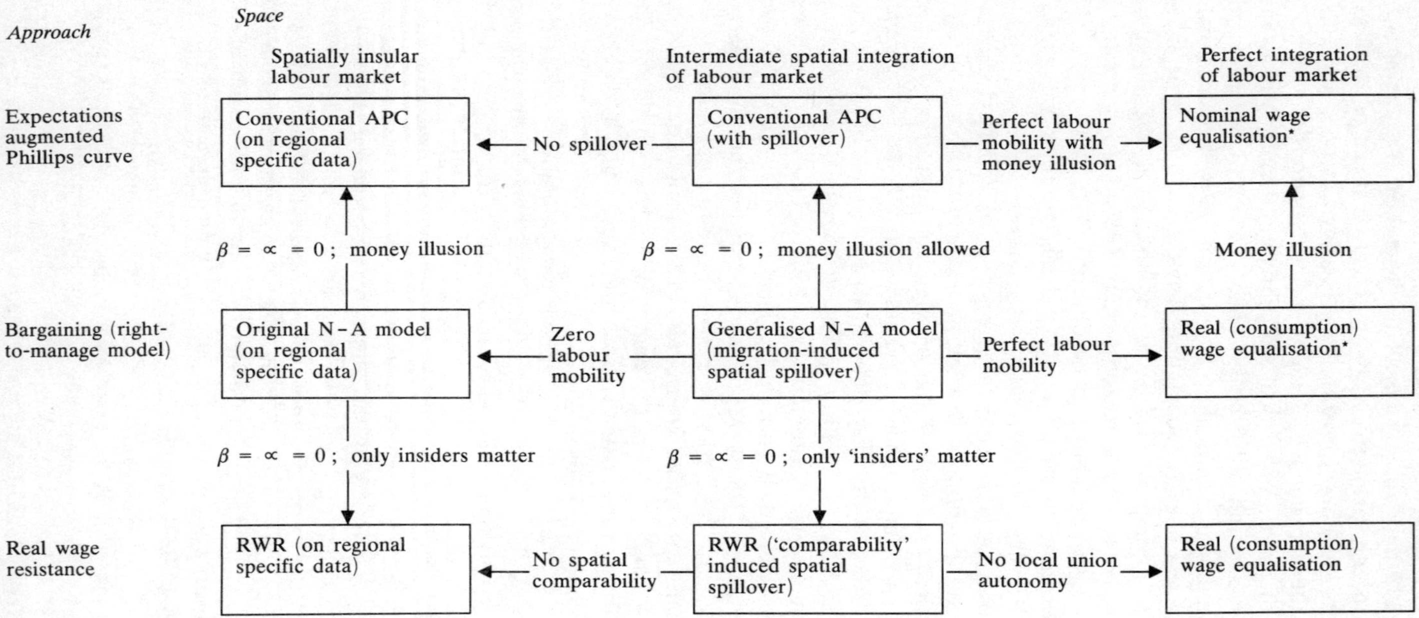

* In fact, perfect labour mobility ensures the equalisation of net advantages. Only if all nonwage advantages were equal would wage equalisation result.

Figure 1. Bargaining theories of regional earnings determination. (The abbreviations are APC augmented Phillips curve, N–A Nickell–Andrews, RWR real wage resistance.)

4 An exploratory econometric analysis

In this section we investigate two models of earnings determination which can be derived as special cases of a suitably reparameterised general Nickell–Andrews model. Variants of the two models are estimated using annual time-series data for Scotland and the United Kingdom from 1961 to 1983. First, each of these is briefly discussed and its relationship to the general model noted, by reference to figure 1. The econometric methodology is then discussed and the results considered. A fuller description of the data is contained in an appendix.

4.1 *The models*

4.1.1 *Real wage resistance models*

The first model we consider is a version of the real wage resistance hypothesis (RWR) which is amended to allow for the possibility of spatial spillover. Specifically, the model implemented is closely related to that used by Lawson (1981; 1982). The essential features are captured by the following expression.

$$\Delta \ln W_{S,t}^{\mathrm{net}} = \Delta \ln \tilde{W}_{S,t}^{\mathrm{net}} + \lambda_1 (\ln \tilde{W}_{S,t-1}^{\mathrm{net}} - \ln W_{S,t-1}^{\mathrm{net}}) + \boldsymbol{\theta}_t \,, \tag{20}$$

where

W_S^{net} is average real net (of tax) earnings in region S,

$\tilde{}$ denotes a target value,

λ_1 is a catch-up parameter,

$\boldsymbol{\theta}_t$ is a vector of variables which can lead to deviations of the level of real net earnings from the target value.

The equation reflects a bargaining model in which unions seek to impose their target real net hourly earnings on employers. In the long run, unions are taken to be successful in achieving their aims, but in the short run there is the possibility that earnings may deviate from the target growth path. In such circumstances there will be pressure for catch up in subsequent periods and the speed with which wages converge on the target growth path will depend on the size of the parameter λ_1. Short-run deviations from target can be interpreted as originating in encroachments on the union's ability to impose its desired wage and such factors may include changes in the level of unemployment. In the long run, of course, these influences disappear. The model is distinguished from the general Nickell–Andrews model in that none of the variables which determine firm utility impinge on the 'bargain' and unions take into account only those members who are currently employed and they ignore 'outsiders'.

This model can accommodate alternative views of the degree of spatial integration of regional labour markets via the determination of the union's target wage. First we consider the case of insular labour markets which is consistent with no 'spatial comparability' effect on earnings (see figure 1). Under such circumstances unions may be concerned to achieve a steady growth in real net earnings per hour (for example, see Lawson, 1982). Hence we can write

$$\ln \tilde{W}^{\text{net}}_{S,t} = \alpha_0 + \alpha_1 t \,, \tag{21}$$

where t is a time trend, and thus

$$\Delta \ln \tilde{W}^{\text{net}}_{S,t} = \alpha_1 \,. \tag{22}$$

Also, real net earnings can be written as

$$W^{\text{net}} = \frac{W(1-\tau_2)}{P_c} = \frac{W\rho}{P_c} \,, \tag{23}$$

where ρ is the retention ratio. Substitution of equations (21)-(23) in equation (20) and reparameterising on nominal earnings change gives

$$\Delta \ln W_{S,t} = \mu_0 + \mu_1 t + \mu_2 \Delta \ln \left(\frac{P_c}{\rho} \right)_t + \mu_3 \ln W^{\text{net}}_{S,t-1} + \boldsymbol{\theta}_t \,, \tag{24}$$

where

$$\mu_0 = (1-\lambda_1)\alpha_1 + \lambda_1 \alpha_0 \,, \qquad \mu_1 = \lambda_1 \alpha_1 \,, \qquad \mu_2 = 1 \,, \qquad \mu_3 = -\lambda_1 \,.$$

The second case allows a degree of spatial integration and hence for the possibility of 'comparability' induced spatial spillover. This implies a specification of the union's (in region S) target earnings as a function of target earnings elsewhere, which are taken to be equal to actual earnings elsewhere for simplicity:

$$\ln \tilde{W}^{\text{net}}_{S,t} = \beta_0 + \beta_1 \ln W^{\text{net}}_{R,t-k} \,, \tag{25}$$

and hence

$$\Delta \ln \tilde{W}^{\text{net}}_{S,t} = \beta_1 \Delta \ln W^{\text{net}}_{R,t-k} \,. \tag{26}$$

As before, we can derive a nominal earnings-change equation and this now takes the form

$$\Delta \ln W_{S,t} = \gamma_0 + \gamma_1 \Delta \ln \left(\frac{P_c}{\rho} \right)_t + \gamma_2 \Delta \ln W^{\text{net}}_{R,t-k} + \gamma_3 \ln W^{\text{net}}_{R,t-k-1} + \gamma_4 \ln W^{\text{net}}_{S,t-1} + \boldsymbol{\theta}_t \,, \tag{27}$$

where

$$\gamma_0 = \beta_0 \lambda_1 \,, \qquad \gamma_1 = 1 \,, \qquad \gamma_2 = \beta_1 \,, \qquad \gamma_3 = \lambda \beta_1 \,, \qquad \gamma_4 = -\lambda_1 \,.$$

The form of the coefficients suggest that we should expect

$$\gamma_3 + \gamma_4 \gamma_2 = 0 \,, \qquad \gamma_1 - 1 = 0 \,.$$

The form of equation (25) is such that the long-run equilibrium may be consistent with persistent regional wage differentials. However, it also nests as a special case the situation when long-run regional wage equalisation occurs. This arises when $\beta_0 = 0$, and $\beta_1 = 1$, yielding:

$$\Delta \ln W_{S,t} = \gamma_1 \Delta \ln \left(\frac{P_R}{\rho} \right)_t + \gamma_2 \Delta \ln W_{R,t-k}^{\text{net}} + \gamma_3 \ln W_{R,t-k-1}^{\text{net}} + \gamma_4 \ln W_{S,t-1}^{\text{net}} + \boldsymbol{\theta}_t , \qquad (28)$$

where we now expect

$$\gamma_1 = 1 , \qquad \gamma_2 = 1 , \qquad \gamma_3 + \gamma_4 = 0 .$$

The final case under this category is that of perfect integration of regional labour markets. In these circumstances there is no local union autonomy and the wage bargain struck at the national level is handed down to the regions. In conditions of uniform consumers' prices and employee taxes, this implies a wage-change equation of the form

$$\Delta \ln W_{S,t} = \alpha_0 + \alpha_1 \Delta \ln W_{R,t} , \qquad (29)$$

where in addition we expect

$$\alpha_0 = 0 , \qquad \alpha_1 = 1 .$$

4.1.2 *Expectations-augmented Phillips curve models* The second class of model is a variant of the familiar expectations-augmented Phillips curve wherein different views of the degree of spatial integration of regional labour markets can be accommodated. The specific form of the model chosen to represent the case of intermediate integration can be shown to nest the alternatives of complete integration or complete insularity.

This model, which allows both for regional specific effects and for spillover influences, is similar to that shown in equation (1) where the log of unemployment in the region is taken to proxy for excess demand, that is,

$$\Delta \ln W_{S,t} = \alpha_0 + \alpha_1 \Delta \ln P_c^e + \alpha_2 \ln U_{S,t} + \alpha_3 \Delta \ln W_{R,t-k} . \qquad (30)$$

If $0 < \alpha_1 < 1$, and $\alpha_2 < 0$, then the model is consistent with the conventional Phillips curve and the presence-of-money illusion, whereas $\alpha_1 = 1$, and $\alpha_2 < 0$ implies the natural rate hypothesis.

Again, a major distinction between this model and the general Nickell-Andrews model is the absence of variables which influence firm utility. However, in this model, 'outsiders' are allowed to influence wage determination via the excess demand term.

This model reduces to the insular labour-markets view when $\alpha_3 = 0$, that is, when there is an absence of wage spillover and only region-specific excess demand and price expectations influence nominal wage change. Alternatively, when $\alpha_1 = \alpha_2 = 0$ the model collapses to the perfectly integrated case wherein no regional specific influences impinge on the wage-determination mechanism.

4.2 *Empirical investigation*

Throughout our empirical investigation we seek to avoid drawing invalid inferences from the results, by assessing the performance of each model according to a number of criteria. First, an estimated model is checked for consistency with the underlying theory by reference to the sign, size, and significance of estimated coefficients. In addition, the estimated model should be consistent with expected parameter restrictions. Failure to achieve consistency with basic theory is taken to imply model inadequacy. A second requirement is that an estimated model should exhibit no evidence of misspecification. Hendry and Mizon (1978) and Hendry (1980) provide strong reasons to suggest that evidence of serial correlation, parameter instability, and forecast inaccuracy can be interpreted as indicating misspecification, and we employ a number of tests designed to evaluate the adequacy of models in those respects.

The recognition that each of our models can be thought of as a single equation from a more general structural model implies the possibility of simultaneous equation bias arising if ordinary least squares estimation is used. We therefore use instrumental variable estimation, and the tests for misspecification and for the validity of parameter restrictions, are consistent with this procedure. The tests are as follows:

(1) The validity of parameter restrictions are tested using the appropriate Wald statistic, this being asymptotically distributed as $\chi^2(n)$ under the null hypothesis that the n restrictions are valid.

(2) Parameter stability (and forecast accuracy) is assessed by means of two tests. The first is that reported by Davidson et al (1978). The models are estimated over the period 1964 to 1981 and used to generate forecasts for 1982 and 1983. The test statistic, DH(2), is based on the sum of the squared forecast errors divided by the standard error of the equation and is asymptotically distributed as $\chi^2(2)$ under the null of parameter stability. We also use a version of the Chow test which is taken to be an $F(2, 18-k)$ under the null hypothesis of parameter stability, where k is the number of explanatory variables in the model.

(3) The presence or otherwise of residual autocorrelation is assessed using a test of the joint significance of the first p residual autocorrelations as proposed by Sargan (1976). We test the cases where $p = 1$, or $p = 1, 2$ and these are reported as S(1) and S(2), respectively. These test statistics are asymptotically distributed as $\chi^2(p)$ under the null hypothesis that the p autocorrelation coefficients are zero.

(4) In addition, we use Sargan's test for the validity of the instruments (Sargan, 1964) and again failure on this test is taken as evidence of misspecification. The test statistic, reported as $I(l)$ is asymptotically distributed as $\chi^2(l)$ under the null of valid instruments where l is the excess of instruments over explanatory variables.

Last, goodness of fit is measured using the simple squared correlation between the actual and fitted values (r^2)[(11)].

4.2.1 *Results* Table 2 contains the results for three variants of the RWR model shown above as equations (24), (27), and (28). For simplicity, data for the United Kingdom as a whole have been used to represent the 'other' region (R) and coefficients should be interpreted in this light. Column 1 lists the results for the case of insular labour markets where the instruments used were a constant, a time trend, $\Delta\ln(P_c/\rho)_{t-i}$, $\Delta\ln U_{t-i}(i = 1, 2)$, and $\ln W^{\text{net}}_{S,t-1}$.

The current change in the log of Scottish unemployment replaces $\boldsymbol{\theta}_t$ but does not appear to exert a significant influence on wage change. Similarly, the time trend is insignificant and so raises doubts about the adequacy of the associated specification for the target wage. Therefore, we conclude this to be an inadequate model.

Next we turn to the intermediate labour-market integration models. In column 2 we list the results for the case where real wage differentials can persist in the long run. The instruments used were a constant,

$$\Delta\ln(P_c/\rho)_{t-i}(i = 1, 2)\,,\ \Delta\ln W^{\text{net}}_{R,t-1}\,,\ \ln W^{\text{net}}_{R,t-1}\,,\ \text{and}\ \ln W^{\text{net}}_{S,t-1}\,.$$

Table 2. Results for real wage resistance models.

Variable[a]	Model[b]		
	1	2	3
Constant	−1.078 (1.420)	−0.283 (0.349)	
Time trend	0.004 (0.006)		
$\Delta\ln(P_c/\rho)_t$	1.118* (0.456)	1.285* (0.183)	1.136* (0.089)
$\Delta\ln W^{\text{net}}_{R,t}$		0.846* (0.217)	0.773* (0.179)
$\ln W^{\text{net}}_{R,t-1}$		0.381 (0.283)	0.530* (0.166)
$\ln W^{\text{net}}_{S,t-1}$	−0.256 (0.323)	−0.443* (0.227)	−0.526* (0.164)
$\Delta\ln U_{S,t}$	−0.053 (0.063)		
r^2	0.778	0.975	0.980
S(1)	0.85	0.44	1.84
S(2)	1.39	1.21	2.20
DH	0.31	4.62	1.66
Chow	0.14	0.86	0.67
I(l)	4.39 (l = 2)	0.86 (l = 1)	3.00 (l = 1)

[a] Dependent variable is $\Delta\ln W_{S,t}$.
[b] Figures in parentheses are asymptotic standard errors and * indicates a significant variable at the 5% level.

(11) All the diagnostics were calculated using TSP (Time Series Processor, TSP International, Stanford, CA; although checks for consistency were conducted on GIVE, General Instrumental Variable Estimation, London School of Economics, where appropriate). Our use of instrumental variable estimation accounts for the chosen measure of goodness of fit.

Given the use of annual data, we thought it reasonable to express the target in terms of current wages elsewhere (that is, $k = 0$). The possibility of simultaneity bias [via mechanisms such as those outlined by Hart (1981)] should be removed by the method of estimation used. We only report the case where $\Delta \ln U_{S,t}$ is excluded, as when included the results again suggested that it had no significant effect on wage change.

There is no evidence of misspecification and the model exhibits a reasonably good fit. We also investigated the validity of the expected parameter constraints that $\gamma_3 + \gamma_4 \gamma_2 = 0$, and $\gamma_1 - 1 = 0$ (see above), and these were found to be acceptable at the 5% level (the Wald test of the joint validity of those restrictions giving a statistic of 5.92). Although all the parameters have the expected sign, both the constant and lagged real net wages for the United Kingdom are insignificant and this is again taken to imply model inadequacy. In column 3 the results for the model where long-run wage equalisation occurs are listed (again we only report the model which excludes $\Delta \ln U_{S,t}$). In this case the instruments used were $\Delta \ln(P_c/\rho)_{t-i} (i = 1, 2)$, $\Delta \ln W_{R,t-1}^{\text{net}}$, $\ln W_{R,t-1}^{\text{net}}$, and $\ln W_{S,t-1}^{\text{net}}$. The model exhibits no evidence of misspecification, fits the data well, and has correctly signed and significant parameters. One qualification is that a test of the joint validity of the implied parameter restrictions that $\gamma_1 - 1 = 0$, $\gamma_2 - 1 = 0$, and $\gamma_3 + \gamma_4 = 0$ marginally fails at the 5% level [$\chi^2(3) = 9.05$, and $\chi^2(3)$ critical value at 5% of 7.82]. Overall then, it would appear that amongst the RWR models, those which allow for some degree of labour-market integration give better results and in particular, the model in which long-run wage equalisation is imposed holds out most promise for future investigation.

The results for the expectations-augmented Phillips curve were as follows:

$$\Delta \ln W_{S,t} = \underset{(0.020)}{0.0043^{\star}} - \underset{(0.163)}{0.065} \Delta \ln P_{c,t} - \underset{(0.013)}{0.015} \Delta \ln U_{S,t} + \underset{(0.172)}{1.245^{\star}} \Delta \ln W_{R,t},$$

$$r^2 = 0.975, \quad S(1) = 0.08, \quad S(2) = 1.90 \qquad (31)$$

$$DH = 3.00, \quad Chow = 0.49, \quad I(2) = 3.53.$$

Expected price change was proxied by actual price change in the current period and the instruments used were $\Delta \ln P_{c,t-i}$, $\ln U_{S,t-i} (i = 1, 2)$, and $\Delta \ln W_{R,t-1}$. This model performs satisfactorily on the basis of the misspecification tests and exhibits a reasonably high degree of fit. However, the sign of the coefficient on the price term is opposite to that conventionally expected, but is insignificant at the 5% level, as is the unemployment term. Although multicollinearity between prices and UK wages may partly explain the performance of prices, a limited search over alternative specifications failed to produce a model in this category which was data consistent and theory consistent.

As noted above, this model nests as special cases both the insular and completely integrated labour-market views. The implied restrictions were tested and, not surprisingly, those required to yield the first view were easily rejected [$\chi^2(1) = 57.0$] whereas those required for the second were accepted [$\chi^2(2) = 2.57$]. This prompted estimation of the model which is consistent with complete integration in the case of the three approaches (given price equalisation) to wage determination shown in figure 1 and the results were as follows:

$$\Delta \ln W_{S,t} = \underset{(0.015)}{-0.016} + \underset{(0.120)}{1.68^*} \Delta \ln W_{R,t} ,$$

$$r^2 = 0.974 , \quad S(1) = 1.75 , \quad S(2) = 1.91 \qquad (32)$$

$$DH = 0.25 , \quad \text{Chow} = 0.12 , \quad I(2) = 5.72 ,$$

where the instruments used were a constant, $\Delta \ln P_{c,t-i} (i = 1, 2)$, and $\Delta \ln W_{S,t-1}$. As can be seen, the diagnostics are satisfactory, with no evidence of misspecification, and the model also fits the data reasonably well. Moreover, we are unable to reject the hypothesis $\alpha_0 = 0$, and $\alpha_1 = 1$ (see above). As noted in passing above, the implications of this model are that no regional specific wage-determination mechanism operates in Scotland. Rather, the rate of growth of nominal wages is handed down from the nation and the model is consistent with either a uniform nominal price of labour, or when prices and employee taxes are constant across space, it is consistent with real wage equalisation. However, the model offers no insight into the wage determination mechanism at the national level.

5 Conclusions

In this paper we have extended recent bargaining theories of earnings determination to accommodate the regional dimension, with a view to clarifying the importance of space and market forces in the pay-determining process. Neoclassical variants of these models, which were shown to accommodate the conventional approach based on spatially disaggregated expectations-augmented Phillips curve as a special case, in general imply regional earnings 'spillover', but this arises primarily through actual and potential labour mobility. Further, the neoclassical approach also incorporates other elements of spatial interaction, which again operate through market mechanisms. More institutionally oriented theories of bargaining also generate spatial earnings spillover, but this occurs directly through a spatial comparability effect, and, of course, the role of market forces is emphasised less in this context.

An exploratory econometric analysis using Scottish time-series data was developed, but the sample size precluded estimation of all but a number of special cases, including that which has formed the basis of past work. Within this admittedly restrictive context the evidence strongly rejected the notion of spatial segmentation in regional earnings determination, but did not allow rejection of the extreme alternative of perfect spatial integration. No evidence of a role for market forces was obtained, and the special case which performed best, in terms of theory and data consistency, was a variant of the real-wage-resistance hypothesis in which target net real earnings in Scotland are determined by those in the rest of the United Kingdom. This tentative evidence in favour of 'institutional' theories of regional earnings determination is reinforced by consideration of the size of the estimated earnings-spillover coefficients. If the selectivity of the migration process is taken into account, even the evidence of labour mobility most sympathetic to the neoclassical perspective (Harrigan et al, 1986) is difficult to reconcile with the unit spillover coefficient. Naturally, however, the limitations of the present econometric analysis militate against emphatic conclusions, and further research into the role of space and market forces in regional earnings determination is clearly called for.

Acknowledgement. The Fraser of Allander Institute staff acknowledge the financial support of the ESRC.

References

Blackaby D H, Manning D N, 1987, "Regional earnings revisited" *Manchester School of Social and Economic Studies* (forthcoming)

Blanchard O J, Summers L H, 1987, "Hysteresis and the European unemployment problem", in *Unemployment, Hysteresis and the Natural Rate Hypothesis* Ed. R Cross (Basil Blackwell, Oxford) forthcoming

Brechling F P R, 1973, "Wage inflation and the structure of regional unemployment" *Journal of Money, Credit and Banking* **5** 335-379

Burton J, Addison J T, 1977, "The institutionalist analysis of wage inflation: a critical appraisal" *Research in Labour Economics* **1** 333-376

Cowling K, Metcalf D, 1967, "Wage-unemployment relations: a regional analysis for the UK, 1960-1965" *Bulletin of the Oxford University Institute of Economics and Statistics* **29** 31-39

Davidson J E H, Hendry D F, Srba F, Yeo S, 1978, "Econometric modelling of the aggregate time-series relationship between consumers' expenditure and income in the United Kingdom" *Economic Journal* **88** 661-692

Harrigan F J, Jenkins I, McGregor P G, 1986, "A behavioural model of migration: an evaluation of neoclassical and Keynesian alternatives" DP-42, Fraser of Allander Institute, University of Strathclyde, Glasgow

Harrigan F J, McGregor P G, 1987, "Price and quantity interaction in a regional economic modelling framework" DP-43, Fraser of Allander Institute, University of Strathclyde, Glasgow

Hart R A, 1981, "Regional wage-change transmission and the structure of regional wages and unemployment", in *Regional Wage Inflation and Unemployment* Ed. R L Martin (Pion, London) pp 17-45

Hart R A, MacKay D I, 1977, "Wage inflation, regional policy and the regional earnings structure" *Economica* **44** 267-281

Hendry D F, 1980, "Predictive failure and econometric modelling in macroeconomics: the transactions demand for money", in *Economic Modelling* Ed. P Ormerod (Heineman Education Books, London) pp 217-242

Hendry D F, Mizon G E, 1978, "Serial correlation as a convenient simplification, not a nuisance: a comment on a study of the demand for money by the Bank of England" *Economic Journal* **88** 549-563

Jackman R, Layard R, 1981, "Trade unions, the NAIRU and a wage inflation tax" DP-100, Centre for Labour Economics, London School of Economics, London

Lawson T, 1981, "Incomes policy and the real wage resistance hypothesis: econometric evidence for the UK, 1955-1979" mimeograph, Growth Project, Department of Applied Economics, University of Cambridge, Cambridge

Lawson T, 1982, "On the stability of the inter-industry structure of earnings in the UK: 1954-1978" *Cambridge Journal of Economics* **6** 249-266

Layard R, Nickell S, 1985, "The causes of British unemployment" *National Institute Economic Review* **111** 62-85

Layard R, Nickell S, 1986, "Unemployment in Britain" *Economica* supplement 53, pp S121-S169

Leontief W, 1946, "The pure theory of the guaranteed annual wage contract" *Journal of Political Economy* 76-79

McDonald R M, Solow R W, 1981, "Wage bargaining and employment" *American Economic Review* **71** 896-908

Martin R L, 1981, "Wage-change interdependence amongst regional labour markets: conceptual issues and some empirical evidence for the United States", in *Regional Wage Inflation and Unemployment* Ed. R L Martin (Pion, London) pp 96-135

Metcalf D, 1971, "The determinants of earnings changes: a regional analysis for the UK, 1960-1968" *International Economic Review* **12** 273-282

Newell A, Symons J S V, 1985, "Wages and employment in the OECD countries" DP-219, Centre for Labour Economics, London School of Economics, London

Newell A, Symons J S V, 1986, "The Phillips curve is a real wage equation" DP-246, Centre for Labour Economics, London School of Economics, London

Nickell S J, 1982, "A bargaining model of the Phillips curve" DP-130, Centre for Labour Economics, London School of Economics, London

Nickell S J, Andrews M, 1983, "Unions, real wages and employment in Britain 1951-79" *Oxford Economic Papers* **35** 183-206

Oswald A J, 1982, "The microeconomic theory of the trade union" *Economic Journal* **92** 576-595

Ross A, 1948 *Trade Union Wage Policy* (University of California Press, Berkeley, CA)

Sargan J D, 1964, "Wages and prices in the United Kingdom: a study in econometric methodology", in *Econometric Analysis for National Economic Planning* Eds P E Hart, G Mills, J K Whitaker (Butterworth, Sevenoaks, Kent) pp 25-54

Sargan J D, 1976, "Testing for misspecification after estimating using instrumental variables" mimeograph, Department of Economics, London School of Economics, London

Thirlwall A P, 1970, "Regional Phillips curves" *Bulletin of the Oxford University Institute of Economics and Statistics* **32** 19-32

Thomas R L, Stoney P J M, 1971, "Unemployment dispersion as a determinant of wage inflation in the UK, 1925-66" *Manchester School of Social and Economic Studies* **39** 83-116

APPENDIX

Data sources

W_S, W_R Average hourly earnings of male manual workers, all industries, from the October Survey for Scotland and the United Kingdom. Source: *Employment Gazette* (various), Department of Employment (HMSO, London)

P_c Consumers expenditure deflater. Source: National Income and Accounts (various) (HMSO, London).

ρ $(1 - \tau_2)$ where τ_2 is employee income taxes. Source: Series for employee income tax reported by Layard and Nickell (1986).

ϕ_S Total Scottish unemployment rate (%). Source: *Employment Gazette* (various), Department of Employment (HMSO, London).

The Structural Element in Regional Unemployment

I R GORDON
University of Kent at Canterbury

1 Introduction

A decade ago various commentators were arguing that the traditional conception of a 'regional problem' in Britain, with north and south differentiated clearly in terms of employment opportunities, had become obsolete in the face of widening intraregional disparities and the emergence of an 'inner-city problem'. Even at the time the evidence for a real economic, rather than political, shift was rather tenuous. In the mid-1980s, however, with the interregional unemployment gap at its widest since the war, the north-south divide seems as real as ever, and the only real change is that the West Midlands has switched sides. The immediate causes of the widening of the differential in unemployment rates are fairly clear; on the one hand, general recession has led to a predictable reduction in labour mobility between regions, with the south 'exporting' a substantial part of its expected increase in unemployment to the traditional regions of emigration; on the other hand, employment trends over the past decade have become conspicuously less favourable in the north, and in the West Midlands; industries and branch plants in both regions have borne the brunt of recession. However, since (apart from the Midlands) the bounds of the depressed regions of the 1980s are so similar to those of the 1930s, it is timely to ask whether this reopening of the north-south gap is a temporary phenomenon, and what it would take to reverse it. An approach to that question is to ask why, despite very large volumes of emigration and fifteen years or so of active regional policy, the depressed regions of the 1930s continued to experience above average unemployment right up to the current depression.

One answer to that question starts from the observation that there have been continuing divergences in employment trends over this period and a persistent tendency to demand-deficiency in the north. The thesis of this paper, however, is that much of the differential in the incidence of unemployment as between north and south is, or has become, structural in character, with implications for the feasibility of various solutions to the problem, although it may not be 'structural' in the sense used by regional analysts since Thirlwall (1969) and Cheshire (1973). An attempt to redefine what may be identified as 'structural' unemployment flies in the face of Machlup's (1958) severe warnings about the misuse of these 'weasel words'. More recently, Standing (1983) has pointed to the confusion caused by the proliferation of, on his count seven, different uses of the concept of 'structural unemployment'. However, provided that alternative meanings are clearly distinguished, it is appropriate to consider whether a conventional category such as this is being applied in a way which is adequate to those real processes which can be identified.

In this paper, I shall be concerned with three basic ideas about the character of structural unemployment, particularly at the regional level, and the relationship between them. The first of these ideas relates structural unemployment to the phenomenon of structural change in *employment*, whether this is seen narrowly in terms of the 'structural component' of the standard shift-share analysis (that is, the question of how favourable or unfavourable the industrial composition of employment is for *net* change) or more broadly in terms of restructuring processes (which may give rise to higher levels of gross change in industrial employment). The second interpretation relates more narrowly to the degree to which at a point in time there exists a *mismatch* between the composition (or structure) of demands for and supplies of labour, as distinct from a quantitative gap between demand and supply. In a third view structural unemployment is seen essentially as an outcome of *labour-market* processes in situations of limited information, and the effects of particular hiring and firing practices on the chanelling of groups of workers into or away from unemployment. Very broadly, the orthodox view among British regional economists has been that structural unemployment should be defined in terms of occupational or industrial mismatch, with an implicit explanation in terms of employment change, on which basis it has appeared relatively unimportant. Equally broadly, the contention of this paper is that, although the phenomenon may be manifested in various sorts of mismatch, it needs to be explained in relation to labour-market processes, and that in these terms it is a more substantial element in the regional unemployment problem.

2 Two approaches to the measurement of structural unemployment

The basic Keynesian classification of types of unemployment—into demand-deficient, structural, and frictional elements—essentially involves a prognosis as to how far aggregate unemployment would respond to various forms of change, particularly policy interventions on the demand side or supply side of the labour market. In practice, however, attempts to quantify these elements have tended to adopt a more static perspective, focusing on the discrepancy between the stocks of vacancies and of unemployed, first in the aggregate and then for particular occupational or spatial subgroups. The rationale for this snapshot approach appears to be an attempt at measurement independent of theory. However, three recognised problems with implementations of this approach all imply the need for a rather more explicit modelling of labour-market processes as a basis for measurement of the three components of unemployment. These problems are the need to identify a point of labour-market equilibrium, or zero demand-deficiency, as a baseline;

the nonindependence of these components; and the fact that all labour submarkets, whether occupational or spatial, are to some degree open. The standard solution to this set of problems (see Cheshire, 1973; Dixon and Thirlwall, 1975; Armstrong and Taylor, 1981) is to define equilibrium as a situation in which the numbers of unemployed and of vacancies are equal; to measure the structural and frictional components at a point of zero demand-deficiency, using either an actual observation, if available, or an extrapolation of regression relationships, if outside past experience; and to treat a somewhat arbitrary set of occupational and/or spatial groupings as if they were closed labour markets. These essentially heuristic responses have the virtue of consistency in the results which they yield, and offer what is probably the most satisfactory implementation of the 'snapshot' approach, avoiding the uncertainties of a more explicit consideration of labour-market processes. In making pragmatic use of unemployment–vacancy relationships to identify the point of zero demand-deficiency, however, some of these causal issues are indirectly raised.

Rationalisation of the unemployment–vacancy relationship requires a model of the relationship between these *stock* variables and labour-market flows. The simplest such model (deriving from Holt, 1970) posits a homogeneous type of labour and an integrated labour market with a random matching between unemployed individuals and job vacancies such that the rate of hirings in any short period is proportional to the stock of each:

$$h = \alpha uv, \tag{1}$$

where
h is the rate of hirings as a proportion of the labour force,
u is the unemployment rate,
v is the vacancy rate.
The coefficient α ($\alpha > 0$) is in this context a direct measure of the efficiency of the matching process. The rate of quits from employment, voluntary and involuntary, is assumed either to be constant or to vary (probably negatively) with the unemployment rate alone:

$$q = \beta - \gamma u, \tag{2}$$

where q is the rate of quits as a proportion of the labour force.
In a short-term equilibrium the level of unemployment and the level of vacancies will each be stable, provided the rates of quits and hirings are equal: in this case the unemployment and vacancy rates are related by

$$u = \frac{\beta}{\alpha v + \gamma}. \tag{3}$$

With a homogeneous labour force there could be no structural unemployment but, if zero demand-deficiency is identified with the point at which $u = v$, the level of frictional employment, u_F, would be given by

$$u_F = \frac{-\gamma + (\gamma^2 + 4\alpha\beta)^{1/2}}{2\alpha} . \qquad (4)$$

In this model, however, the overall level of unemployment is more naturally factored into multiplicative rather than additive components: at their simplest these comprise a pressure-of-demand factor, based on the *ratio* of unemployment rate to vacancy rate, and a frictional factor (which would also include any structural unemployment), based on the *product* of the unemployment and vacancy rates. The observed unemployment rate is the geometric mean of these two orthogonal factors:

$$u = \left(\frac{u}{v}\right)^{1/2} (uv)^{1/2} . \qquad (5)$$

If, as Holt (1970) assumes, the rate of quits were effectively independent of the level of unemployment (that is, $\gamma = 0$), the product term also would be independent of the unemployment and vacancy rates, defining a specific $u - v$ curve:

$$uv = \frac{\beta}{\alpha} . \qquad (6)$$

The ratio term, on the other hand, simply identifies the position on such a curve, taking the value of 1 at the point which is conventionally identified as zero demand-deficiency and expressing the actual level of unemployment as a ratio of that benchmark.

Holt (1970) introduces the possibility of structural unemployment by positing a number of discrete classes of labour with no possibility of movement or substitution between them, once workers and vacancies have been allocated across the occupational classes. In this case, the basic model may be applied separately to each class to determine the level of demand-deficient plus frictional unemployment in each. Since the $u - v$ curve is convex, however, the aggregate unemployment and vacancy rates obtained by averaging those in the occupational classes will necessarily be *above* the $u - v$ curve for the classes, to an extent reflecting the variance in their unemployment and vacancy rates. The distance from this curve, measured on the unemployment axis, provides an alternative measure of structural unemployment.

The aggregate rate of hirings in such a segmented market is reduced both by the compartmentalisation of submarkets and by imbalances in the distribution of unemployment and vacancies:

$$h = \alpha cmuv , \qquad (7)$$

where

c is an index of compartmentalism, $0 > c \geqslant 1$,

m is an index of occupational mismatch, $0 > m \geqslant 1$.

The product of these two indices, representing the expected rate of hirings relative to that in a homogeneous market, may be simply calculated from

$$cm = \sum_{o} \hat{u}_o \hat{v}_o \,, \tag{8}$$

where $\hat{u}_o$, $\hat{v}_o$ are, the proportion of total unemployment and total vacancies, respectively, in occupational class o.

Nickell (1982) and Jackman and Roper (1985) show that the mismatch index on its own may be approximated by

$$m = \sum_{o} (\hat{u}_o \hat{v}_o)^{1/2} \,. \tag{9}$$

This index represents the minimum level of unemployment (as a proportion of the actual) consistent with the maintenance of the existing rate of hirings in each occupational class. From it may be derived a proportional measure of structural unemployment, $1/(m-1)$, which should be independent of the level of demand-deficient unemployment, in contrast to the 'snapshot method' under which the two are negatively related.

At the point of zero demand-deficiency, to which 'snapshot' estimates of the level of structural unemployment relate, the Holt model will always produce much lower estimates of the numbers involved. The reason is that, in the Holt model, unemployment and vacancies are expected to vary in inverse proportion to each other within any submarket so as to maintain a constant rate of hirings, whereas in the 'snapshot' method they are assumed to be independent of each other. If the Holt assumptions are correct, transferring the unemployed from demand-deficient occupations to fill vacancies in excess-demand occupations would produce a situation of zero demand-deficiency in both much sooner than implied by the 'snapshot' method (see example in table 1). At the least the Holt model exposes the fallacy in the static approach of treating the stock of vacancies simply as a measure of the demand for labour rather than as a joint outcome, with the stock of unemployed,

Table 1. Illustration of two alternative estimates of structural unemployment.

Occupation	Original situation		After elimination of structural unemployment			
	unempl.	vacancies	snapshot version		Holt version	
			unempl.	vacancies	unempl.	vacancies
A	20	40	20	20	28	28
B	30	40	30	30	35	35
C	50	20	20	20	32	32
Total	100	100	70	70	95	95

of the matching process within particular labour markets. On this count, the 'Holt' estimates must be seen as more realistic indicators of structural imbalance.

If the Holt model is to be applied to an *open* labour market such as a region, however, some modifications are required. In particular, the hiring and quit functions need to be redefined to relate to the proportion of recruits and quitters who come from (in the first case) or go to (in the second) that particular labour market. In both cases it is reasonable to assume that this proportion depends, in the same way, on the relative sizes and accessibility of the labour markets within and outside the region concerned—or its internal and external 'labour potential'. But the proportion of vacancies filled by candidates from within the region would also depend on the relative unemployment rate in the external catchment area and on the relative attractiveness to employers of the two sources of labour supply. The internal hiring and quit functions for an unsegmented market may then be written as

$$h_{ii} = \alpha u_i v_i \frac{\Pi_{ii}}{\Pi_{ii} + \Pi_{ie}} f_i \left(\frac{u_i}{u_e}, \frac{l_i}{l_e} \right), \tag{10}$$

where the subscripts i and e denote the internal and external labour areas, and

Π_{ie} is the labour 'potential' of area e for area i,
l is an index of perceived labour 'quality',
f is an increasing function, and

$$q_{ii} = \beta \frac{\Pi_{ii}}{\Pi_{ii} + \Pi_{ie}} . \tag{11}$$

The elasticity of the hiring rate with respect to relative unemployment and relative labour quality should vary with the openness of the labour market, tending to increase up to the point at which internal and external potential are equal. The conditions for stability in the vacancy and unemployment rates are now, first, equality in the internal hiring and quit rates and, second, equality between the rate of net labour migration, and employment growth less natural change in labour supply (see Burridge and Gordon, 1979). The first condition on its own yields the $u-v$ relationship

$$v_i = \frac{\beta}{\alpha u_i} f_i \left(\frac{u_e}{u_i}, \frac{l_e}{l_i} \right) . \tag{12}$$

In this case, the vacancy rate depends not only on the internal unemployment rate, but also on that in the hinterland: hence the demand-deficient element of unemployment cannot be computed for any region without reference to the level of unemployment obtaining in the other regions with which it exchanges migrants. This open-market version of the Holt model thus offers a rationalisation for the empirical results obtained by Thirlwall (1975), who found regional unemployment rates to vary not only with their own vacancy rates but with each other's unemployment rates also[1].

In the case of a segmented labour market, the mismatch and compartmentalisation factors would again enter the model [as in equation (7)], but some measure of comparative labour quality would remain appropriate. The mismatch and the labour quality factors are *both* appropriately regarded as contributing to the incidence of 'structural' unemployment, since they reflect an interaction between the composition of employers' demands and available labour supply. There are two or three differences in their roles, however. The least significant is that mismatch factors are defined in relation to conventional occupational or industrial classifications, whereas compartmentalisation factors may involve various other qualitative dimensions of labour. More important is that the second type of factor is intrinsically *comparative*, reflecting the competitive character of the interactions between regional labour markets, and accounting for the low level of unemployment in some as the obverse of high unemployment in others. Related to this is the fact that it reflects essentially subjective *judgments* made by employers with imperfect information, rather than the apparently objective and deterministic distinctions between skills implied by measures of occupational mismatch. These are issues to be taken up again in section 4 of this paper. But first it will be useful to consider what the static classification and the Holt flow model imply about the regional incidence of structural unemployment in Great Britain.

3 Estimates of structural unemployment in the British regions

In the previous section, two more-or-less orthodox approaches to the assessment of levels of structural unemployment were outlined, one based on a static comparison of the distribution of unemployment and of vacancies, the other on their pattern of interaction over time as demand fluctuated. Both approaches essentially assume closed labour markets, but we noted some possible extensions to the second approach, based on the Holt model, to accommodate interregional labour migration.

The standard definition of structural employment at the regional level, based on the static or 'snapshot' approach, involves computing the excess of unemployment over vacancies in all of the occupational or industrial groups for which there is such an excess, in a situation of overall balance between unemployment and vacancies in that region. Structural unemployment is then the amount by which unemployment and vacancies could both be reduced if unemployed individuals from demand-deficient occupations were inserted into vacancies in excess-demand occupations.

[1] In this case, however, it is clear that vacancy rates are not simply measures of demand or independent predictors of unemployment, as Thirlwall assumed.

As such, its scale would clearly appear less if measured at times of general excess or deficiency in demand, although hypothetical measures can be computed from such data with a comparison of occupational *shares* in the stocks of unemployment and vacancies (see Jackman and Roper, 1985). Two practical problems arise in the computation of estimates of structural unemployment on this basis. The first involves the incomplete coverage of official statistics, particularly of unfilled vacancies but also of unemployment (notably among married women). Estimates based on the 1977 National Survey of Engagements and Vacancies suggest that only about one third of vacancies are notified to employment offices, and this proportion varies substantially between sectors and regions, and over time (Jackman and Roper, 1985, pages 11 and 45). A proportion of those seeking work are omitted and this proportion also has fluctuated over time: on average it has been around one third, although some compensating deduction should be made for those registered unemployed who are not seeking work.

The second issue concerns the appropriateness of the occupational categories employed. Various degrees of disaggregation have been adopted in different studies between the full set of 396 occupations distinguished by the Department of Employment (DE) up to 1979 (Armstrong and Taylor, 1981) and the eighteen broad occupational groups for which data were published up to 1982 (Jackman and Roper, 1985). Larger estimates of the structural component are, of course, obtained with finer disaggregations, although Armstrong and Taylor (1981, page 120) suggest that the estimates are reduced only by a third if the eighteen groups are used instead of the 396 specific occupations. A comparison with 1980 data (now for males and females combined), indicates that the estimated number of structurally unemployed (on Jackman and Roper's proportional definition) would be further reduced by less than a fifth if only two occupations were distinguished: 'general labourers' and others.

A more fundamental problem raised by Mickelwright (1984) concerns the use of DE occupational classifications of the unemployed, which are based not on a last or normal occupation but on local officers' judgments as to the occupations 'most appropriate for finding a job'. In particular he points out that the DE classify *many* more of the male unemployed as 'general labourers' than would be warranted by their last job, and that this discrepancy increased sharply as unemployment rose during the 1970s. Thus we find that, whereas in 1979 about one third of the unemployed were classed by DE as 'general labourers', unpublished data from the Labour Force Sample Survey show that only 4% were last employed in this occupation. In a real sense it appears to be the experience of unemployment which makes men 'general labourers', more than the status of 'general labourer' making men unemployed. This is an important issue of causality to which I shall return in the next section, but its implications may be more for the interpretation of estimates of the structurally unemployed than for their computation. The Department's definitions of occupations used to classify vacancies and the unemployed are formally consistent with each other, *and* there is no reason to doubt that in terms of placement prospects those classed as 'general labourers' are general labourers[(2)].

Jackman and Roper (1985) compute a number of indices of structural imbalance, one of which (identified as I_1) is in effect an attempt to apply the 'snapshot' method to time series, by examining the occupational mismatch between *shares* of unemployment and vacancies. When appropriate corrections are made to the vacancy series, their estimates indicate that the number of structurally unemployed as a proportion of non-demand-deficient unemployment at the national level fluctuated between 35% and 42% during the years 1963 to 1982. Regional estimates for the years 1974 to 1982 show significant variations from an average of 34% in the South East to a high of about 44% in the North West. The range has fluctuated markedly, however, falling from about 16% in 1974/75 to 7% in 1979 and rising again to 12% in 1981/82. Scotland and the South West were exceptional in each showing a downward trend over the period, and by 1982 had a similar degree of occupational mismatch to the South East. Overall there is some positive association between these estimates of structural unemployment and relative unemployment levels, but it is clearly not very strong. Nor on these estimates could the structural component account for more than a small part of the long-standing tendency for unemployment rates in the north to be more than double those prevailing in the South East.

The more realistic estimates of structural unemployment derived from the Holt model tend to be even lower, although being defined in proportional terms they assume more importance as general unemployment levels increase. At the national level, another of Jackman and Roper's (1985) indices (I_3), again based on an adjusted vacancy series, indicates that structural imbalance would have accounted for only between 10% and 15% of prevailing unemployment levels in the years 1963 to 1982. Similar estimates for regions (with unadjusted data for 1980) imply twice as much structural imbalance in the East Midlands, Wales, North, North West, or Yorkshire and Humberside as in the southern regions or West Midlands, with Scotland in between. But this differential would have accounted for only about 7% of the numbers unemployed in the northern regions (equivalent to about $\frac{1}{2}$% in the unemployment rate at this time). Even in recession times the Holt model indicates that structural unemployment can be a real phenomenon, but it remains only a minor element in interregional differentials.

(2) As W I Thomas argued "if men define situations as real they are real in their consequences" (Janowitz, 1966, page xi).

We turn therefore to consider the other components of regional unemployment, notably the balance between demand-deficient (DD) and non-demand-deficient (NDD) unemployment. The standard approach to this question is exemplified by Jackman and Roper (1985) who report the results of a set of unemployment–vacancy rate regressions using corrected data series for the years 1964 to 1984. Their estimates of the points at which unemployment and vacancies would have been equal suggest that the NDD rate has shifted upwards over the years, but at the midpoint of the series in 1974 the national rate stood at 3.9%. The NDD rates for most regions appeared very close to this average but were rather higher in the North West (4.1%), and lower in the South East (3.5%), Yorkshire and Humberside (3.4%), and East Midlands (2.8%). The small scale of variations and (with some exceptions) the ordering of regions appear broadly consistent with estimates of the effects of structural imbalance at the regional level. However, these regressions treat the regions in isolation from each other and from national demand conditions, although the conditions under which in the past particular regions have experienced or approached the NDD rate would differ very greatly. Indeed, the apparent similarity of all these regional regressions may be quite misleading, reflecting a situation in which regional unemployment is related more to national than to regional vacancy rates (Gordon, 1977). At the least, Thirlwall's (1975) results indicate that NDD estimates for regions may be substantially altered if regional interdependences are allowed for.

To test this hypothesis a set of regional regressions were undertaken for the years 1963 to 1984 using an open-labour-market version of the Holt model [compare equation (12)]:

$$\ln(u_{i,t}) = a_0 + a_1 \ln(v_{i,t}) + a_2 \ln(u_{e,t}) + a_3 \ln(u_{i,t-1}) + a_4 t + \varepsilon_{i,t}, \tag{13}$$

where

t is time in years,

ε is an error term,

$a_0, ..., a_4$ are coefficients to be estimated.

The lagged unemployment variable is included here to capture the effects of the procyclical fluctuations in hirings rates which are responsible for the characteristic anticlockwise rotation of $u-v$ observations around the locus of the equilibrium $u-v$ curve (Bowden, 1980). The external, or hinterland, unemployment rates were an average of unemployment rates in each other region weighted by their shares of labour migration to and from a particular region[3]. The vacancy rates incorporate Jackman and Roper's (1985) estimates of the appropriate corrections for nonregistration. No corrections have been made to the unemployment rates. A simple time trend is included in the absence so far of adequate

[3] These weights, based on the decomposition of interregional flows in Gordon and Molho (1987c) are shown in the appendix.

substantive explanations of the continuing outward drift in the $u-v$ relationship (Layard and Nickell, 1985).

The results, estimated by three-stage least squares, are shown in table 2. It can be seen that the external unemployment rate is significant in each of the regions except the South East. The region's own vacancy rate is significantly negative in five of the regions, but apparently positive in Wales. In the other six regions, the coefficient on the vacancy rate is about half the value estimated in equivalent national regressions, or analyses which treat particular regions in isolation. This shortfall reflects the elasticity of external sources of supply in the face of regional fluctuations in labour demands. A similar shortfall is evident in the coefficients obtained on the lagged unemployment rate and on the time trend, although the results for the latter showed marked regional variations.

Table 2. Regional regressions with logged unemployment rates 1963–84.

Independent variable	Coefficient (and *t*-value) in regression for[a]						
	SE	SW	M+YH	NW	N	W	SC
Regional vacancy rate[b] (logged)	−0.547	−0.307	−0.208	−0.291	−0.121	0.289	−0.310
	(3.8)	(4.1)	(2.4)	(4.9)	(1.9)	(1.8)	(8.2)
Unemployment rate:[b]							
external (logged)	0.319	0.452	0.855	0.540	0.590	1.097	0.547
	(1.5)	(4.0)	(5.5)	(6.6)	(5.2)	(6.5)	(9.5)
lagged (logged)	0.240	0.000	0.065	0.256	0.291	−0.116	0.228
	(3.0)	(0.0)	(0.9)	(5.1)	(4.2)	(1.0)	(6.1)
Time	0.031	0.048	0.023	0.017	0.002	−0.004	0.007
	(2.0)	(3.9)	(1.5)	(2.1)	(0.1)	(0.3)	(1.0)
Constant	1.037	1.194	0.280	0.812	0.625	0.239	0.905
	(2.2)	(5.8)	(1.1)	(5.0)	(3.1)	(0.8)	(8.3)
Proportionate standard error	0.089	0.094	0.120	0.067	0.086	0.088	0.049
R^2	0.992	0.989	0.989	0.995	0.989	0.989	0.996
Number	22	22	22	22	22	22	22

Note: The seven-equation system was estimated by three-stage least squares using the SAS procedure SYSREG. Current unemployment and vacancy rates were treated as endogenous. The additional variables used as instruments were employment changes in the seven regions and time squared. The *R*-squared values and standard errors are derived from the second stage of the estimation procedure. Time is measured in years with 1975 equal to 0.5.

[a] The regions are SE South East (including East Anglia); SW South West; M+YH Midlands plus Yorkshire and Humberside; NW North West; N North; W Wales; SC Scotland.

[b] Unemployment and vacancy rates are both for adults and relate to September each year. The unemployment series are unadjusted, but vacancy data have been grossed up on the basis of estimates in Jackman and Roper (1985).

At the second stage in this estimation procedure there was strong evidence of both temporal and spatial autocorrelation in the residuals. This appeared to reflect some error in the weighting matrix used to construct the measure of external unemployment rates, and the problem was effectively controlled at the third stage of the estimation procedure. Despite this problem it may be noted that the equations fit very well and a number of firm qualitative conclusions can be drawn from them.

In particular, the regression results show very clearly that a region's NDD rate, at which its unemployment and vacancy rates are equated, cannot be identified independently of assumptions about the levels of unemployment obtaining in other regions. Realistic interregional comparisons can only be made by solving the system of regional $u-v$ equations to identify the set of NDD rates which are consistent with zero demand-deficiency in all other regions. Estimates of this set of rates for the midpoint of our series in 1974/75 are presented in table 3. As in Thirlwall's (1975) forecasting exercise, the recognition of regional interdependence exposes much more sharply the underlying divergences in labour-market performance(4). Thus it appears that the

Table 3. Estimates for non-demand-deficient regional unemployment rates.

Region[a]	NDD rate[b] (%)	NDD relative to South East[b]	DD relative to South East[c]	u/v ratio[d]
SE	3.2	100	100	0.18
SW	3.9	124	140	0.32
M+YH	3.6	114	142	0.43
NW	4.5	141	168	0.65
N	5.6	176	182	0.88
W	7.6	239	109	1.12
SC	4.7	147	193	1.28

[a] See table 2 for definition of regions.

[b] The non-demand-deficient (NDD) rates are derived by solving the system of equations in table 2 (and the identities defining the external unemployment rates) for the set of values of regional unemployment equalling the regional vacancy rate at time $t = 0$ (midway between 1974 and 1975).

[c] The demand-deficient (DD) index of relative demand-deficiency was derived by dividing an index of relative unemployment rates in 1974–75 by the NDD index.

[d] The unemployment/vacancy ratio relates to the rates as defined for the regressions in table 2.

(4) Thirlwall's estimates of an interdependent system using data for the period 1951–72 can be solved to yield a similarly divergent set of NDD estimates. However, he rejected that interpretation of his results on the grounds that previous estimates had shown the NDD rate not to differ markedly between regions.

traditional high-unemployment regions of the North and West would have had substantially higher rates of unemployment than the South East even if demand-deficiency (and excess demand) had been eliminated everywhere. Indeed, if unemployment rates are factored into DD and NDD components (as in table 3), the first appears to account for about half of the variation between regions. Wales is the extreme case in this regard but in this instance alone the DD index is quite out of line with the standard indicator of demand pressure, the *u/v* ratio, and this result must be regarded as very suspect. If the system is solved for a year towards the end of the observation period, the level of NDD rates which emerges is about half as high again, with a similar pattern of regional differentials, although with proportionately smaller increases in the North, Scotland, the South East, and North West. Over the two decades covered by these regression analyses the NDD component of unemployment has grown substantially, but it has been a consistently important element in the unemployment gap between core and periphery. Why this should be so requires an explanation in terms going beyond the limited issue of occupational mismatch.

4 Regional variations in labour-market disadvantage

The analysis in the previous section suggested that structural unemployment, as traditionally defined in terms of occupational mismatches, has been an even smaller component of the regional unemployment problem than the standard literature (for example, Cheshire, 1973; Dixon and Thirlwall, 1975) had indicated. At the same time, it has been argued that this literature has substantially underestimated the contribution of non-demand-deficient unemployment in total to regional unemployment differentials. On the conventional three-way classification of unemployment that should imply that there are considerable differences in levels of frictional unemployment between the peripheral regions and the South East. The implication that there is some generalised discrepancy in the efficiency of labour-market operations between such broad regions is not a helpful one, however. I wish to argue that much of this component is also appropriately regarded as 'structural', particularly in relation to the considerations of labour-market 'competitiveness' introduced at the end of section 2. In this section of the paper, I shall try to relate this rather abstract notion of competitiveness to more concrete evidence about labour-market processes and to derive some operational measures of regional variations in labour-market disadvantage. In the final section, I will consider whether any useful implications can be drawn from this analysis for the consideration of appropriate and feasible policy responses to the widening gap in regional unemployment rates.

The very limited scale of occupational imbalance should be no great surprise. Until 1980 at least, the degree of industrial variance in employment trends had been fairly stable for some time and was certainly no worse than that resulting from textile and mining contractions in the 1950s and 1960s which were accommodated within low levels of national unemployment (Layard and Nickell, 1985). Moreover, it is evident that there is considerable mobility of labour both between occupations and between industries. As with geographical mobility, much of this is relatively 'short-distance' between neighbouring occupations, but the rippling effects even of limited shifts are capable of yielding substantial readjustments in the distribution of labour supply. Further, there is very little evidence of any substantial discontinuities in the occupational structure posing effective barriers to mobility (Gordon and Molho, 1987b). The normal situation in terms of occupational as well as geographical mobility is one involving a highly responsive equilibriating system (Gordon and Molho, 1987a). In occupational terms, the principal exception to this pattern is right at the bottom of occupational structure where the unemployment rate among general labourers (even on the Labour Force Survey definition) is significantly higher than would be expected in terms of relative rates of employment change, job turnover, etc.

An important factor contributing to this potential for flexibility in the labour force is that most occupations are not characterised by high degrees of occupationally specific skill, such as tend to be assumed in analyses of occupational mismatch. Blackburn and Mann (1979) showed that the operational skills needed for most male manual jobs were very limited and capable of being supplied by most manual workers. 'Skill' requirements were more a matter of cooperation and responsibility, with a skilled position being essentially one of trust. Similarly, Oliver and Turton (1982) showed that what employers mean by 'skill' is as much a question of perceived behavioural characteristics, notably reliability, stability of work record, experience, and responsibility, as of more specific abilities. Another sort of study (Cousins and Curran, 1982) has shown that the vast majority of men working in unskilled manual jobs have previous experience of other kinds of work, often of skilled manual jobs—and not exclusively of obsolete skills either. It would appear, therefore, that inhibitions to occupational movement arise largely from the essentially relativistic perceptions of employers as to individuals' behaviour and tacit skills (Manwaring, 1984) rather than the absence of specific and objectively identifiable mental or physical capacities. In the face of a tightening labour market, employers are likely not only to increase the incentives for new recruits but also to have to revise the screening criteria which they use in attempting to identify suitable and acceptable workers. If there are limits to the speed at which expectations are revised or a downward spiral in the careers of the redundant (Norris, 1978), there may possibly emerge a minority of workers who are not reabsorbed into expanding types of work before symptoms of excess demand appear. In the main, however, we might expect to find that occupational mismatches were limited in scale but that there were marked differences in degrees of 'competitiveness' between groups of workers. The effect would be a concentration of unemployment among the disadvantaged groups, not because they could not *do* many of the jobs currently in demand but because at the prevailing level of demand they could not *compete* successfully for them. Within the context of a closed labour market their unemployment would be essentially a question of demand-deficiency; in an open labour market, however, the unemployment associated with concentrations of these groups may be seen as structural in character.

The screening procedures of employers involve a range of heuristics relating both to acceptability and to suitability, in which 'gut feeling' plays an important and idiosyncratic role. Jenkins's (1986) study of recruitment practices highlights the importance of appearance, manner and attitude, and maturity as primary selection criteria, but labour-market history appeared equally important in the recruitment of manual workers. Employers may well anticipate adverse selection in relation to the characteristics of those seeking employment as against those retained in employment (Akerlof, 1976; Stiglitz, 1985). Recruitment is an inherently chancy business in which employers usually have to rely on a series of cues and stereotypes to make predictions about likely performance on the job. The same is true for the Employment Service when it undertakes preinterview screening of those submitted for vacancies, or when it decides who is to be categorised as a 'general labourer'. This decision may be critical not because there is no demand for such workers but because a consequent restriction to unstable jobs is, especially in a weak labour market, a step towards subemployment and increasing spells of unemployment (Norris, 1978).

This type of analysis suggests that the competitive prospects of an individual within any labour market are likely to depend less on their occupation or demonstrable skills than on a combination of characteristics, some natural but mostly acquired, and most only indirectly captured by standard measures of 'personal characteristics'. The labour force in a region may appear as more or less 'competitive' according to the proportion of its workers who are disadvantaged on such criteria[(5)]. To see how far there are such differences between regions, we must start by identifying a set of predictors of individuals' chances of being unemployed. For this purpose, logit analyses of the incidence of unemployment among males in each region were undertaken using unpublished data from the 1981 Labour Force Survey. The variables considered included

(5) 'Competitiveness' as used here is the other side of the coin to the uneven pressure of competition which Mattson and Weibull (1981) see as affecting the prospects of job searchers. The difference in our open labour-market analysis is that competition occurs between as well as within areas.

Table 4. Logit estimates for probability of males being unemployed, 1981 (source: unpublished Labour Force Survey data).

	Coefficients[a]						
	SE	SW	M + YH	NW	N	W	SC
Age and status:							
16–19	0.478 (3.5)	0.735 (2.4)	0.074 (0.6)	0.226 (1.3)	−0.179 (0.7)	−0.006 (0.0)	0.127 (0.6)
20–24	0.284 (2.5)	0.416 (1.5)	0.149 (1.4)	0.458 (3.1)	0.103 (0.5)	0.283 (1.3)	0.551 (3.3)
25–29[b]	–	–	–	–	–	–	–
30–49	−0.407 (4.2)	0.204 (0.9)	−0.430 (4.7)	−0.328 (2.5)	−0.512 (3.1)	−0.511 (2.7)	−0.259 (1.8)
50–54	−0.450 (3.2)	−0.056 (0.2)	−0.507 (3.9)	−0.606 (3.2)	−0.706 (2.8)	−0.685 (2.4)	−0.769 (3.5)
55–59	−0.528 (3.7)	0.060 (0.2)	−0.514 (3.9)	−0.592 (3.1)	−0.417 (1.8)	−0.327 (1.3)	−0.171 (0.8)
60–64	0.600 (4.4)	0.835 (0.2)	0.241 (1.8)	0.363 (1.9)	0.466 (2.0)	0.148 (0.5)	−0.004 (0.0)
Married	−0.443 (5.1)	−0.690 (3.8)	−0.574 (6.5)	−0.388 (3.0)	−0.607 (3.8)	−0.505 (2.7)	−0.802 (5.4)
Living with parents	−0.108 (1.0)	−0.324 (1.3)	−0.254 (2.3)	−0.219 (1.4)	−0.275 (1.4)	−0.470 (2.0)	−0.608 (3.4)
Registered disabled	0.992 (6.2)	0.446 (1.2)	0.798 (5.2)	0.595 (2.5)	0.434 (1.3)	1.071 (2.7)	0.078 (0.2)
Ethnic origin:							
Afro-Carribean	1.012 (6.9)	1.273 (1.6)	0.740 (3.9)	0.037 (0.1)	na	na	na
Asian	0.917 (6.2)	0.458 (0.4)	0.912 (6.7)	0.893 (3.5)	1.376 (1.9)	na	na
Mixed or 'other'	0.474 (1.9)	0.406 (0.5)	0.788 (2.5)	0.306 (0.5)	na	na	na
Tenure:							
owned outright	0.462 (4.7)	0.341 (1.8)	0.129 (1.4)	0.286 (2.2)	−0.347 (1.7)	−0.080 (0.4)	−0.106 (0.5)
mortgager[b]	–	–	–	–	–	–	–
council tenant	0.852 (10.9)	0.822 (4.9)	0.918 (12.6)	1.181 (11.2)	0.819 (5.8)	1.000 (6.2)	1.032 (6.4)
new town tenant	0.948 (3.9)	–	1.738 (7.8)	1.628 (4.5)	0.459 (0.7)	0.698 (2.2)	0.892 (3.4)
housing association	1.088 (6.0)	0.490 (0.8)	0.975 (4.3)	0.768 (2.2)	0.188 (0.5)	1.946 (3.1)	0.786 (3.5)
private rented	0.159 (1.5)	−0.265 (1.1)	0.142 (1.2)	0.387 (2.1)	−0.076 (0.3)	−0.284 (1.0)	−0.451 (1.9)
Qualification:							
degree	0.056 (0.3)	0.467 (1.3)	−0.167 (0.8)	−0.377 (1.2)	−0.908 (1.6)	−0.297 (0.6)	−0.534 (1.3)
unspecified	0.802 (4.5)	0.682 (2.0)	0.858 (5.6)	0.798 (3.1)	0.444 (1.2)	0.227 (0.5)	0.167 (0.5)
none	0.752 (10.6)	0.567 (3.8)	0.626 (9.5)	0.520 (5.6)	0.512 (4.2)	0.432 (3.1)	0.609 (6.1)

Table 4 (continued)

	Coefficients[a]						
	SE	SW	M+YH	NW	N	W	SC
Socioeconomic group:[b]							
personal service	0.100 (0.4)	−0.289 (0.4)	0.592 (2.2)	0.753 (2.4)	0.581 (1.3)	−0.081 (0.1)	0.712 (2.5)
semiskilled manual	0.122 (1.4)	0.080 (0.5)	0.250 (3.5)	0.237 (2.2)	0.238 (1.7)	−0.077 (0.5)	0.075 (0.6)
unskilled manual	0.572 (5.2)	0.987 (4.5)	0.760 (7.8)	0.931 (7.5)	1.025 (6.3)	0.924 (5.0)	0.988 (7.2)
unclassified	3.296 (37.1)	3.860 (18.2)	4.262 (35.4)	4.366 (24.2)	4.061 (16.3)	4.048 (15.5)	4.168 (22.2)
Industry:[c]							
employment stability (10%)	−0.480 (6.2)	0.107 (0.7)	−0.451 (5.8)	−0.507 (4.6)	−0.473 (3.5)	−0.502 (3.3)	−0.740 (6.5)
employment growth (10%)	−0.291 (6.4)	−0.289 (3.0)	−0.358 (8.4)	−0.296 (4.9)	−0.299 (3.7)	−0.289 (3.3)	−0.253 (3.7)
Constant	−4.317 (24.4)	−3.296 (9.1)	−3.665 (20.2)	−3.813 (14.3)	−3.075 (9.4)	−3.266 (8.6)	−3.949 (13.4)
Number of unemployed	1558	359	1949	1028	565	447	824
rate (%)	8.0	7.4	11.7	13.8	14.5	13.8	13.4

[a] See table 2 for definition of regions. The dependent variable includes those seeking work plus the 'other economically inactive' excluding the permanently sick and disabled. Coefficients are on a logarithmic basis: the exponential of any value represents the proportional change in the relative odds of unemployment against employment associated with that characteristic. Bracketed values in the main part of the table are asymptotic t-statistics. (na = not applicable.)

[b] Omitted categories in dummy variable regression. The omitted categories for ethnic origin, qualification, and socioeconomic groups may be summarised as 'whites', other qualifications, and other SEGs (white-collar, skilled, agricultural, etc).

[c] The employment stability variable was based on the number of individuals in each industry remaining with the same firm during the 12 months preceding the survey, expressed as a proportion of the average numbers employed at the time of the survey and 12 months previously: the mean value was 86% for males with a standard deviation of 4%. The employment growth variable was based on the change in numbers employed in each industry in the 12 months preceding the Labour Force Survey: the mean value was −3% with a standard deviation of around 7%. Zero values for the two variables represent perfect stability in employment and no change in numbers. Values of −1 represent 90% stability and a decrease of 10% in employment.

a range of indicators of socioeconomic status, housing class, education, ethnic origin, age, family status, qualifications achieved, sector of employment, and disability. Two measures of the industry of last employment were used, one relating to its rate of employment growth or decline, and the other to the rate of turnover among its workers. The first was interpreted as a situational factor like region of residence, whereas the second was seen as reflecting the individual worker's relative power and competitiveness in the labour market. Since the significance of some of these indicators could vary according to context, separate logit analyses were undertaken for each region, to see whether, for example, public sector housing was as strongly correlated with the chances of unemployment in a region where 70% were in this sector as in a region where 30% were. In fact, as the results in table 4 indicate, that did prove to be the case (with more than double the risk compared with an otherwise comparable mortgager in all regions), and in general the estimated effects of particular characteristics were quite consistent across regions. That in itself validates the logit approach with its assumption that these factors exert a multiplicative rather than additive effect on the chances of being unemployed rather than employed. The results show that there is a wide range of characteristics which appear to produce a substantial effect on an individual's competitiveness in securing and retaining employment. These include both more-or-less natural attributes such as age or ethnic origin, and others which are more clearly influenced by experience in particular labour markets, for example lack of formal qualifications and having last worked in an unskilled or unstable job.

To see how far regional labour forces might differ in the proportion of workers disadvantaged in terms of these criteria, a common version of the logit function was used to classify Labour Force Survey respondents in terms of their relative likelihood of being unemployed. The growth industry variable and the regional constants were omitted, as situational rather than individual characteristics, but the 'stability' of the last job was retained, as a crucial element in an individual's work history. The results of this classification exercise are reported in table 5. Three categories of workers have been distinguished, including a highly disadvantaged group who although only about 5% of the labour force accounted for a third of total unemployment. This group appear to be rather evenly represented in each region, and their distribution certainly does not account for the higher unemployment levels of the North and West. But within the main body of the labour force some significant regional differences are evident, with fewer of the disadvantaged in the four 'core' regions and proportionately more in Scotland, Wales, and the North. The differences are again not such as to account directly in compositional terms for the higher unemployment in the latter regions. However, they are at least consistent with the hypothesis that their workers are relatively disadvantaged in competing for employment opportunities, and that this competitive disadvantage is a cause of higher levels of non-demand-deficient unemployment. The number of regions for which we currently have estimates of the level of non-demand-deficient unemployment is too small to test this hypothesis directly, or to indicate how much of the gap in unemployment rates is explicable in these terms. Other factors do also have to be taken into account; for example, those characteristics of a region which may make its jobs particularly attractive to migrants from elsewhere, thus reducing its residents' share in the flow of new hirings. However, the evidence from the Labour Force Survey does suggest that the competitive position of workers in the regions of high unemployment may be an important factor in their persistently higher levels of unemployment.

Table 5. Proportions of competitively disadvantaged male workers by region, 1981.

Region[a]	Percentage of male workers[b]		
	relatively advantaged	disadvantaged	highly disadvantaged
SE	67.6	27.1	5.3
SW	71.6	24.5	3.9
M+YH	65.9	29.2	4.9
NW	66.9	27.2	5.9
N	60.0	35.0	5.0
W	61.2	33.5	5.3
SC	50.2	44.1	5.5
Great Britain unemployment rate	4.3	14.6	67.4

[a] See table 2 for definition of regions.

[b] The classification of male workers in this table is based on a common version of the logit function estimated in table 4, omitting regional constants and the industrial growth variable.

5 Conclusion

This paper has been an attempt to relate to each other two rather different perspectives on labour-market processes—an orthodox Keynesian view of the components of unemployment and a somewhat more sociological treatment of labour-market segmentation—and to develop the particular implications for each of *open* labour-market systems such as those which characterise regional economies. Its conclusions are substantially less clear-cut than those offered by the traditional *classifications* of types of unemployment, but the apparent simplicity of the latter is misleading and it is necessary to take rather more account of the processes underlying observed distributions of unemployment and vacancies. This involves first a formal recognition of the potential for induced mobility between areas and occupations in response to changing opportunities, and then a more substantive consideration of the circumstances of competition for different groups of workers in the labour market. The first of these steps is the simpler and it has been possible to show, in section 4 of this paper, how it alters the standard picture of the components of regional unemployment, demonstrating that regional labour markets differ in more ways than simply the level of demand-deficiency. The second step has been tackled only in a more exploratory way, in section 5, but it has been shown that there are a common set of factors which affect individuals' employment prospects in all regions, and significant differences in how regional labour forces rank on them. In this way we have started to fill out the rather abstract notion that there is a structural component to regional unemployment in terms of the competitive position of their labour force.

The basis of this approach is the 'job competition' thesis, advanced by Thurow (1972), which maintains that, since new workers have generally to be paid the same rate as existing employees, competition for vacancies depends essentially on the perceived suitability of candidates. As we have noted, this is a problematic judgment for employers to make and much may depend on past labour-market history. Hence, if it is the case, as we have suggested, that workers in the regions of traditionally high unemployment score rather lower on the index of labour-market advantage, that may be as much a consequence as a cause of the history of unemployment in a region. Indeed the coexistence of high levels of both demand-deficient and non-demand-deficient unemployment in those regions might suggest that the one was the cause of the other, or that over a period of years the one got converted into the other. One piece of evidence consistent with that interpretation has been the slower movement of individuals out of the 'unskilled' category in the regions of high unemployment (Buck and Gordon, 1987).

The practical significance of this issue relates to the question of how far, or at what speed, high levels of regional unemployment originating from employment decline can be reversed, either by conventional regional policy or by the encouragement of emigration. Past experience offers little guidance here and a closer examination of regional labour-market processes is needed to see whether other manpower policies can assist in restoring the competitive position of workers in the regions. The simple implications which may be drawn from this analysis, are that, even with an active policy, progress in lowering regional unemployment is likely to be slow, requiring more persistence than has been evident in the past, but that in the absence of such a policy, sustained decline in labour demand is likely to have compounding effects on the quality of labour supply.

Acknowledgements. This paper is based on work supported by the Economic and Social Research Council as part of a project on Metropolitan Labour Market Analysis. I am grateful to the Office of Population Censuses and Surveys and the ESRC Data Archive for access to the Labour Force Survey, and to Ian Molho and Leslie Curry for comments on an earlier version of this paper.

References

Akerlof G A, 1976, "The market for 'lemons': quality uncertainty and the market mechanism" *Quarterly Journal of Economics* **84** 488-500

Armstrong H, Taylor J, 1981, "The measurement of different types of unemployment", in *The Economics of Unemployment in Britain* Ed. J Creedy (Butterworth, Sevenoaks, Kent) pp 99-127

Blackburn R M, Mann M, 1979 *The Working Class in the Labour Market* (Macmillan, London)

Bowden R J, 1980, "On the existence and secular stability of $u-v$ loci" *Economica* **47** 35-50

Buck N, Gordon I R, 1987, "The beneficiaries of employment growth: an analysis of the experience of disadvantaged groups in expanding labour markets", in *Critical Issues in Urban Economic Development, Volume 2* Ed. V H Hausner (Oxford University Press, Oxford) pp 77-115

Burridge P, Gordon I R, 1979, "Unemployment in the British metropolitan labour areas" *Oxford Economic Papers* **33** 274-297

Cheshire P C, 1973 "Regional unemployment differences in Great Britain" *National Institute of Economic and Social Research, Regional Papers II* (Cambridge University Press, Cambridge) pp 1-40

Cousins M J, Curran M, 1982, "Patterns of disadvantage in a city labour market", in *Diversity and Decomposition in the Labour Market* Ed. G Day (Gower, Aldershot, Hants) pp 49-65

Dixon R J, Thirlwall A P, 1975 *Regional Growth and Unemployment in the United Kingdom* (Macmillan, London)

Gordon I R, 1977, "Regional interdependence in the UK economy", in *Structure, System and Economic Policy* Ed. W Leontief (Cambridge University Press, Cambridge) pp 111-122

Gordon I R, Molho I I, 1987a, "Equilibrium and disequilibrium in occupational unemployment rates", mimeo, Urban and Regional Studies Unit, University of Kent, Canterbury

Gordon I R, Molho I I, 1987b, "Occupational mobility and inter-occupational distance", mimeo, Urban and Regional Studies Unit, University of Kent, Canterbury

Gordon I R, Molho I I, 1987c, "The changing structure of inter-regional migration in Great Britain", mimeo, Urban and Regional Studies Unit, University of Kent, Canterbury

Holt C C, 1970, "How can the Phillips curve be moved to reduce both inflation and unemployment?", in *Microeconomic Foundations of Employment and Inflation Theory* Eds E S Phelps, and others (Norton, New York) pp 224-256

Jackman R, Roper S, 1985, "Structural unemployment" DP 233, Centre for Labour Economics, London School of Economics and Political Science, London

Janowitz M (Ed.), 1966 *On Social Organization and Social Personality* (University of Chicago Press, Chicago, IL)

Jenkins R, 1986 *Racism and Recruitment* (Cambridge University Press, Cambridge)

Layard R, Nickell S, 1985, "The causes of British unemployment" *National Institute Economic Review* issue 111, pp 62-85

Machlup F, 1958, "Structure and structural change: weaselwords and jargon" *Zeitschrift für Nationalekonomie* **18** 280–298

Manwaring T, 1984, "The extended internal labour market" *Cambridge Journal of Economics* **8** 161–187

Mattson L, Weibull J, 1981, "Competition and accessibility on a regional labour market" *Regional Science and Urban Economics* **11** 471–497

Micklewright J, 1984, "Male unemployment and the Family Expenditure Survey 1972–80" *Oxford Bulletin of Economics and Statistics* **46** 31–53

Nickell S, 1982, "The determinants of equilibrium unemployment in Britain" *Economic Journal* **92** 555–575

Norris G M, 1978, "Unemployment, subemployment and personal characteristics: (b) job separation and work histories: the alternative approach" *Sociological Review* **25** 327–347

Oliver J M, Turton J R, 1982, "Is there a shortage of skilled labour?" *British Journal of Industrial Relations* **20** 195–200

Standing G, 1983, "The notion of structural unemployment" *International Labour Review* **122** 137–153

Stiglitz J E, 1985, "Information and economic analysis: a perspective" *Economic Journal, Supplement* **95** 21–41

Thirlwall A P, 1969, "Types of unemployment with special reference to 'non demand-deficient' unemployment in Great Britain" **16** 20–49

Thirlwall A P, 1975, "Forecasting regional unemployment in Great Britain" *Regional Science and Urban Economics* **5** 357–374

Thurow L C, 1972, "Education and economic equality" *The Public Interest* **35** 66–81

APPENDIX

Table A.1. Weights used to construct estimates of the external unemployment rate.

Region	Weights							Total
	SE	SW	M+YH	NW	N	W	SC	
SE		0.258	0.349	0.138	0.078	0.082	0.095	1.00
SW	0.577		0.198	0.070	0.044	0.054	0.056	1.00
M+YH	0.529	0.134		0.113	0.075	0.058	0.091	1.00
NW	0.428	0.098	0.231		0.082	0.055	0.107	1.00
N	0.367	0.091	0.232	0.123		0.043	0.143	1.00
W	0.447	0.131	0.207	0.097	0.050		0.067	1.00
SC	0.370	0.097	0.233	0.134	0.118	0.047		1.00

Key: SE South East including East Anglia; SW South West; M+YH Midlands plus Yorkshire and Humberside; NW North West; N North; W Wales; SC Scotland.

Unemployment within Enterprises in Centrally Planned Economies: A Regionalised View

J S KOWALSKI
Universität Karlsruhe

1 Unemployment within enterprises; causes and consequences

Officially there is no unemployment in the centrally planned economies (CPEs). Everyone who wants to find work may realise this wish. To give one example: in January 1983, in the middle of an unprecedented economic crisis in Poland, when production levels had fallen substantially and much industrial capacity was idle, the Central Labour Exchange Office in Warsaw registered 240 000 vacancies in industry facing 400 applicants looking for a job. By the end of 1984 the number of those looking for a job had risen to 5 000, but there were still 262 000 registered vacancies (*Statistical Yearbook for Poland*, 1985, page 71). What is more, in all the CPEs apart from Hungary there are laws forcing people to enter regular employment, laws which prescribe more or less severe punishments for avoiding being employed.

This 'full-employment' situation has been one of the main sources of satisfaction for the central planners. Indeed, from the outset of the economic crisis, which spread throughout the CPEs during the 1970s (Drewnowski, 1982), this lack of unemployment remained the only point at which it could have been maintained that the planned economies showed some superiority against the market ones. The central planners concede almost readily that the CPEs are less efficient in many respects, but "... we provide everybody with a job, nobody is on the streets".

One of the aims of this paper is to qualify this statement. It is true, but only in a limited sense. There is virtually no open unemployment, but in all the CPEs there exists what has been called 'unemployment within enterprise' (UWE) (Wiles, 1979; Kornai, 1980). And, as I shall show, this concealed unemployment is regionally differentiated, like the open unemployment of market economies.

A considerable part of the labour force in socialist enterprises (both management and workers) remains idle for all or part of the working day. This happens not because they are particularly lazy or workshy but rather is an inherent consequence of the way that the CPEs function[(1)].

Before I proceed to analyse the reasons for this state of affairs, let me acknowledge that the concept of 'unemployment within enterprises' is necessarily a fuzzy one. It is impossible, when looking at a given

[(1)] I am of course aware that the work ethic in the CPEs is rather weak. But since (as I believe) people themselves are not very different in various political systems, the reasons for the weak work ethic must also be inherent in the system.

enterprise, to determine precisely how many people belong to this category at any moment. There is always a borderline group of persons who are occasionally doing something during the day. The situation may also change very rapidly, and the amount of UWE may fluctuate from hour to hour within the enterprise.

It has been said above that the reasons for UWE lie in the functioning of the CPEs. Why is this so? My explanation derives from a theoretical model initially developed by Kornai (1980; 1982), and has been extended to include explicitly the role of political decisionmaking mechanisms in the CPEs (Kowalski, 1983; 1986). The approach used in the model is positive, not normative, showing how the CEPs function in *reality* and not how they *should* function according to their design principles. The key premises of the model may be briefly summarised as:

(1) CPEs are shortage economies, in which widespread chronic shortages, not only in consumer markets, but also in interindustry trade, are the normal situation, influencing the long-term and short-term behaviour of firms and individuals.

(2) Firms have soft budget constraints, that is, they can spend more money than they earn or get in repayable credits. Combined with their experiences of shortages, and a drive to overfulfill plans to earn good marks from superiors, this leads to hoarding of all possible inputs, which thus get siphoned out of the market.

(3) Money and prices play no role in the decisionmaking of firms, either in the short run or the long run, because of the softness of budget constraints.

(4) Soft budget constraints are accompanied by 'voluntaristic', lawless, and unplanned decisionmaking. This stems from the political system, which frees top decisionmakers from any legal control. 'Centrally planned economies' are in reality very unplanned systems (Kowalski, 1983). Lawlessness, in the sense that it is possible for key actors in the economy to disregard legal norms (like plans), is the characteristic feature of the CPEs.

(5) A key role in the functioning of the economy is played by those levels of performance which, at a certain point of time, and in a given place, people consider to be 'normal' (for example, a three-year wait for a car, a three-month delay in executing a purchase order for inputs, a three-hour queue to get bread, and so on). While such variables remain at these normal levels, the economic system remains in a non-Walrasian equilibrium, with socially accepted levels of shortages, investment, production consumption, and growth. Deviations from these normal levels, however, act as signals and activate various adjustment mechanisms (Kowalski, 1986).

Labour is treated by the managements of enterprises just like any other input. Managers, feeling no financial constraints, but facing uncertain allocations and rationing, try to build up reserves, hoarding labour as well as other inputs. Since the mid-1960s, when external reserves of labour were exhausted as a consequence of rapid industrialisation (Kuklinski, 1982), acute shortages of labour have been experienced by the managers in the CPEs. This has further reinforced their drive to secure safe supplies of labour by hoarding it within their enterprises.

There is no contradiction between the recognition of a chronic shortage of labour and the statement that the managers build up reserves of it, by hiring people when they are not actually needed. Indeed shortage and slack (that is unproductive reserves of resources) coexist and reinforce each other. In fact, in the words of Kornai (1980, page 255):

> "the more frequent and intensive the labour shortage, the greater will be the internal slack, namely the unemployment on the job. By trying to build up reserves of labour, the managers help to create 'sucking out' effect on the labour market and thus lead to the situation where if they really need a specific kind of work force, it is impossible to find it."

UWE labour hoarding is not, however, as tends to be the case in market economies, simply a reflection of instability in product demand, but is greatly exacerbated by supply-side problems, such as shortages of complementary inputs, machine breakdowns, lack of spare parts, and absenteeism.

The UWE has very serious psychological and economic consequences. Being on the job without really having anything to do results in boredom, and a conviction that one's time is being wasted. Demotivation and demoralisation follow. In economic terms these lead to decreased labour productivity, discipline, and morale. Why should one try to be punctual if there is no work to do? Why should one work intensively if experience suggests that one's product may get no further than the next production stage when shortages of something will stop production? Since as a rule there is no direct link between individual work effort and earnings, even a purely material motivation to work well will be lacking. Another consequence of UWE is widespread 'blackwork', a shadow economy, conducted by people officially on the job, who are actually working privately for customers inside or outside the enterprise.

In many respects, the long-term psychological and economic consequences of UWE in the CPEs parallel the phenomena of frustration and alienation observed among the openly unemployed in Liverpool or Bremen. It is of some interest then to ascertain whether there are spatial variations in UWE which are as significant as those that have been found for open unemployment in the market economies.

2 Hidden unemployment—an attempt at evaluation

2.1 *Methodology*

Whether the scale of UWE is actually comparable with that of unemployment in the market economies is a complex and almost unresearched problem. Everybody knows that UWE exists; sociologists and economists in the CPEs are aware of it and warn of its negative impacts, but no systematic estimates are available of the actual number of people involved. Some experts (for example, Wiles, 1979) believe that the overall level of UWE is between 20% and 30% of employment. In administrative jobs the UWE levels may reach 50%, although we should note that similar observations have been made about public bureaucracies in Western countries.

My objective in this paper is to evaluate *differences* between regions in the incidence of UWE. The method used here will not allow us to estimate absolute *levels* of UWE in the various regions. However, it does make it possible to judge which regions at particular times experienced higher or lower levels of UWE than other regions.

The procedure is based on an analysis of the degrees of productive utilisation (DPU) in each region, defined in a specific way below. The results are then checked against regional indicators of change in labour productivity. The analysis has been conducted for forty-nine regions in Poland (voivodships) for 1976, 1978, and 1982. Because of limits on data availability and problems related to price changes, it has been limited to the industrial sector only.

The conceptual basis of this study involves a comparison of regional production with regional input potentials (for a detailed account see Funck and Blum, 1980; 1982; Blum, 1982; 1983; for an application to the Polish case see Blum and Kowalski, 1984; 1986). Two basic assumptions are made:

(1) Regional production capacities are determined by a set of *regional input potentials* including locational factors, infrastructure capacities, and other immobile inputs which are unevenly distributed over space.

(2) Other *attractable input factors*, are combined with input potentials in fixed proportions, according to an underlying production technology.

Provided that the attractable input factors are available in appropriate quantities, actual regional output, as well as production capacity are determined solely by the regional input potentials. Then, with a Cobb–Douglas-type production function, regional product, P_{it}, is given by

$$P_{it}(\hat{v}_{it}) = a_0 \prod_{j=1}^{m} \tilde{v}_{jit}^{a_{jt}} , \qquad a_0 > 0 , \quad a_j \neq 0 , \tag{1}$$

where

i indicates the region, $i = 1, ..., n$,

j indicates the input potential, $j = 1, ..., m$,

t is the time period, $t = 1, ..., T$,
$\hat{v}_{it}$ is a vector of input potentials in region i at time t,
$\hat{v}_{jit}$ is the jth element in the vector,
a_o is a constant term,
a_j is the production elasticity coefficient.
With any shortages of materials, or other attractable input factors, however, production will be proportionately lower.

In addition to fixed capital and transport infrastructure (represented by the density of roads and railways), employment has also been treated as a regional input potential, on the assumption that, under the housing and labour market conditions of a CPE, labour is effectively immobile between regions. Hence shortages of attractable inputs will entail unemployment of labour as well as capital.

The parameters of this Cobb–Douglas production function were estimated cross-regionally with a regression of industrial output on the four sets of input potentials. By taking the estimated parameters for the country as a whole, measures of 'natural regional production' can be derived, by inserting the value of input potentials in given regions into the equation. The actual regional production is compared with the natural one and their ratio is defined as the degree of productive utilisation in the region (DPU). Note that the natural production level corresponds to the production level which would be achieved if all input potentials in a region were employed in an average way for all regions in the country. Then the DPU may be considered to be a measure of the deviation of the economic performance of a given region from the national standard.

Given our assumption of a common production function in each of the Polish regions, a below-average DPU in a particular region implies that its input potentials are relatively underemployed or misused in comparison with other regions. The DPU may thus serve as an indicator for the level of hidden unemployment within enterprises. Admittedly, low DPU may reflect underemployment of fixed assets as well as of labour, but it should be clear from the first section that underemployment of fixed assets and of labour coincide and that underemployment is manifested externally in the widespread shortages of materials and lack of the 'free' labour force. Hence it may be assumed that underemployment of fixed assets means high UWE.

The general hypothesis is that UWE will be higher where enterprises tend to be less successful in ensuring supplies of materials and other attractable inputs. At a regional level, the hypothesis in this paper is that the stronger more developed regions should record lower UWE levels than weak agriculturally dominated ones, as a result of uneven interregional competition for assignment of resources. Stronger industrial regions, which are usually ruled in the CPEs by politically more potent lobbies, succeed better than the weak ones in securing inputs for 'their' enterprises, thus lowering UWE relatively (a detailed discussion of the sectoral and regional decisionmaking mechanisms is to be found in Kowalski, 1986).

2.2 *Results*

Figure 1 shows the results of the DPU analysis for 1976, 1978, and 1982. It has been possible to provide the results for all three years on a single map because in almost every case the regions maintained their relatively low (or high) DPU levels throughout the period under investigation. The threshold values, 1.10 and 0.90, used as indicators of extremely high or low DPU levels, respectively, have been arbitrarily chosen from the range of DPU values.

Let us consider the map in detail. In the group of regions with high DPU levels, and implicitly low hidden UWE, we find the strong industrial

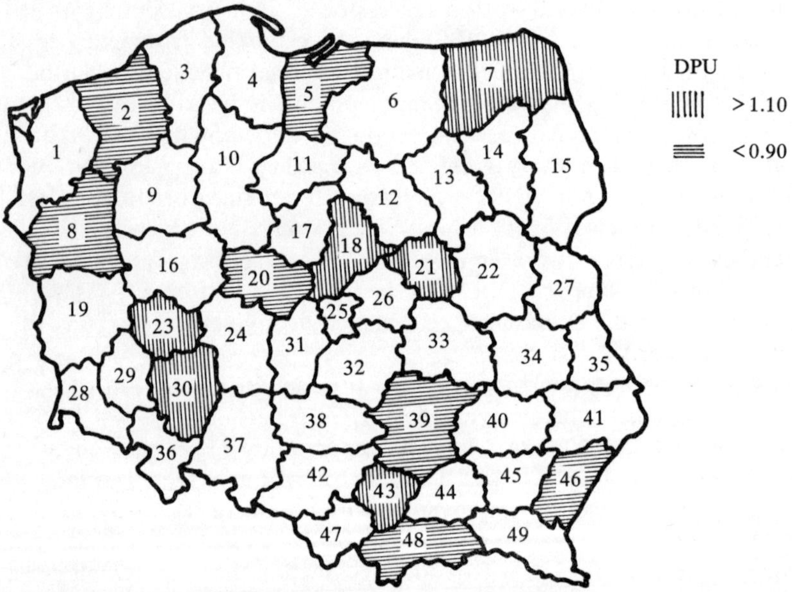

1 Szczecińskie
2 Koszalińskie
3 Słupskie
4 Gdańskie
5 Elblaskie
6 Olsztyńskie
7 Suwalskie
8 Gorzówskie
9 Pilskie
10 Bydgoskie
11 Toruńskie
12 Ciechanowskie
13 Ostroleckie
14 Łomzyńskie
15 Białostockie
16 Poznańskie
17 Włocławskie
18 Płockie
19 Zielonogórskie
20 Konińskie
21 Warszawskie
22 Siedleckie
23 Leszczyńskie
24 Kaliskie
25 Łodzkie
26 Skierniewickie
27 Bielskopodlaskie
28 Jeleniogórskie
29 Legnickie
30 Wrocławskie
31 Sieradzkie
32 Piotrkowskie
33 Radomskie
34 Lubelskie
35 Chełmskie
36 Walbrzyskie
37 Opolskie
38 Czestochowskie
39 Kieleckie
40 Tarnobrzeskie
41 Zamojskie
42 Katowickie
43 Krakowskie
44 Tarnowskie
45 Rzeszowskie
46 Przemyskie
47 Bielskie
48 Nowosadeckie
49 Krosnieńskie

Figure 1. Extremely low and high levels of degree of productive utilisation (DPU), 1976, 1978, 1982.

and administrative centres (Warsaw, Wroclaw, Krakow) as well as a number of regions dominated by agriculture. The second group is smaller, including only two regions. On the other hand, in the group of regions with low DPU, and thus suspected of having relatively high UWE, we see almost exclusively weak agricultural voivodships. This seems to support the hypothesis that the politically stronger industrial-administrative centres should be better able to furnish their enterprises with attractable inputs than the weak ones, and that, as a consequence, levels of UWE should be lower there than in the weak regions.

It should be noted here that in the above reasoning it is assumed that there are no significant differences between the strong and weak regions in the quality of actual organisation of work within industrial enterprises. It is true that the strong regions have more assets, but there is absolutely no evidence that enterprises in economically and politically strong regions are better managed, organised, or motivated than elsewhere. Also I feel able to disregard possible regional differences in the 'age' of fixed assets and their embodied technology, since in the CPEs these should be much smaller than in the market economies. The crucial point then is the differential ability of some regions to siphon off the resources from the central assignment pool, so that their production capacities and labour do not remain idle.

In addition to the analysis of DPU levels, another approach to regional UWE comparison has been explored, based on differences between rates of growth of industrial production and employment. It is postulated that in those regions where these differences are relatively small, enterprises have hired more persons who remain unproductive than elsewhere. Of course, interregional differences in the economic structure must also affect those differences to some degree, insofar as various industries record different productivity of labour. But from other studies (Blum and Kowalski, 1984; 1986) it is known that the Polish regions have a much more even economic structure, from the point of view of the shares of various branches in industry as a whole, than, for example, the West German ones. Differences in the price movements for the various groups of commodities could also be disregarded (with one exception mentioned below) as they were more or less similar in all industries. Hence, if we compare two regions, one with a high and the other a low difference between the rate of growth of production value and the rate of growth of employment, the second region could be expected to have a higher UWE level than the first.

The results of these computations for the periods 1976-78 and 1978-82 are shown in figure 2, with each map showing only those regions with low differences, that is, those with high imputed UWE levels.

The content of the map in figure 2(b) is of very limited value insofar as it relates to a period of enormous collapse in production levels and rapid price movements, which cannot be discounted as easily as we have done above. It has only been included for illustrative purposes. As a matter of interest it should be noticed that the strongest industrial region—Katowice—is included among the high UWE regions in figure 2(b).

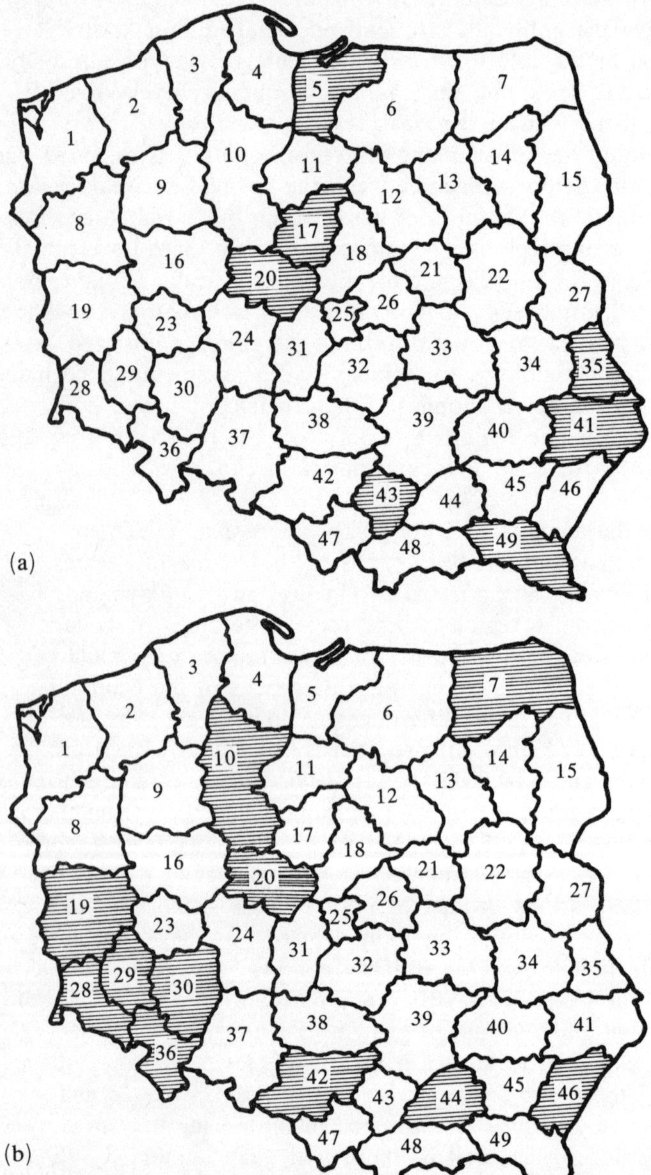

Figure 2. Regions (voivodships) with high unemployment within enterprises for (a) 1976–78, (b) 1978–82 (see figure 1 for key).

This is patently against the hypothesis, but is easily explained. This region is an exception, specialising greatly in coal and steel, two commodities whose prices rose much slower than average industrial prices from 1980. Hence the result implies nothing about resource use.

Figure 2(a) is more interesting, since it relates to a period when the assumptions are much more realistic. It shows some differences from figure 1, but one essential similarity: with a single exception all the regions with small differences in the two growth rates are weak agricultural ones. This supports the reasoning put forward above and is consistent with the results of the DPU analysis.

3 Conclusion

My results are very tentative and only as good as the theory behind them. They tend generally not to contradict this theory, that is, they point to the probability of higher UWE levels in the state industrial enterprises of the weak regions compared with the politically dominant industrial regions. The latter manage to obtain more mobile inputs and are thus better able to use their production capacities and labour.

This conclusion is also consistent with investigations showing that in the stronger regions living standards and production capacities have risen faster than in the weak ones (Ciechocinska, 1985; Lodkowska, 1985; Kowalski, 1986). The only exception to this trend is to be found in the early 1980s, that is, during the economic crisis, when the strong regions were even worse 'hit' than the weak ones. It remains to be seen if a return to 'normalcy' in the economy will reinstate the dominant position of the strong regions.

References

Blum U, 1982, "Effects of transportation investments on regional growth" *Papers of the Regional Science Association* **49** 169-184

Blum U, 1983, "Bestimmungsgründe der regionalen Wirtschaftsstruktur" DP2/1983, Institut für Wirtschaftspolitik und Wirtschaftsforschung, Universität Karlsruhe, 7500 Karlsruhe 1

Blum U, Kowalski J S, 1984, "Regional production in Poland—a study of efficiency and inefficiency in regional perspective" DP1/1984, Institut für Wirtschaftspolitik und Wirtschaftsforschung, Universität Karlsruhe, 7500 Karlsruhe 1

Blum U, Kowalski J S, 1986, "On the efficiency of regional production in Poland, 1976-1982" *Annals of Regional Science* **20** 12-32

Ciechocinska M, 1985, "Trends in changes of living standards in Poland (1960-1981)" *Przegląd Geograficzny* **57**(1-2) 15-35

Drewnowski J (Ed.), 1982 *Crisis in the East European Economy* (Croom Helm, Beckenham, Kent)

Funck R, Blum, U, 1980, "Die Berücksichtigung von Wachstums- und Struktureffekten in den Richtlinien für Wirtschaftliche Vergleichsrechnungen im Strassenwesen" final report of a project for the Ministry of Transportation; Institut für Wirtschaftspolitik und Wirtschaftsforschung, Universität Karlsruhe, 7500 Karlsruhe 1

Funck R, Blum U, 1982, "Regional effects of investments in the transport infrastructure" mimeo, Institut für Wirtschaftspolitik und Wirtschaftsforschung, Universität Karlsruhe, 7500 Karlsruhe1
Kornai J, 1980 *Economics of Shortages* (North-Holland, Amsterdam)
Kornai J, 1982 *Growth, Shortage and Efficiency* (University of California Press, Berkeley, CA)
Kowalski J S, 1983, "On the relevance of the concept of the Centrally Planned Economies" *Jahrbuch für Sozialwissenschaft* **2** 255-266
Kowalski J S, 1986, "Regional conflicts in Poland: spatial polarization in a centrally planned economy" *Environment and Planning A* **18** 599-617
Kuklinski A, 1982, "Space, economic and regional studies in Poland" United Nations Center for Regional Development, Publications Section, Marunouchi 2-4-7, Naka-ku, Nagoya 460, Japan
Lodkowska G, 1985, "Spatial differentiation of local living standards and conditions in Poland" *Przegląd Geograficzny* **57**(3) 319-339
Statistical Yearbook for Poland 1985, Główny Urząd Statystyczny, Warszawa
Wiles P, 1979, "*Die Parallelwirtschaft*" Bundesinstitut für Ostwissenschaftliche Studien, Köln

Part 2

Urban Labour-market Processes and Inequality

Areal Heterogeneity and Labour Returns

L CURRY
University of Toronto

1 Heterogeneity

1.1 *Importance*

The ambiguity involved in designating areas homogeneous or heterogeneous is one of the most pervasive of geographical fundamentals. A territory can be one or the other according to the scale at which it is examined: this does not necessarily mean uniformity locally with diversity increasing with scale, although such a situation is common. Heterogeneity is closely tied to another fundamental, the relative closedness of local space. Again it need not happen that this increases with increasing scale, although it often does. Together these two principles permeate much of human geography but we shall be concerned here with their effect on labour markets.

1. Since a homogeneous region at one level is almost always heterogeneous at a lower or a higher level, the notion of density becomes arbitrary and has to be related to the mobility of the economic agents involved. The whole theory of trade, for example, or of spending patterns is rooted in these shifting sands.

2. A development project occurring in some area will provide positive benefits to some places, negative benefits to others, and be neutral elsewhere. This will almost always happen. It is a basic fact of life: some parts gain, some lose. In these circumstances Pareto optimality is virtually useless as a geographic welfare criterion because the scale of the area of calculation is essentially arbitrary. Even the development of trade will leave some areas worse off, even if there is aggregate gain.

3. The reverse is also true when it comes to paying for public goods, establishing equity levels, etc. Transfer payments and spatial freedom of movement of agents are part of the integrating role of higher order political authorities but, of course, are extremely blunt instruments.

4. Since political boundaries are essentially arbitrary nets dropped over economic resources, the objective functions established by the controlling units can be helpful or harmful to particular places. For example, the fortunes of the coffee economy in Venezuela would be quite different were it not situated next to a major petroleum exporting area.

1.2 *Theoretical significance*

My problem is very simple: how to specify the spatial relations between worker and job opportunities. This apparently purely technical issue is bound up with a number of important theoretical concerns. Present theory is unarticulated and ad hoc. To discuss the spatial structure of supply, demand, imports, exports, and flows of a commodity in price equilibrium we resort to predetermined regions. Similarly, in the theory of trade we note the ratios of labour, capital, and land in given regions. Yet we know that labour supply is not fixed, in the study of commuter travel, for example. Again, labour demand can only be assumed known when technology and prices are known, but these are variables in the trade problem. Each subsystem can be handled fairly formally, but there is no way to put the subsystems together. The obvious route is to follow Beckmann and Puu (1985) in embracing the continuous viewpoint. The two planks of the divergence-convergence laws (excess supply, demand) and the gradient (prices) provide an easy passage to flow fields with reference to commodity balances as well as transport costs and their minimising. This approach can provide great insight but does appear simplistic in its reliance on movements up slopes in the uniform plane or in spaces which can be transformed to it. Excess supply of a commodity can be defined if agents' supplies are known and vice versa, but how can we solve for both simultaneously?

With the spatial price equilibrium regional model and its continuous analogue it is possible to specify excess demand categorically. But this is only because atomistic competition is assumed. In fact, markets are the result of literal or metaphorical bargaining from positions of power based on degrees of monopoly. And, because there are no spatial boundaries in existence, the extent of monopoly here depends on the amount of competition nearby, just as the stability of a domino here depends on that of another there. It is this circumstance which determines the relative returns of labour and capital which are given for fixed regions in trade theory.

1.3 *In labour markets*

Heterogeneity in the economy has been previously considered in terms of bargaining power in fixed regions (Curry, 1985). The bargaining powers of heterogeneous agents and of opportunities are based on the degree of competition they are experiencing. Consider the agents in a tiny area and array them in terms of the degree of specialisation of their skills. Assume that all agents can perform tasks requiring the lowest skills and that some (and perhaps all) can work in successively more specialised (and progressively more differentiated) tasks. An agent obtains the highest return for its uniqueness in relation to other agents and for the universality of its skills relative to all opportunities. For high returns an agent will have only a small population of comparable agents and a large population of comparable opportunities. An opportunity pays only low returns when its needs are unique relative to other opportunities, and also when its needs are universal relative to the set of agents. The situation for agents is shown in figure 1. Variety of skills increases as degree of specialisation of skills increases. The greater the variety, the less the degree of competition among agents and thus the higher the remuneration. The slope of the remuneration–specialisation curve OO′ categorises factor heterogeneity in this tiny autarkic fixed area. The degree of homogeneity of opportunity requirements can be handled in similar fashion, with the difference that increasing competition between opportunities for agents leads to increasing and not decreasing remuneration to agents (figure 2).

In taking account of the spatial configuration of the large number of postulated tiny areas, assume that the slopes of a population of OO′ curves are independently randomly distributed so that the spectrum describing their areal differentiation is flat. Agents can move to opportunities in other unit areas and this will increase competition between agents. This mixing will reduce areal differentiation at small scales with progressively less effect at large scales. Prevailing commuter distances will determine the maximum scales affected (figure 3). Mixing due to the location of opportunities in adjacent areas will act similarly. The search of agents is likely to be biased towards greater variety of agents (and more homogeneous opportunities); maximum agent entropy and minimal opportunity entropy are thus desired. On the other hand, the lack of homogeneity of opportunities reduces the number of opportunities and thus the opportunity over agent (O/A) density and so the returns paid. The search of an opportunity is biased towards

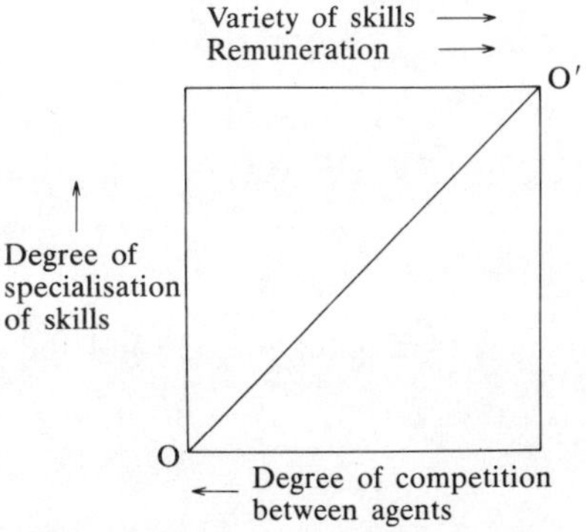

Figure 1. Agents' remuneration under competition.

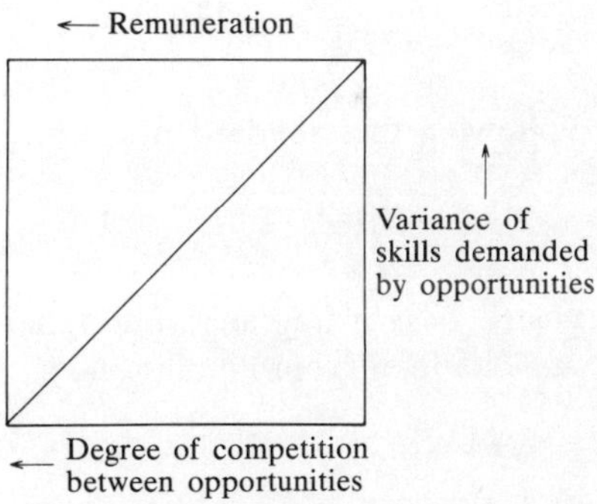

Figure 2. Remuneration of opportunities under competition.

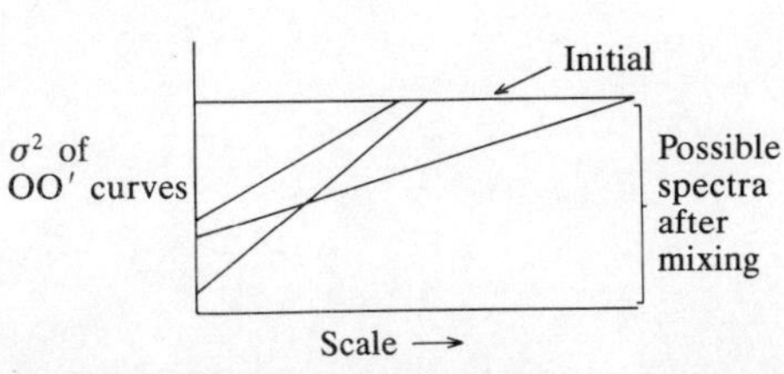

Figure 3. Areal differentiation by scales under mixing.

greater variety of opportunities and more homogeneous agents: the opportunity prefers maximum opportunity entropy and minimum agent entropy.

2 Distribution of incomes

2.1 *Maximum entropy approach*

First I shall look at a couple of aspatial models of the distribution of incomes, the first by Badger (1980) using only entropy-maximising methods. The distribution of incomes among all of the people of an area probably provides the best index of their bargaining power, since it captures the results of all the legal and customary practices which assign people to roles which determine their productivity and rent-gathering status. It is unfortunate that statistics only appear to be available for nations so that the more interesting aspects, their geography, are lost. The approach to be adopted is inferential using entropy maximising, appealing here to the ignorance of the analyst. In general, let there be a finite number of discrete values $x_1, x_2, ..., x_n$ having probabilities $P(x_1)$, $P(x_2)$, ..., $P(x_n)$, the latter to be inferred. A number of constraints of the form

$$\sum_t P(x_t)\,[f_t(x_t)] = C_j, \qquad j = 1, 2, ..., m, \tag{1}$$

are known. One of these is obtained by recalling that this is a probability problem,

$$\sum_t P(x_t) = 1\,. \tag{2}$$

Following the standard procedure of Jaynes, we obtain

$$P(x_t) = \exp[-\lambda_0 - \sum_{j=1}^{m} \lambda_j f_j(x_t)]\,, \tag{3}$$

where λ_0 is a Lagrange multiplier obtained from equation (2) and the λ_j are obtained from equation (1);

$$\exp(\lambda_0) = \sum_t \exp[-\sum_j \lambda_j f_j(x_t)]\,, \tag{4}$$

because this is a straightforward normalisation. A well-known parameter is the measure of income inequality, σ_u^2,

$$\sigma_u^2 = \sum_{t=1}^{n} [U(x_t) - \overline{U(x_t)}]^2\, P[U(x_t)] = C_1\,, \tag{5}$$

where

$$\overline{U(x_t)} = \sum_{t=1}^{n} U(x_t)\, P[U(x_t)]\,, \tag{6}$$

$U(x_t)$ is some function of x_t and C_1 is a constant. From equations (3) and (4),

$$P[U(x_t)] = \exp\left\{-\frac{[U(x_t)-\overline{U(x_t)}]^2}{2\sigma_u^2}\right\}$$

$$\times\left\langle\sum_{t=1}^{m}\exp\left\{-\frac{[U(x_t)-\overline{U(x_t)}]^2}{2\sigma_u^2}\right\}\right\rangle^{-1}, \tag{7}$$

$1/2\,\sigma_u^2$ being the Lagrangian multiplier.

The function of x, $U(x)$ which is to be used is now taken up. Because the income probabilities for the USA, displayed as a cumulative distribution on logarithmic probability paper, have a shallow inverted S-shape,

$$U(x_t) = \exp\left(-\frac{C}{x_t}\right)^d \tag{8}$$

is used. The inflection point occurs at

$$x_I = C\left(\frac{d}{1+d}\right)^{1/d}. \tag{9}$$

Badger used 'average societal utility function' arguments here which do not seem either acceptable or necessary. The inflection point approximately divides off the top 5% of incomes having about 20% of total income. It would appear more in keeping with the Jaynes formalism to introduce some parameter measuring concentration beyond that measured by σ^2 and obtain the appropriate multiplier. The final result is

$$P[U(x_t)] = \exp\left(-\frac{1}{2\sigma_u^2}\right)\left\{\exp\left[-\left(\frac{C}{x_t}\right)^d\right]-\overline{U(x_t)}\right\}^2$$

$$\times\left\langle\sum_{t=1}^{n}\exp\left(-\frac{1}{2\sigma_u^2}\right)\left\{\exp\left[-\left(\frac{C}{x_t}\right)^d\right]-\overline{U(x_t)}\right\}^2\right\rangle^{-1}. \tag{10}$$

Evidently the only constraints on the distribution of income which need to be appealed to are the mean, the variance, and some higher moment truncated below the top 5% of incomes. Since we can describe the distribution of incomes knowing only these parameters, explanation needs only to account for these values. The average represents general productivity and the increases above the inflection point for the 5% imply a lack of homogeneity in the population presumably caused by privileges of property ownership, or power, or talent which can be remunerated. It is the degree of spread as shown in the variance which is the interesting parameter and represents the degree of mixing, of mobility, of separate layering of bargaining groups. This is a rather strange result considering that there is such a lively process going on beneath these figures. I next consider the sort of distribution one would get by assigning occupations to technologies in a random fashion.

2.2 *Occupations into technologies*

Again ignoring spatial aspects, we can approach the distribution of incomes of occupations in terms of the technologies in which they are generated. It is useful to retain here a convention in biology and in economics which has definitional convenience. Under the competitive exclusion principle two different species cannot occupy the same niche; economics, with a push from mathematical programming, asserts a single technology organises a given mix of resources. It is reasonable to assume that incomes are decided by the number of persons in an occupation and the amount of demand for them by technologies. We need to 'derive' the technological structure of the economy or, more realistically, make some plausible guess about it.

Let technologies be composed of subcomponents and we shall assume occupations are listed according to their degree of specialisation: in the simplest interpretation, let there be K occupations ranked in terms of their monopoly power, with occupation r, the least specialised, occurring in all of r subtechnologies, so that occupation 1 is present in only one. Obviously, simply to exist, each occupation must be in at least one subtechnology and each subtechnology must have at least one occupation; there could be many members of an occupation. Assign the rth occupation on an independently random basis to one of r subtechnologies and keep doing this until it appears in all of the others. When this has been done for all occupations, technologies (not subcomponents) will be defined in terms of the occupations composing them, including the relative numbers of members of each. The values of the parameters of the resulting geometric distribution can be obtained. No generating mechanism is suggested.

Some results are (Cohen, 1966):

1 The number of technologies in which occupation r appears has an expected value of approximately $K^{-1}\sum(K+1-q)^{-1}$ $(q = 1, ..., r)$. The variance of this measure is $K^{-3}\sum(q-1)(K+1-q)^{-2}$ $(q = 1, ..., r)$.

2 On average, the less specialised the occupation, the greater the number of its members. However, there is no necessity for this always to be true because of random fluctuations, corresponding to the numbers needed within a technology (that is, factor coefficients).

3 The average number, H_j, of members that occupation r will have in technology j, is given by

$$E(H_j) = 1 + \sum_{o=j}^{r-1} (K-o)^{-1} , \qquad (11)$$

where o counts the number of members required to satisfy r types.

4 Let the number of members of an occupation be a variable and let T_o be the number of technology types containing at least one occupation

member if o members are assigned as above:

$$\left.\begin{aligned} E(T_o) &= K[1-(1-K^{-1})^o]\,, \\ \mathrm{var}(T_o) &= K^2\left[1-\left(\frac{2}{K}\right)^o-\left(1-K^{-1}\right)^{2o}\right] \\ &\quad +K\left\{\left(1-\mathrm{K}^{-1}\right)^o-\left[1-\left(\frac{2}{K}\right)^o\right]\right\}. \end{aligned}\right\} \qquad (12)$$

These results are useful as displaying the likelihood of particular opportunities obtaining particular occupation members and vice versa, other things being equal. This type of result would be part of a theory of locational decisions of firms.

5 The expectation of the number, T_r, of allocations necessary to reach r distinct technologies is $E(T_r)$ for an occupation, given earlier; the expected number of allocations for all occupations is the end of the game,

$$E\left(\sum_{r=1}^{K} T_K\right) = K^2\,. \qquad (13)$$

3 Access and monopoly power

The owner of an opportunity in a centre can give an initial estimate of the labour-supply curve by assuming that possible competitors pay various wages and attract various volumes of workers relative to him or her. For any given wage he or she pays there must be a range of possible wages the competitors could pay and this will provide a probability distribution of supply for a given wage. The wage A has paid produces a certain level of supply only when B and C's wages are given. Possible supply will be quite different from realised supply; a worker although ending up at A will still affect B and C, since he or she can always switch. The more that workers are capable of switching the more they are taken into account; with poor accessibility to other opportunities workers cannot switch and are beaten down by monopoly power. The better the accessibility to all opportunities the greater the gap between possible and realised supply (that is, the more there is double, triple, etc counting) and wages will be high.

The difference between actual and possible numbers of workers being employed at a centre is a function of geographical arrangements and so can be handled analytically for specific spatial distributions. We shall posit uniformly spaced employment centres on an uneven labour distribution and so allow the passing on of density effects over space. Obviously, integration over space depends on the distance apart of centres and thus the extent to which cumulation can occur. In reality, it is highly likely that employment is positively correlated with labour availability and, if this were perfect, the effects of this model would disappear. Consequently another model is briefly summarised to stress the role of friction.

3.1 *Morse on inventories*

Consider first a parable. A person joining a queue for service will have his or her waiting time determined by what has happened previously, perhaps hours ago. Arrivals may be quite sparse in that entry period but the time to completion can be long because of a previous dense period which is only slowly losing its effect on the queue size. Equally, this sparse period can affect a future dense period. To specify the conditions of the queue we need to know the density function describing arrivals with its parameters and that for service as well as the queue discipline. The spatial analogy is quite close, save that the first-come, first-served discipline which is often natural in the temporal case is rarely so in spatial labour markets—people do not go to the nearest available job opening. Also, instead of individual servicing, jobs tend to be clustered, not necessarily showing any covariation with homes, at least at lower scales.

Let there be territory in which the labour supply, of some mean density, S, is isotropically distributed so that the space each person has is an independent random variable. Employment centres are spaced at a fixed distance Q apart so allowing numbers to vary and areal differentiation to occur. There is some maximum distance, μ, apart beyond which workers will not travel, $\mu \geqslant kQ$, $(k = 1, 2, ...)$. The distance travelled for constant numbers of workers as we move away from a datum point is a random variable, $\tilde{N}$, representing the possible number of workers which can be tapped. We shall discuss this in terms of $\mu - \tilde{N} = i$ (figure 4) (Morse, 1955). The probability that n distance increments occur in a distance Q is a Poisson distribution,

$$\mathrm{U}_n(Q) = \frac{S^n \exp(-S)}{n!}, \tag{14}$$

where S is the mean density of workers. Note that the use of a Poisson distribution of distances between events refers to an 'inverse Poisson process' where counts per quadrat are negative exponential (Curry and McDougall, 1972). Let P_i be the steady-state probability that $\tilde{N} = \mu - i$. Since this is homogeneous space, P_i at some distance, v, will be the same as at $v + Q$ for every value of v. P_j, the probability of having a supply area of $\mu - j$ at distance $v + Q$, is related to P_i by the conditional probabilities, M_{ij}, of transition from state i to state j in distance Q.

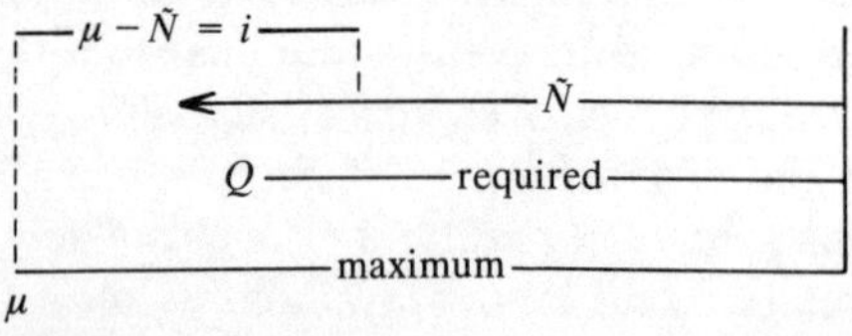

Figure 4. Relationships of specified distances (μ is maximum distance and $\tilde{N}$ is a random variable).

With $\mu - N$, that is, $i < Q$, if n distance increments are encountered between v and $v+Q$ the state of the system at $v+Q$ is $i+n = j$. The probability of this occurring is U_{j-i}. If $(k+1)Q > \mu - \tilde{N} \geqslant kQ$, then k centres requiring an extra distance of kQ are possible at distance v; if n distance increments are encountered between v and $v+Q$, the market distance, $\tilde{N}$, is $\mu - i + kQ - N$. The state of the system is thus given by $i - kQ + N = j$ and the probability of its occurring is U_{j-i+kQ}.
The state of the system is $i(0 \leqslant i)$.
The state probabilities are given by

$$P_j = \begin{cases} \sum_{i=0}^{j} U_{j-i} \sum_{k=0}^{\infty} P_{i+kQ}\,, & j < Q\,, \\ \sum_{i=0}^{Q-1} U_{j-i} \sum_{k=0}^{\infty} P_{i+kQ}\,, & j \geqslant Q\,, \end{cases} \tag{15}$$

with the transition elements

$$M_{kQ+i} = \begin{cases} 0\,, & j < Q\,, \\ U_{j-i}\,, & j \geqslant Q\,, \end{cases} \tag{16}$$

and matrix

$$\mathbf{M} = \begin{bmatrix} U_0 & U_1 & U_2 & \cdots & U_{Q-2} & U_{Q-1} & U_Q & \cdots \\ 0 & U_0 & U_1 & \cdots & U_{Q-3} & U_{Q-2} & U_{Q-1} & \cdots \\ 0 & 0 & U_0 & \cdots & U_{Q-4} & U_{Q-3} & U_{Q-2} & \cdots \\ & \vdots & & & & \vdots & & \\ 0 & 0 & 0 & \cdots & U_0 & U_1 & U_2 & \cdots \\ 0 & 0 & 0 & \cdots & 0 & U_0 & U_1 & \cdots \\ U_0 & U_1 & U_2 & \cdots & U_{Q-2} & U_{Q-1} & U_Q & \cdots \\ 0 & U_0 & U_1 & \cdots & U_{Q-3} & U_{Q-2} & U_{Q-1} & \cdots \\ & \vdots & & & & \vdots & & \end{bmatrix}. \tag{17}$$

In this problem we are clearly interested only in the steady-state results, that is, independent of any initial conditions. Using the transition probability matrix $\mathbf{M}$, we have, after n transitions,

$$\left.\begin{aligned} \mathbf{P}(n) &= \mathbf{P}(0)(\mathbf{M}^n)\,, \\ \mathrm{P}_j(n) &= \sum_i \mathrm{P}_i(0) M_{ij}^n\,, \\ (\mathbf{M}^n)_{ij} &= \sum_k (\mathbf{M}^{n-1})_{ik} M_{kj}\,. \end{aligned}\right\} \tag{18}$$

However, $\mathbf{M}^n$ approaches a limiting form independent of n as n is increased indefinitely. In this form, rows are identical, that is,

$$(\mathbf{M}^n)_{ij} \to \mathrm{P}_j(n \to \infty), \qquad \forall\, i\,. \tag{19}$$

In this steady state, the probability, $\mathrm{P}_j(n)$ is given by

$$\left.\begin{aligned} \mathrm{P}_j(n) &= \sum_i \mathrm{P}_i(0)(\mathbf{M}^n)_{ij} \to P_j \qquad (n \to \infty)\,, \\ \mathbf{P}(n) &\to \mathbf{P}(\infty) = [P_1, P_2, ..., P_s]\,, \end{aligned}\right\} \tag{20}$$

where the P_j are the steady-state probabilities:

$$P_j = \sum_{i=1}^{s} P_i M_{ij}\,. \tag{21}$$

The Ps from the s equations above are solved as

$$P_j = \begin{cases} \displaystyle\sum_{i=0}^{j} \frac{U_{j-i}}{Q}, & j < Q\,, \\ \displaystyle\sum_{j=0}^{Q-1} \frac{U_{j-i}}{Q}, & j \geqslant Q\,. \end{cases} \tag{22}$$

Since the state function has a value of x_i in state i, the expected value of x under steady-state conditions is given by

$$E(x) = \sum_i x_i P_i\,. \tag{23}$$

In our problem,

$$\begin{aligned} E(\tilde{N}) &= \sum_j (\mu - j) P_i \\ &= \mu - S - \tfrac{1}{2}(\mathrm{Q} - 1)\,, \end{aligned} \tag{24}$$

and the variance of x is given by

$$\sigma^2(x) = \sum_i P_i x_i^2 - E^2(x)\,. \tag{25}$$

Again in our problem,

$$\begin{aligned} \sigma^2(N) &= \sum_j (\mu - j)^2 P_j - E^2(\tilde{N}) \\ &= S + \tfrac{1}{12}(Q-1)^2\,. \end{aligned} \tag{26}$$

It is evident that for centres to be evenly spaced, they are likely to be of significantly different sizes and unlikely to be performing identical functions. For centres of constant size, however, bargaining relations will depend on the mean worker-density, S, the stipulated maximum distance apart of centres, μ, and, of course the chosen distance, Q. The fraction of area for which workers can reach a centre for given Q and μ is given by

$$\begin{aligned} \sum_{j=0}^{\mu-1} P_j &= \frac{1}{Q}\left\{\sum_{n=0}^{\mu-1} (\mu - \eta)\frac{S^n \exp(-S)}{n!} - \sum_{n=0}^{\mu-Q-1} [(\mu - Q) - n]\frac{S^n \exp(-S)}{n!}\right\} \\ &= \frac{1}{Q}[\mu \mathrm{D}_{\mu-1}(S) - (\mu - Q)\mathrm{D}_{\mu-Q-1}(S)]\,, \qquad \mu > Q\,, \end{aligned} \tag{27}$$

with

$$D_m(x) = \frac{1}{m+1} \sum_{n=0}^{m} (m+1-n) \frac{x^n \exp(-x)}{n!}, \tag{28}$$

a tabulated function. This fraction is almost 0 for $S > (\mu + \mu^{1/2})$, and is almost 1 for $S < [\mu - Q - (\mu - Q)^{1/2}]$.

The autocovariance function, $\rho_t(\tilde{N})$, is a measure of how the state function $\tilde{N}$ representing the distance travelled for a constant number of workers tends to return to its average value after it has, by chance, fluctuated away from it. If, say, the population tends to be dense in one area, N will be small; since centres are to be equally spaced at distance Q, it may be several centres away before we get back into phase with the average N on which Q will be based. In general,

$$\begin{aligned} \rho_n(x) &= \sum_i [P_i x_i - E(x)][P_{i+n} x_{i+n} - E(x)] \\ &= \sum_i [P_i x_i - E(x)][P_j x_j - E(x)] \\ &= \sum_i P_i x_i P_j x_j - E^2(x) \\ &= \sum_i P_i x_i \mathbf{M}_{ij}^n x_j - E^2(x)\,. \end{aligned} \tag{29}$$

For lag 0, that is, $n = 0$, ρ_n is of course equal to the variance of the state function, that is, in our problem,

$$\rho_o(\tilde{N}) = S + \tfrac{1}{12}(Q-1)^2\,; \tag{30}$$

for $n = 1$,

$$\rho_1(\tilde{N}) = \sum_{k=0}^{\infty} \sum_{j=0}^{Q-1} P_{kQ+j}(kQ+j)[j + \tfrac{1}{2}(1-Q)]\,, \tag{31}$$

where P_{kQ+j} is the probability of having a supply area of $\mu - (kQ+j)$ at distance $\nu + Q$. Whereas a Poisson series characterised by the independence of its variables has no autocorrelation, summing N variables will produce dependence. Since the system is Markovian, autocorrelation will decline exponentially so that only the value for lag 1 is required. It may be seen that the distance apart of the centres, Q, will determine the degree to which fluctuations persist in space, which might have been expected.

There must be a relation between spatial autocovariances in factor returns and the variance of incomes in a region. Obviously autocovariance for lag 0 is the variance of the sample. For a totally homogeneous surface, increasing the size of the area sampled will increase the variance encountered to only a small extent. Given that there are B distinct wage levels since there are B occupations, to obtain $\alpha\beta$ of them ($\alpha \leqslant 1$) the expected sample size is $B \ln(1-\alpha)^{-1}$ (Curry, 1967). For an independently random spatial distribution, derivatives are independent and scale component equally likely and the function describing their contribution to total areal differentiation is flat. With local mixing, differentiation goes down, that is, covariance goes up at small scales, whereas total variance goes down. Thus, as dependence is introduced, variance is reduced.

3.2 *Spatial friction*

It is this autocovariance which is the incisive variable. We have assumed workers go to their nearest centre regardless of price, which we do not believe. However, by doing this we have a measure of the way in which centres influence each other. A region of dense population implies a large fluctuation in the density surface. Each centre here will have a large gap in its possible-realised numbers, so that wages will be low. Possible numbers are measured by some multiple of $\tilde{N}$, the distance for a given number of people. Actual numbers are measured by the same multiple of Q, the equal spacing of centres adopted allowing numbers to vary. We can take the lag-1 autocovariance as an overall description of wage differentiation. Thus, in a sparse region, centres are protected from each other and prices are high.

We take up now the importance of spatial friction mentioned earlier (Haken, 1978). Take the same process as before but in one dimension and consider here the departure from the average degree of competitiveness which, since there is no drift, trends in a positive or negative direction with equal probability overall. Given an impulse of strength ϕ at location j where there is an intensity of l_j and a gradient of $\delta(l-l_j)$, the force of the impulse in direction ± 1, $\psi(l)$, is given by $\phi\delta(l-l_j)(\pm 1)$. With a friction constant of Y, that is, the difficulty of influencing neighbouring areas, and a gradient of V, the friction force is $-YV$. Consequently, the change in gradient is $\dot{V} = -YV+\psi(l)$. If we assume a Poisson process, the autocovariance function $< \mathrm{u}(l)\mathrm{v}(l') >$, $(l > l')$, can be shown to equal $(\phi^2/\partial y)\exp(-y|l-l'|)$. This shows how quickly the gradient loses its memory: it loses it altogether at $1/Y$. The degree of departure, $(\sim\phi^2)$, from the overall average is determined by the dissipation $(\sim Y)$. If $Y = 0$, this leads to extreme areal differentiation.

In this case, we have abandoned any spatial integration to concentrate on a frictional effect. It should be noted that the friction depicted here is the inverse of that affecting the movement of workers. If a worker finds it easy to move, his or her friction will be low, but the friction affecting the transmission of departures from the (zero) average will be high.

4 Areal transfer function approach

I shall now attempt to model the circumstances directly in theoretical vein where isotropy is assumed and the object is to make general statements about an area. Let it be composed of many small regions and let there be two maps, one of workers within a particular range of skills constituting an occupation, and the other of a set of opportunities requiring these skills (we ignore the edge effect of classification). Form the opportunity/agent ratio for each region and then, by cascaded averaging and differencing, form the scale components of this map. This is the transfer function linking the two maps made of Z-transforms and can operate by simple multiplication. Now choose a distance-weighting function representing the probabilities that a worker in that occupation would travel certain distances to secure a job. We cannot have this function wage dependent and shall regard it as representing recruitment practices in terms of local information flows producing a diffusive type flow. Obtain the Z-transforms of this function and multiply it by that of the map ratio. We now see how the areal differentiation of the ratio changes through the possibility of workers being willing to move. The joint transfer function represents the scale components of relative wage rates if there are no substitution effects.

Repeat this procedure for each of a number of occupations, using different spread functions where necessary. Now introduce feedback between all pairs of these joint transfer functions, which could involve direct substitution, with weights assigned to represent the degree to which workers could switch or be switched. Feedback is again simple multiplication in the Z-transform domain. We now have complex adjustments occurring with the final result incorporating considerable interplay between the mixes of occupations. Presumably, multiplications should be continued until a steady state is reached, although it is probably the manner of change which would be most interesting. Note that any data one can obtain on substitution coefficients for occupations will already have taken distance relations into account. However there is not much we can do about this. Figure 5 shows a flow diagram of the relationships.

To return to the two maps at the beginning, let the map of workers be related to the map of jobs by an impulse-response function made up of weights, h_k, such that (Curry, 1983),

$$x_w = \sum_{k=0}^{\infty} h_k y_{w-k} . \qquad (32)$$

Use of the Z operator $\mathrm{Z}^{-k}\mathrm{f}(w) = \mathrm{f}(w-k)$ gives

$$x_w = \sum_{k=0}^{\infty} h_k \mathrm{Z}^{-k} y_w$$

$$= \mathrm{H}(\mathrm{Z}) y_w , \qquad (33)$$

where H(Z) is the transfer function defined so that

$$x_w = y_w (1 + h_1 \mathrm{Z}^{-1} + h_2 \mathrm{Z}^{-2} + \ldots) . \qquad (34)$$

We can then move directly to the difference equation generalising the output map from this input map,

$$y_w = x_w - a_1 x_{w-1} - a_2 x_{w-2} - \dots . \tag{35}$$

If we introduce the spread operator by its transfer function, say

$$y_w = x_w(1-bZ^{-1}) = H_g(Z)x_w , \tag{36}$$

the combination is

$$y_w = [c_1 H_r(Z) + c_2 H_g(Z)]x_w , \tag{37}$$

so that the joint operator is

$$x_w = \frac{y_w}{1-(c_1 a_1 + c_2 b)Z^{-1} - (c_1 a_2)Z^{-2}} . \tag{38}$$

We can then have this transfer function feed back into that of other occupations as they will feed back into this one. Corresponding difference equations can be obtained at each successive stage and the a_i examined.

Without going into a lot of algebra, it is possible to convert the transfer functions in the scale of areal differentiation domain into impulse-response functions in the distance domain and from these obtain the equations which might have generated such curves, that is, obtain the coefficients of, say, a second-order difference equation.

I have stressed that we want to generalise about the whole maps and this is why I assumed stationarity. If this is obviously untrue, we can

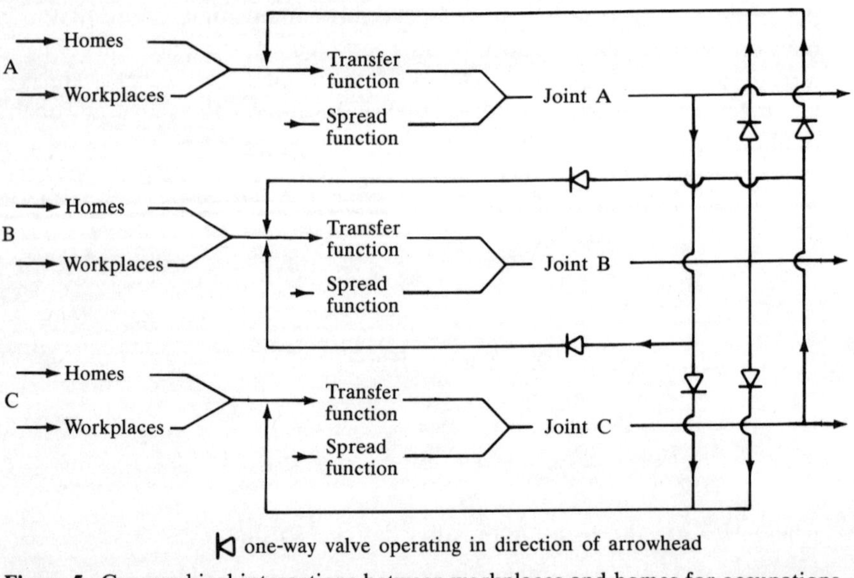

Figure 5. Geographical interactions between workplaces and homes for occupations A, B, C.

still carry out a similar type of analysis but must lose in elegance because we have to go into much greater geographical detail. In the cascaded averaging and differencing routine, each data point obtained its own transfer function and these were then averaged for the whole map. But we can keep them separate. The analysis is the same, repeating it for each data point. Finally we can move back into the distance domain and out of transforms. There would be severe problems at the map edges, but taking the analysis over a larger area than really required would mitigate them. A strictly distance-based spread operator might not be so plausible as it was for the whole map. And going into the generating equations does not seem useful. But in principle the analysis could be done and so it is not necessary to (a) treat areas with very determinate patterns as stationary or (b) treat only areas which are reasonably homogeneous.

References

Badger W W, 1980, "An entropy-utility model for the size distribution of income", in *Mathematical Models as a Tool for the Social Sciences* Ed. B J West (Gordon and Beach, New York) pp 87-120

Beckmann M J, Puu T, 1985 *Spatial Economics: Density, Potential and Flow* (North-Holland, Amsterdam)

Cohen J E, 1966 *A Model of Simple Competition* (Harvard University Press, Cambridge, MA)

Curry L, 1967, "Central places in the random spatial economy" *Journal of Regional Science* **7** (supplement) 217-238

Curry L, 1983, "Elements of spatial statistical systems analysis" *Professional Geographer* **35** 149-157

Curry L, 1985, "Factor returns and geography" *Geografiska Annaler(B)* **67** 69-81

Curry L, McDougall E B, 1972, "Statistical spatial analysis and remotely sensed imagery" unpublished final report to US Geological Survey; copy available from the author

Haken H, 1978 *Synergetics* (Springer, Berlin)

Morse P M, 1955, "Stochastic properties of waiting lines" *Journal of the Operations Research Society of America* **3** 255-261

Decentralisation in the London Region: Some Policy Simulations

I J MOLHO
University of Newcastle upon Tyne

1 Introduction

The pattern of decentralisation which may be observed in most parts of the British urban and regional system involves a complex set of interdependencies between movements in population and employment, reflecting both housing and labour market processes. These processes have substantial implications in terms of the prospects of urban and rural areas alike, and the welfare of their inhabitants. One possible approach to the issue is to regard such patterns of decentralisation as reflecting dynamic tendencies toward some underlying spatial equilibrium in the distribution of population and jobs. The complexity of the interactive processes involved, however, coupled with the difficulty of identifying the underlying equilibrium, make it very difficult to assess the likely effects of any policy initiative aimed at alleviating spatial economic imbalance. Thus, within the content of the general flux of economic and social forces, it is not at all clear what the ultimate effect might be on such imbalances of policies such as local job creation, public housebuilding, or the stimulation of private house construction.

The pattern of decentralisation in Great Britain is by now well documented (for example, see Keeble, 1976; Fothergill and Gudgin, 1982; Kennett, 1982; Owen et al, 1984; Vickerman, 1984). In order to answer such policy questions, even in qualitative terms, however, it is necessary to construct a more explicit behavioural model of the underlying processes. Authors of various studies have posited the notion that 'people follow jobs' or, alternatively, that 'jobs follow people', and have attempted to test the direction of causality (Steinnes, 1982). Others have set out a view of population and employment dispersal as mutually reinforcing processes, and suggested that cumulative causation of this kind may even lead to a progressive destabilisation of the urban economic base (Eversley, 1973).

A number of attempts have been made to construct empirical models of labour and housing market systems in metropolitan areas located within a regional and national context (Gordon and Lamont, 1982; Congdon, 1983), which implicitly embody such cumulative processes. Unfortunately, because of their very complexity, these cannot be directly interpreted in terms of the likely effects of government policy. First, important nonlinearities in the estimated relationships are a block to the direct inversion of such systems to yield simple reduced forms, where the effects of changes in exogenous variables on endogenous ones may be directly observed. Second, and more importantly, the presence of important spatial *interactions*, fundamental to the process involved, implies that a change in any one particular area, will set up ripple effects which will ultimately affect to varying degrees every other area in the system. More formally, such models cannot be handled in terms of *vectors* of endogenous and exogenous variables (taking on assigned values for each area), since all the areas are intimately related to each other via *matrices* of spatial interactions. These are very real problems which need careful attention before the important policy issues can be adequately addressed.

In this study I seek to use and adapt an existing model of labour and housing market interdependencies (from Gordon and Lamont, 1982), first to *solve* the system, and then to simulate the model under a variety of different policy scenarios. The analysis relates to the period 1966–71, and covers Greater London and its surrounding Outer Metropolitan Area (OMA). This period is of interest, partly because the data available permit the marrying together of the 1966 and 1971 Censuses in a way which it is impossible to do for the 1981 Census, and also because decentralisation from London was at its height at this time. The implications of the changes that have occurred in this process since the early 1970s are considered in the concluding section of this paper.

In the next section of this paper are outlined the broad features of the model used here, and section 3 is a consideration of the framework from the point of view of competing explanations of dispersal from London. In section 4, a methodology for solving the model is presented, and section 5 presents the results of the simulation exercises. Section 6 provides a summary and conclusion.

2 The model

Gordon and Lamont's (1982) original model of labour and housing market interaction in the London region was used essentially as a framework for the investigation of a number of specific hypotheses about causal processes, and no attempt was made to solve the whole system. As originally specified, there were a number of unsatisfactory features which became apparent when it was translated into a simulation model, and these have required adaptation and reestimation of a number of equations, to improve both their fit and the stability of the system. Some other inadequacies remain, as will become apparent in section 4. However, the basic form of the model is clearly appropriate for the simulation of intrametropolitan change, incorporating as it does not only interaction between housing and labour market variables but also the interaction between areas which follows from the shifting patterns of migration and commuting.

Migration flows are specified in terms of an extended form of gravity model which separated migrants according to the search field they operate within:

$$M_{ij} = \sum_s M_{ij}^s = \sum_s A_i^s B_j^s \exp(-\beta^s D_{ij}) \,, \tag{1}$$

where

M_{ij} signifies the number of migrants moving from area i to area j over a specified period,

s indicates the search field they operate within,

A_i, B_j reflect attraction and repulsion factors attached to the areas of origin and destination, respectively,

D_{ij} represents physical distance between origin and destination,

β is a parameter measuring sensitivity of migrants to distance.

In an analysis of migration patterns in and around the London area (including exchanges with other parts of Great Britain[(1)]), three principal migration streams were found, corresponding to national, regional, and local fields of search. Each of these search fields was associated with particular underlying *motivations* for movement, related to employment, environment and housing, and housing alone.

The push and pull factors for each stream were then specified as functions of independent variables, with equations of the form

$$\ln\left(\frac{A}{P}\right)_i^s = \alpha_0^s + \sum_h \alpha_h^s X_{ih} \,, \tag{2}$$

$$\ln\left(\frac{B}{P}\right)_i^s = \gamma_0^s + \sum_k \gamma_k^s Y_{ik} \,, \tag{3}$$

where

P represents a population-size deflator,

$\boldsymbol{X}_h$, $\boldsymbol{Y}_k$ are vectors of independent variables,

α_h, γ_k are corresponding parameters.

Actual rates of inflow and outflow, in this gravity model formulation, also depend on the push and pull factors for each other area, and thus on any changes which they experience in the independent variables.

The labour-market subsystem in the model (defined only for men in this version) consists of the pair of *national* stream migration-equations (for pushes and pulls), an unemployment equation, and an equation determining the rate of employment growth in each area. Outward migration in this stream principally reflected mobility characteristics of the local population, particularly in terms of skill structure. Inward migration, on the other hand, was determined by rates of employment growth (averaged across local travel-to-work areas), the perceived attractiveness of the area as measured by residential preference scores, and the availability of privately rented furnished accommodation.

(1) The migration matrix consisted of seventy-one areas in London and the OMA, plus forty-one areas covering the rest of Great Britain, the fineness of the definitions being progressively less, the further away from London.

Unemployment affected national stream migration, both as an inducement to leave and as a deterrent to entry. Employment growth rates were determined principally by the multiplier effects of net migration (in all three streams) and by the local industrial structure(2). Unemployment was determined in the model by rates of local employment change, and their average across the relevant travel-to-work area, with the difference between them reflecting the effects of induced commuting changes. Local unemployment rates also reflected the pattern of housing tenure in an area, residential density, the natural growth of labour supply, and the skill structure of the local population.

The housing-market system consisted of four migration equations (that is, push and pull factor equations for each of the two housing-related migration streams), plus two house-construction equations (one for the public and one for the private sector), and an equation determining house prices. The migration equations for the regional and local streams depended upon growth in housing-construction rates, the distribution of house tenures in an area, environmental attractiveness, and house prices. Private-sector house-construction rates depended principally upon the pressure of *demand* for housing, as captured by natural growth in the local population and net migration (in all three streams) into the area. Local authority housebuilding on the other hand mainly reflected the existing tenure pattern, housing stress, and slum clearance. The house-price equation was specified as a supply function, but the estimated supply elasticity was very high and prices appeared principally to reflect land availability and wage costs in construction.

The housing and labour market systems interacted with each other via the following principal routes:

(1) all forms of net migration (whether induced by labour-market conditions or otherwise) stimulated employment growth by local multiplier effects on labour demand, as well as adding to the stock of local labour supply;

(2) all forms of net migration contributed to the pressure for local housebuilding;

(3) the mix of house tenures affected the attraction of the area for all forms of in-migration, as well as acting as a potential constraint on out-migration, thus, on both counts, affecting house construction, employment growth, and unemployment rates.

A full listing of the model is given in appendix A.2 of this paper, and appendix A.1 gives an explanation of the changes which have been introduced in the version used for this simulation.

(2) A shift-share variable was included for this purpose, constructed according to the *national* growth rates of industries present in the local economy.

3 Decentralisation

The housing and labour market interactions embodied in the model involve a combination of positive and negative feedback loops, with the mode of change of the regional system depending essentially on the balance between these two forms of link. This applies particularly to the case of decentralisation of population and employment, which has been the most obvious characteristic of the region in the last quarter of a century, and the policy issues relating to its possible modification, through the stimulation of employment growth and house construction in the inner areas.

We start by considering the positive feedback loops which would tend to make decentralisation self-sustaining. In the Gordon and Lamont (1982) model the bulk of the outward-moving population is concentrated in the regional and local migration streams, attracted to the outer metropolitan areas *not* so much by the availability of jobs, as by the availability of housing (particularly for owner-occupation), and the better quality of environment. This pattern is self-reinforcing in the model, insofar as net in-migration induces further housebuilding which serves to attract more migrants to an area. The process also has repercussions for the labour market, with in-migration stimulating local demand and generating additional employment in the area. The generation of job opportunities in the outer metropolitan area in turn serves to induce in-migration in the national *job-related* stream, thus setting up a further self-reinforcing chain. The decentralisation of *population* and the decentralisation of *jobs* thus appear to be mutually supportive processes. The social selectivity of outward movement may further increase the tendency to mutual reinforcement. This cannot be tested within the present aggregate version of the model, but we should expect to find that the operation of the housing-market constrains *outward* movement among the less skilled manual workers, particularly in the regional stream. As a result a residual of unskilled manual workers would tend to be left in the inner city, forming black spots of unemployment in these areas. The rising unemployment rates in the inner city would then serve further to induce dispersal away from the urban core.

Against this tendency to self-sustaining change, the principal set of negative feedbacks in the system involves the links between unemployment, migration, and commuting. Unemployment increases the tendency to out-migration from an area, but population losses, from whatever cause, as well as induced increases in out-commuting, serve in turn to lower unemployment. We might expect a similar negative loop to operate between land availability and movement of population or employment, particularly if land constraints in London play the crucial role suggested by Fothergill and Gudgin (1982). However, in the estimated equations, land availability appeared *not* to affect patterns of employment growth substantially. To some extent, this may reflect difficulties of measurement, as well as the rather aggregative fashion in which employment change is treated in the model[3]. In the estimated equation, however, of greater importance than land availability appeared to be rates of local demolitions, which were associated with job losses, and which appeared to index a variety of problems associated with premises in the older industrial areas. The main impact of land availability per se was as a supply-side influence on house prices; however, the impact of house prices in the rest of the estimated system was also fairly slight, perhaps because it is the expectations of *future* house prices which are most relevant for residentially motivated migrants. Whatever the cause, the weak effects of land prices and house prices in the model mean that there is little advantage in seeking formally to complete this loop by making land availability itself endogenous, as a function of shifts in population and employment.

In most respects, the model is a formalisation of a fairly traditional perspective on the decentralisation process, in which the inner city is seen as an increasingly less desirable location both for households and for firms (for example, see Foreman-Peck and Gripaios, 1977; Hare, 1986). Perhaps the main differences lie, first, in the separation made between streams of migration involving distinct sets of motive and constraint, and the recognition that the principal outward streams from London are related more directly to the *housing* market than to the labour market; second, the view of the decentralisation of population and employment as mutually *reinforcing* processes with cumulative effects, in which the spatial distribution of *opportunities* plays a crucial role; and, last, the explicit recognition of interdependencies between the housing markets and labour markets in this process, for example, insofar as housing-related moves can generate jobs (as well as construction activity) in the outer areas and job-related moves can also stimulate housebuilding.

One important limitation of the model lies in the fact that, whereas decentralisation is a long-term process, the model is essentially cross-sectional, relating to changes over a particular five-year interval (1966–71). This five-year period may represent a passing phase in a cumulative process of change and is not necessarily an appropriate base from which to draw conclusions about appropriate policies for the late 1980s. However, it is argued here that, in recognising the interdependencies involved, the model provides a suitable starting point for at least qualitative assessment of the effects of different policies in a complex system of labour markets and housing markets. In the concluding section of this paper, the degree to which circumstances have *changed* since 1971 will be discussed, together with the possible implications of these changes for the simulation results.

(3) No distinction is made between different sectors of industry, part-time or full-time jobs, or job losses and job gains—only the net aggregate change is measured.

In principle, the model could be employed to produce longer-term simulations by solving it for successive five-year periods. However, many of the *independent* variables in the analysis (for example, land availability, residential density, etc) would not remain exogenous in the long term. A possibly more important example is the skill-structure variable, which acts in the model as an exogenous determinant of both migration and unemployment. Clearly, in the long run the skill structure of the local population in an area will be affected by successive waves of migration and thus be endogenous in terms of the self-selection of population groups living in an area (Evans and Richardson, 1981). Even more fundamentally, it may be argued that the occupational mix in an area reflects as much the characteristics of accessible *jobs* as they reflect the characteristics of the residents who fill those jobs. Depending upon the degree of demand deficiency at a particular time and place, potentially highly skilled workers may be forced to take unskilled jobs, and thus become labelled as unskilled (Norris, 1978). The treatment of skill-structure variables as exogenous must thus be highly questionable, particularly over the longer term, and, for these reasons, the simulation results presented must be viewed only as a guide to the likely effects of policy in the short to medium run.

Weighing against these limitations, the main strengths of the model lie in its explicit treatment of *space*, with spatial interactions being handled by the gravity equations in the case of migration, and averaged growth rates in employment across travel-to-work areas in the case of commuting. These very strengths do, however, serve to complicate the interpretation of results and represent a block to simple solution methods.

4 The solution method

The main problem involved in simulating the model, outlined in section 2 and listed in the appendix, was that, whereas many of the endogenous and exogenous variables such as unemployment or house prices took the form of *vectors* with single values for each area, the variables capturing spatial interactions (such as migration) take on the form of *matrices*, with each cell in the matrix reflecting the intensity of interaction between pairs of areas. No standard computer package or any simple optimisation algorithm was found which was capable of dealing with such a situation.

The solution method devised for the purpose started by treating as exogenous such variables as net migration which depended upon the simulation of interactions, though they are in fact *endogenous* in the model. When a solution had been generated on this basis for the housing and labour market system[(4)], the values obtained for the migration push and pull factors [equations (2) and (3)] in each stream could then

[(4)] NAG routine E04JAF was used for this purpose.

be inserted into the estimated gravity models [of the form of equation (1)] to predict the complete migration matrix[5]. By summing and differencing the predicted inflows and outflows, *predictions* of the pattern of net migration in each stream could then be generated. These were then treated as exogenous once again, and used to resolve the model. Iteration continued by solving for the push-pull factors, predicting net migration, resolving the model, and so on.

The problem thus becomes one of finding that pattern of net migration in each stream, which, when inserted into the model, yields a set of migration push and pull factors which reproduce the original vectors of net migration. At each iteration, a criterion (F) was constructed, measuring the degree to which the net migration variables changed between iterations[6].

$$F = \sum_k \sum_i (\hat{x}_{ik} - \tilde{x}_{ik})^2 , \qquad (4)$$

where i indicates the area, k the variable [since there is more than one net migration stream in the model—also see footnote (6)], $\hat{x}$ indicates a current predicted value, and $\tilde{x}$ indicates the predicted value of the variable in the previous iteration.

The calculated value of F was then used as the convergence criterion for the simulation model, as well as being used to guide the *direction* in which the net migration variables changed. Each time the criterion fell in value, an improvement was deemed to have occurred, and the new set of net migration variables would be inserted back into the model. If that led to a further improvement, the process would be repeated. If not, then a *fraction* of the total step would be tried[7]. If this still did not produce an improvement in F, movements in the reverse direction would be tried. In cases in which all attempts to generate an improvement failed, then a deterioration would be accepted temporarily, and improvements from the new position would be tried. Although this procedure proved rather laborious computationally, it generally proved possible to generate a solution, with values of F of less than 0.25 (accumulated over all the areas and all the variables) being accepted as constituting convergence.

(5) The push and pull factors for areas outside Greater London and the OMA were implicitly treated as fixed throughout the analysis in generating the predicted net migration figures for each stream.

(6) In the adapted framework, migration *potentials* were also included as determinants of second and third stream migration (see appendix), and since these also change between iterations, they were also included in the calculation of F. In a separate subroutine, changes in the travel to work area employment growth term were also calculated, but these proved generally stable.

(7) That is, a variable would be constructed of the form $\tilde{x} + a(\hat{x} - \tilde{x})$ where $0 < a < 1$, and a was chosen experimentally.

Tests using different initial starting values for the net migration variables suggested that the solution thereby attained was also unique, at least over the broad neighbourhood which was covered.

5 Results

Three different sets of simulations were run, and the results of these are presented in tables 1–3. The model predicts values of the endogenous variables for each of the seventy-one districts in the analysis (including the thirty-two London boroughs), as well as for each cell in the matrices of the three migration streams. These results have therefore been aggregated for the purposes of presentation. Summary statistics are presented for the endogenous variables and for *net* migration (as calculated from the predicted gross flows matrices) for three broad concentric zones: Inner London, Outer London, and the Outer Metropolitan Area[(8)]. The 'base run' presented in the tables shows the results of solving the model as it stands, with actual (1971) values for the exogenous variables.

Table 1. Simulation results: job-creation scheme.

Variables[a]	Base run[b]			5% boost to employment growth in Inner London[b]			Difference[b]		
	IL	OL	OMA	IL	OL	OMA	IL	OL	OMA
U	0.052	0.028	0.023	0.048	0.026	0.022	−0.004	−0.002	−0.001
MECH	−0.128	0.008	−0.025	−0.081	0.001	−0.024	0.047	0.007	0.001
WECH	−0.100	−0.049	−0.030	−0.065	−0.026	−0.021	0.035	0.023	0.009
PHCN	0.019	0.042	0.052	0.018	0.045	0.052	−0.001	0.003	0.000
LHCN	0.063	0.037	0.035	0.063	0.037	0.035	0.000	0.000	0.000
PRICE	7087	6396	5802	7087	6399	5803	0	3	1
NET1	−0.003	−0.013	−0.002	0.008	−0.009	−0.002	0.011	0.004	0.000
NET2	−0.029	−0.037	0.000	−0.036	−0.036	0.001	−0.007	0.001	0.001
NET3	−0.089	0.059	−0.001	−0.098	0.066	−0.001	−0.009	0.007	0.000
$\sum$NETS	−0.121	0.009	−0.003	−0.126	0.021	−0.002	0.005	0.012	0.001
ΔC[c]							0.026	−0.016	−0.015

[a] See appendix A.2 for full variable definitions: U is unemployment rate; MECH is local rate of employment change; WECH is travel-to-work area employment change; PHCN is private construction; LHCN is local authority construction; PRICE is average house price; NET1-3 are net migration in the national, regional, and local streams, respectively; ΔC is change in net balance of commuting. All variables except PRICE are expressed as proportions. Results for PRICE have been unlogged.

[b] IL is Inner London; OL is Outer London; OMA is Outer Metropolitan Area.

[c] Estimates calculated 'off the model' on the basis of a regression model of the impact of differential employment growth (MECH − WECH) on the change in the net balance of commuting.

(8) Results for individual boroughs are available on request from the author.

A number of features may be noted here. First, and most conspicuously, decentralisation of *employment* is evident in terms of differential rates of job loss in the zones, the highest losses being observed in Inner London. In terms of employment growth within travel-to-work radius, the predicted pattern is a simple one, with more favourable trends as one moves from inner to outer areas. Decentralisation of *population* tends to be concentrated in the more localised residential migration streams, that is, streams two and three. The fact that the sum of net flows for all

Table 2. Simulation results: housebuilding programmes.

Variables	Effect of 1% increase in LHCN in Inner London[a]			Effect of $\frac{1}{4}$% increase in PHCN in Inner London[a]		
	IL	OL	OMA	IL	OL	OMA
U	0.000	0.000	0.000	0.000	0.000	0.000
MECH	0.001	0.000	0.000	0.001	−0.001	0.000
WECH	0.001	0.001	0.000	0.001	0.002	0.001
PHCN	0.001	0.000	0.000	0.002	0.000	0.000
LHCN	0.010	0.000	0.000	0.001	0.000	0.000
PRICE	2	−1	0	3	0	−1
NET1	−0.001	0.000	0.000	−0.002	−0.001	0.000
NET2	0.001	−0.001	0.000	0.001	−0.002	−0.001
NET3	0.000	0.000	0.000	0.002	−0.001	0.000
$\sum$NETS	0.000	−0.001	0.000	0.001	−0.004	−0.001

Notes: see table 1.

[a] Results are presented in term of *differences* from the base run.

Table 3. Simulation results: supply-side policies.

Variables	Mobility assistance. Assisted employment moves in: Inner London			Mobility assistance. Assisted employment moves in: all areas			Retraining schemes 5% fall in UNSK in Inner London		
	IL	OL	OMA	IL	OL	OMA	IL	OL	OMA
U	−0.003	0.000	0.000	−0.003	−0.002	−0.001	−0.012	0.000	0.000
MECH	0.000	0.000	0.000	0.000	0.000	0.000	−0.001	−0.001	0.000
WECH	0.000	0.000	0.000	0.000	0.000	0.000	0.000	0.000	0.000
PHCN	0.000	0.001	0.000	0.000	0.000	0.000	0.000	0.000	0.000
LHCN	0.000	0.000	0.000	0.000	0.000	0.000	0.000	0.000	0.000
PRICE	0	0	0	0	0	0	0	0	0
NET1	0.000	0.000	0.000	0.000	0.000	0.000	−0.002	−0.001	0.000
NET2	0.000	0.000	0.000	0.000	0.000	0.000	0.001	0.000	0.000
NET3	−0.001	0.001	0.000	0.000	0.000	0.000	0.000	0.000	0.000
$\sum$NETS	−0.001	0.001	0.000	0.000	0.000	0.000	−0.001	−0.001	0.000

Notes: see tables 1 and 2.

three areas is negative reflects the fact that population is leaving London and the OMA as a whole, for the Outer South East and East Anglia. Unemployment shows the characteristic urban gradient of high unemployment in the inner city, progressively falling off the farther one moves from the centre. In all these respects, the base solution successfully reproduces observed patterns of variation in the region without having recourse to any directly spatial indicators among the exogenous variables.

The predicted effects of an autonomous boost to employment growth in each borough of Inner London of 5% (amounting to over 50000 jobs) are shown in the second column of table 1, and the difference between the two runs is shown in column 3. The boost to employment in the inner city obviously also generates job opportunities for outer-city residents, and this is reflected in an increase in 'travel-to-work area' employment growth (WECH) in Outer London and the OMA as well as in Inner London.

Three main labour-market effects emerge from this simulation. First, national stream migrants (NET1) are attracted to the inner *and* the outer city (as a suitable residence base from which to travel to work)[9]; second, there is a substantial shift in the net balance of commuting (ΔC) toward the inner city; and, last, there is some reduction in unemployment both in the inner and the outer city. The unemployment effect in Inner London is very small, however, and the bulk of the impact seems to be absorbed in the commuting response, reflecting the substantial take-up of inner-city jobs by outer-city residents. In the model there is no *direct* link between the predicted changes in unemployment and those in the various components of labour supply and demand, since the unemployment equation is cast in the form of equilibrium *levels* rather than within-period changes. Nevertheless, comparison of the predicted changes in commuting, unemployment, national stream migration, and employment growth for Inner London suggests a substantial degree of consistency. There is clearly a problem, however, insofar as the substantial commuting response ought to 'export' much of the benefits of the job-creation scheme to the outer city, whereas inspection of the results reveals this not to be the case; the observed reduction in outer-city unemployment, and the inflow of national stream migrants, is insufficient to balance the outflow of commuters. The main reason for this anomaly ultimately lies in the fact that the migration response implicit in the unemployment equation would appear to be substantially greater than that which is actually observed in NET1, and there is no constraint built into the model to ensure consistency between the two. Further work is required in terms of *modelling* to settle this issue which clearly goes beyond the scope of this paper.

(9) Mover–stayer and vacancy-chain effects have been suppressed on this simulation, on the basis that these represent rather longer-term adjustment mechanisms, as opposed to the simple impact effects simulated here.

To turn to the housing-market effects of the policy some interesting interdependencies are in evidence, stemming from the attraction of national stream migrants to the inner *and* the outer city as suitable residential areas from which to commute to work. In the *outer* city, a chain reaction is produced insofar as such migrants serve to stimulate private house construction there. Such householding serves to attract *residential* migrants to the area (NET2) and (NET3), stimulating further housebuilding, and so on. In the *inner* city, by contrast, any potential stimulation of local housebuilding is 'siphoned off' by the currents of residential movement to the outer city, resulting from the growth of housing opportunities there. Essentially, the two areas may be seen as competing for these localised migrant streams, with the outer city coming off slightly the better.

These housing-market effects have further repercussions on the labour market, insofar as losses of residential migrants lead to a fall in local demand in the inner city. It is this phenomenon, then, which explains why a small fraction of the initial boost of 5% in inner-city employment growth gets 'crowded out' in the final equilibrium, settling at an increase of 4.7%. On the other hand, the *outer* city benefits from the increased demand due to inward residential migration, in the form of positive multiplier effects adding around $\frac{1}{2}$% to the local employment-growth rate.

One final point to emerge from the results presented in table 1 is that, although employment growth does attract national stream migrants to the inner city, the losses in residential migration serve largely to offset this gain in population, leaving the aggregate pattern of dispersal from the inner city not much affected by the policy.

Table 2 presents the results of simulating a series of *housing-market* policies, constructed in the form of *changes* induced from the base run by the relevant policy[(10)]. In the first simulation, local authority housebuilding (LHCN) in the Inner London area was stimulated by an additional 1%. The impact of this was fairly slight, however, partly reflecting the weak effect of local authority housebuilding on the rest of the model, as well as the fact that the connections that *are* present tend to be offsetting, that is, local authority house construction has a *perverse* effect on residential migration, but is complementary to *private* housebuilding, which has the expected effect on local migration.

The effects of private-sector housebuilding can be seen more clearly in the second simulation, where a fairly small boost of an additional $\frac{1}{4}$% was applied to PHCN[(11)]. The effect is a clear reduction of net migration out of Inner London, in the residential streams.

(10) It is notable that in all these simulations, little variation in house prices (PRICE) is in evidence. This reflects the fairly slight connections in the estimated model between house prices and the other endogenous variables.

(11) However, this increase as a *proportion* of private-sector house construction amounts to nearly 15% on top of the value of PHCN in Inner London in the 'base run'.

The final set of simulations were intended to examine the effects of what might be termed 'supply-side' labour-market policies, in contrast to the more demand-side labour-market policies considered in table 1. Two main forms of such policies were considered, first, mobility assistance, and second, retraining schemes.

The treatment of mobility assistance must necessarily be indirect, since there is no obvious single route whereby such policies might enter the model. The policy was effected by raising the responsiveness of national stream migrants to the flow of job opportunities in different areas[12]. Such a policy would be equivalent to assisting migrants (possibly in financial terms) to move to areas of greater job opportunities. The sensitivity of national stream migrants to job opportunities affects patterns of unemployment via the coefficient on (travel-to-work) employment growth in the unemployment equation. The greater the impact of such employment growth in reducing unemployment, the less effective the implicit mediating effects of national stream migration. The effects of reducing this coefficient by 30% (implying a greater sensitivity of migrants to job opportunities) are shown in table 3[13]. In one version of the simulations (column 2), only moves originating in the Inner London area were assisted in this way, and this had the effect of reducing inner-city unemployment without affecting unemployment elsewhere in the region. Effectively, therefore, job losses in the inner city are more efficiently equilibrated out in this simulation.

In another version (column 3) employment-related moves in *all* areas were assisted. The notion here is less one of specifically attempting to shift population out of the areas of high unemployment to districts of greater job opportunities, and more one of attempting to improve the functioning of local labour markets *in general*, in matching population with employment growth. The effect of this is to retain the lower

(12) National stream migrants are the most clearly responsive to job opportunities, and they have the greatest *effect* on unemployment too, since such migration entails an immediate change of workplace. Some simulations were also tried on the residential stream, however, since these streams may also affect unemployment insofar as housing moves may involve a change of workplace at a later date. Boosting rates of residential out-migration from the inner city had the effect of heightening the pattern of decentralisation in these simulations, but leaving the pattern of unemployment unaffected, since dispersal also leads to a reduction in employment growth in the inner city.

(13) Strictly speaking, the coefficient on WECH in the first-stream migration equation ought also to be adjusted to be brought into line with the revised coefficient in the unemployment equation. It is difficult to deduce what the effect of such an adjustment will be on *net* migration in order to bring the migration and unemployment effects into harmony, however. Since the impact of such an adjustment would only have *indirect* additional effects on unemployment via induced multiplier effects on the rate of employment growth, this adjustment of the influence of employment growth on migration was not performed.

unemployment rates in Inner London achieved in the earlier run (targetted specifically on the inner city), but also to reduce unemployment in the outer areas as well. Although these policy simulations would appear to be broadly as effective as the job-creation scheme discussed earlier in alleviating inner-city unemployment, therefore, it is not clear what the practical problems of carrying out such a policy might be, nor the costs involved both in financial terms to the government, and in more general welfare terms for the people affected.

The final 'supply-side' policy simulation which was tried was a form of retraining scheme, incorporated into the model by reducing (exogenously) the proportion of unskilled manual workers in the inner-city boroughs by 5%. When interpreting these results it is important to bear in mind, as discussed earlier, that the presence of unskilled manual workers may not be a purely 'supply-side' phenomenon. Such variables arguably reflect as much about the characteristics of jobs on offer as they do about the workers who fill them. If a retraining scheme gives workers skills for which there is inadequate local demand they might still be forced afterwards to take unskilled jobs, thus leaving the observed skill structure unchanged.

With these caveats in mind, the impact of an actual reduction in the proportion of unskilled workers among inner-city residents would be to affect unemployment in two ways, according to the model. First, this is because unskilled manual workers have a higher probability of becoming unemployed, and, second, since they also have a lower probability of leaving the area. Reducing the proportion of unskilled manual workers in the inner city has the expected effect of reducing net national stream migration into the area (as a result of a higher out-migration rate) and bringing down inner-city unemployment. The reduction in unemployment is quite substantial as compared with reductions achieved in the previous simulations. The important qualification that must be borne in mind in this kind of 'retraining scheme' is that it needs to be accompanied by measures to ensure that the right higher grade *jobs* are on offer to meet the needs of the newly retrained workers.

6 Conclusions

Perhaps the most important factor to have changed since the period 1966–71 from the point of view of the analysis presented here is that decentralisation in the South East has slowed down, particularly in terms of population. The main question is whether or not this reflects a permanent change to the broad trends of dispersal, or simply a temporary adjustment in the rate of diffusion. One potential contributory factor has been the rising level of national unemployment, inhibiting the overall volume of migration. To the extent that this environment is a temporary one, then one might expect decentralisation to be resumed once national unemployment returns to its earlier levels. In the case of London, however, as has already been emphasised, the dispersal of population has been more closely related to *housing-market* developments than to labour-market conditions. The slowdown in decentralisation from London would appear to be caused (see Buck et al, 1986) not so much by increasing 'housing opportunities' in the inner city, but by decreasing opportunities elsewhere, given the depressed state of house production nationally in the later 1970s and early 1980s. A reversal of these conditions is therefore likely to produce a resumption of dispersal. Buck et al concluded (1986, page 47) that

> "Beyond the short term, the safest assumption, whatever the policies pursued in Greater London, is that Greater London as a whole, and the inner areas in particular, will once again experience substantial population losses in their exchanges with outer areas of Southern England."

The simulations presented here suggest that there are no simple solutions to the problems of unemployment in Inner London, even if decentralisation is slowed. This goes for both demand-side and supply-side policies, whether in the labour market or in the housing market. This is not to say that the policies are not worthwhile; that would require an investigation into the costs involved, and some assessment of whether the benefits exceed the costs in social welfare terms. The point is simply that the problems are deep-seated and cannot easily be relieved by short-term measures. Whether the problems are likely to remain intractable into the long term is a much more difficult question, which cannot be answered simply by reference to the model used here.

Clearly, the various policies examined here are not mutually exclusive, and a package of policy measures is likely to be more successful than any single policy applied in isolation. From this point of view, it makes sense to distinguish between policies which attempt to alleviate inner-city unemployment by shifting population to more prosperous areas ('workers to the work'), from policies which attempt to *retain* as far as possible the existing urban base and stimulate employment in these areas ('work to the workers').

In terms of the first policy ('workers to the work'), this would appear to be successful in some measure in reducing Inner London unemployment only in its effects on *employment-related* migrants. In contrast, the decentralisation of residential migrant streams appears to affect inner-city employment growth (via the loss in local demand) about as much as it disperses labour supply, thus leaving unemployment virtually unchanged(14). At any rate, the results suggest that the residential migrant streams are more responsive to *private*-sector housebuilding than to public-sector housebuilding programmes, although private development is less easily directed by policymakers.

(14) See footnote (12) above.

In terms of 'work to the workers' policy, there is clearly evidence to suggest that, to a substantial degree, job creation in the inner city is accommodated by migration and commuting adjustments rather than by direct reductions in unemployment. This is the problem of successfully targetting policies at an areal level.

Although superficially the most successful 'policy' tried here in terms of the effect on inner-city unemployment lay in reducing the proportion of unskilled manual workers resident in the inner city, it is apparent that such a variable is itself likely to be the outcome of labour-market processes—it is a *symptom* of the way the labour market works, rather than a genuine cause. As such, a simple exogenous reduction in this variable is rather too glib an answer to the problems of the inner city, and begs questions of how workers become labelled 'unskilled manual', and how they come to accumulate in large concentrations in the inner city. Such questions involve not only important *spatial* interdependencies, but also interdependencies in the *occupational* structure, and interactions between supply and demand in spatial and occupational submarkets.

Clearly, there is a need for further work in this area. The fact that conditions have changed since 1971 is likely to have affected to some degree the impact of different policies; job-creation schemes may be more effective now, for example, as a result of higher national unemployment inhibiting supply-side adjustments. There is also a need to examine the relative *costs* of the different policy options in relation to the predicted benefits. The question of occupational structure and dynamics within local labour markets is clearly an important area which deserves closer attention. In addition, it would also be of interest to incorporate as far as possible a wider range of policies into the analysis—there is no obvious way of introducing Enterprise Zones, for example, into the model as it stands. Finally, some assessment of the *longer term* prospects and policies is obviously required.

The model used here is clearly not suited to address such questions. Nevertheless, an important feature of the results presented here lies in the clearly evident patterns of interdependency which *are* built into the model, both between labour and housing markets, and between areas in general. Although these interactions considerably complicated the structure of the model (as well as the problem of solving the model), they appear to play an important role in evaluating the effects of policy. From the point of view of improving the model, one important lesson that emerges from the simulations lies in the need to *ensure* consistency in the quantitative size of effects in different parts of the system. This is crucial because the major contribution of a simulation model of this type will be in tracking the complex chain of effects which follow either from housing-market or from labour-market interventions in a metropolitan region.

Acknowledgements. This paper is based on work supported by the Economic and Social Research Council as part of a project on Metropolitan Labour Market Analysis at the University of Kent. The author is grateful to Ian Dobbs, Ian Gordon, Corinne Mulley, and William Rees for helpful discussions and comments. All errors remain my responsibility.

References

Buck N, Gordon I R, Young K, 1986 *The London Employment Problem* (Clarendon Press, Oxford)

Congdon P, 1983, "A model for the interaction of migration and commuting" *Urban Studies* **20** 185-195

Evans A, Richardson R, 1981, "Urban unemployment: interpretation and additional evidence" *Scottish Journal of Political Economy* **28** 107-124

Eversley D, 1973, "Problems of social planning in London" in *London: Urban Patterns, Problems and Policies* Eds D Donnison, D Eversley (Heinemann Educational Books, London) pp 1-50

Foreman-Peck J, Gripaios P, 1977, "Inner city problems and inner city policies" *Regional Studies* **11** 401-412

Fothergill S, Gudgin G, 1982 *Unequal Growth: Urban and Regional Change in the UK* (Heinemann Educational Books, London)

Gordon I R, 1985, "A Poisson model of accessibility effects on migration rates" discussion paper, Urban and Regional Studies Unit, University of Kent, Canterbury, Kent

Gordon I R, Lamont D, 1982, "A model of labour-market interdependencies in the London region" *Environment and Planning A* **14** 237-264

Gordon I R, Molho I J, 1985, "Women in the labour markets of the London region: a model of dependence and constraint" *Urban Studies* **22** 367-386

Hare P, 1986 "The London industrial strategy: a review article" *Scottish Journal of Political Economy* **33** 188-192

Keeble D, 1976 *Industrial Location and Planning in the UK* (Methuen, Andover, Hants)

Kennett S, 1982, "Migration between British local labour markets and some speculation on policy options for influencing population distributions" in *Population Change and Regional Labour Markets* OP 28, Office of Population Censuses and Survey, St Catherine's House, 10 Kingsway, London WC2B 6JP, pp 35-53

Molho I J, 1984, "A dynamic model of inter-regional migration in Great Britain" *Journal of Regional Science* **24** 317-337

Norris G M, 1978, "Unemployment, subemployment, and personal characteristics" *Sociological Review* **25** 89-108

Owen D W, Coombes M G, Gillespie A E, 1984, "The 'urban-rural shift' and employment change in Britain, 1971-81", discussion paper, Centre for Urban and Regional Development Studies, University of Newcastle upon Tyne, Newcastle upon Tyne

Steinnes D, 1982, "Do 'people follow jobs' or do 'jobs follow people'? A causality issue in urban economics" *Urban Studies* **19** 187-192

Vickerman R, 1984 *Urban Economies* (Philip Allan, Oxford)

APPENDIX A.1

Adapting the model

In general the two-stage least squares estimates of the model presented by Gordon and Lamont (1982) were used here. There were three main modifications to the model.

(1) The unemployment equation was reestimated to include explicitly the effects of net second-stream and third-stream migration into an area. The original framework included various *determinants* of these into the unemployment equation, but since these are fixed and exogenous, this procedure was not helpful for the purpose of model simulation, since it does not allow changes in the pattern of net migration in these streams (resulting from 'policy shocks', for example) to feed back into the unemployment equation.

(2) Three independent pieces of information suggested that the original weights in the calculation of the travel-to-work employment-growth variable (WECH) placed undue emphasis on *internal* as compared with *external* changes in the commuting hinterland. These were (a) the *positive* estimated coefficient on MECH in the unemployment equation, (b) the overreaction of commuting to the differential between MECH and WECH (Gordon and Molho, 1985), (c) the estimation of a significant *negative* coefficient on MECH in the pull-factor equation for national stream migration. The weights used in calculating WECH were therefore adjusted accordingly, and the model reestimated with the new variable.

(3) The equations determining migration push–pull factors in the second and third streams were reestimated. Three main changes were introduced. First, the equations were reweighted according to migration *potential* in these streams, since the original set of weights were found to contain errors which effectively excluded certain areas from the estimation. Second, migration *potentials*, π, were also introduced as determinants of second-stream and third-stream migration, constructed as:

$$\pi(A_i^s) = \sum_{j \neq i} B_j^s \exp(-\beta^s D_{ij}) , \qquad \pi(B_i^s) = \sum_{j \neq i} A_j^s \exp(-\beta^s D_{ij}) .$$

The theoretical underpinning for the inclusion of these variables stems from the fact that the original gravity model [equation (1)] restricts the elasticity of movement volume to accessibility to be equal to 1 (Gordon, 1985). To the extent that there exists any duplication of opportunities as we move away from the periphery to the centre, however, we might expect this elasticity to be somewhere below 1. The estimated coefficients on the migration potentials are therefore likely to be negative in sign, reflecting the extent to which the elasticity is in fact less than 1. This problem would not seem to matter in relation to the national migration stream, since these flows are based on broadly national coverage and migration potentials are likely to be broadly constant across any one particular metropolitan area. For the other streams, however, a significant negative coefficient was estimated, which improved the fit of the model substantially.

The third and final modification was that the *form* of certain of the relationships was changed. Previously the relations had been specified as log-linear throughout, as in the form of equation (2) and (3). For the private house contribution variable (and to a lesser extent the residential preference score), however, the relationships were found to tail off significantly over higher values of these variables. The best shape of this relationship was found approximately by including the variables in negative exponential form as $\gamma \exp(-\lambda x)$, where the parameter $-\lambda$ was estimated by a grid search technique[(15)]. Once again, this alteration clearly improved the fit of the model. The final estimated equations used in the simulation model are listed in appendix A.2 (the equations which have been modified are marked with an asterisk).

[(15)] The first derivative of this function is given by $-\lambda\gamma \exp(-\lambda x)$, indicating that the gradient flattens off for increasing values of x. The negative sign on λ implies that the coefficient γ ought to be positive for a downward-sloping relationship, and negative for an upward-sloping one. For the equation determining the second-stream push factor, the estimated value of λ is very high (that is, -170) on the house-construction variable. Plotting this relationship produced something akin to a spline function, with a threshold around 0.03, up to which point private housebuilding strongly affects out-migration, but beyond which very little effect is observed. Around twenty-six values for private housebuilding out of the seventy one were observed *below* the threshold point.

APPENDIX A.2

The labour market

Notes: t-statistics are given in parentheses. The equations were estimated with two-stage least squares. The number of observations was 71.

$$\ln\left(\frac{A^1}{P}\right) = \underset{(0.81)}{0.276 + 2.697\mathrm{U}} - \underset{(-0.01)}{0.0004\mathrm{WKLYE}} - \underset{(-1.81)}{2.2689\mathrm{UNSK}}$$
$$+ \underset{(0.39)}{0.0525\mathrm{LRENTED}} - \underset{(-0.90)}{0.2857\mathrm{URENTED}} + \underset{(1.01)}{0.4843\mathrm{FRENTED}}$$
$$- \underset{(-0.72)}{0.6080\mathrm{NATCH}} + \underset{(1.67)}{2.8784\mathrm{DEFENCE}} + \underset{(1.94)}{0.2425} \ln\left(\frac{B^1}{P}\right)$$
$$+ \underset{(0.43)}{0.0081\mathrm{RSPRF}}\ .$$

$$* \quad \ln\left(\frac{B^1}{P}\right) = -1.1107 - \underset{(-0.91)}{2.5660\mathrm{U}} + \underset{(2.29)}{0.1471\mathrm{WKLYE}} - \underset{(-0.07)}{0.0870\mathrm{UNSK}}$$
$$+ \underset{(0.35)}{0.0412\mathrm{LRENTED}} + \underset{(1.48)}{0.4029\mathrm{URENTED}} + \underset{(2.64)}{1.0954\mathrm{FRENTED}}$$
$$+ \underset{(1.73)}{0.0307\mathrm{RSPRF}} + \underset{(4.75)}{2.3540\mathrm{WECH}} + \underset{(1.85)}{0.2161} \ln\left(\frac{A^1}{P}\right).$$

$$* \quad \mathrm{U} = -0.0711 - \underset{(-3.81)}{0.0736\mathrm{WECH}} + \underset{(1.52)}{0.0085\mathrm{LRENTED}} + \underset{(1.25)}{0.0177\mathrm{URENTED}}$$
$$+ \underset{(2.90)}{0.0700\mathrm{FRENTED}} - \underset{(-1.15)}{0.0010\mathrm{RSPRF}} + \underset{(1.55)}{0.00019\mathrm{RSDNS}}$$
$$+ \underset{(1.25)}{0.0134\mathrm{PRICE}} + \underset{(1.89)}{0.1353\mathrm{NATCH}} + \underset{(6.19)}{0.2374\mathrm{UNSK}}$$
$$+ \underset{(1.46)}{0.2961\mathrm{AGE65}} + \underset{(3.69)}{0.0499\mathrm{NET1}} + \underset{(1.48)}{0.0266\mathrm{NET2}}\ .$$

$$\mathrm{MECH} = 0.0057 + \underset{(1.32)}{0.5697\mathrm{NET1}} + \underset{(1.48)}{0.4308\mathrm{NET2}} + \underset{(2.33)}{0.7082\mathrm{NET3}}$$
$$+ \underset{(0.92)}{0.4404\mathrm{NHCN}} + \underset{(1.30)}{0.0005\mathrm{IDC}} + \underset{(0.12)}{0.0036\mathrm{LAND}}$$
$$+ \underset{(1.71)}{0.8081\mathrm{MSTRGR}} + \underset{(0.45)}{0.2719\mathrm{NATCH}} - \underset{(-0.97)}{0.0449\mathrm{EARNINGS}}$$
$$- \underset{(1.55)}{1.6693\mathrm{DEMC}}$$

The housing market

$$
\begin{aligned}
* \ \ln\left(\frac{A^2}{P}\right) = {} & -0.1817 + \underset{(1.23)}{0.6108}\exp(-170\,\mathrm{PHCN}) + \underset{(0.63)}{2.1575}\,\mathrm{LHCN} \\
& + \underset{(1.66)}{2.8727}\,\mathrm{NHCN} - \underset{(-3.22)}{1.4030}\,\mathrm{LRENTED} + \underset{(0.40)}{0.4424}\,\mathrm{URENTED} \\
& - \underset{(-2.17)}{2.1444}\,\mathrm{FRENTED} + \underset{(1.85)}{0.0649}\exp(-\mathrm{RSPRF}) \\
& + \underset{(0.49)}{0.3960}\,\mathrm{PRICE} - \underset{(-0.63)}{2.8041}\,\mathrm{DEMC} - \underset{(-0.24)}{0.4379}\,\mathrm{HOUSING} \\
& + \underset{(1.17)}{0.1757}\,\mathrm{EARNINGS} + \underset{(1.08)}{1.0666}\,\mathrm{NET1} \\
& - \underset{(-4.36)}{0.06348}\,\pi(A^2)\,.
\end{aligned}
$$

$$
\begin{aligned}
* \ \ln\left(\frac{B^2}{P}\right) = {} & -2.5050 + \underset{(0.65)}{2.0721}\,\mathrm{PHCN} + \underset{(1.16)}{4.3362}\,\mathrm{LHCN} + \underset{(1.26)}{3.7212}\,\mathrm{NHCN} \\
& + \underset{(0.03)}{0.0165}\,\mathrm{LRENTED} - \underset{(-0.10)}{0.1045}\,\mathrm{URENTED} + \underset{(1.39)}{1.7434}\,\mathrm{FRENTED} \\
& + \underset{(1.60)}{0.1216}\,\mathrm{RSPRF} - \underset{(-1.06)}{0.9732}\,\mathrm{PRICE} - \underset{(-0.04)}{0.0634}\,\mathrm{WECH} \\
& - \underset{(-2.95)}{0.0006}\,\pi(B^2)\,.
\end{aligned}
$$

$$
\begin{aligned}
* \ \ln\left(\frac{A^3}{P}\right) = {} & -8.0389 + \underset{(5.04)}{5.5792}\exp(-3\,\mathrm{PHCN}) + \underset{(0.98)}{6.0051}\,\mathrm{LHCN} \\
& - \underset{(-2.95)}{8.6176}\,\mathrm{NHCN} + \underset{(0.60)}{0.5009}\,\mathrm{LRENTED} - \underset{(-1.39)}{2.8346}\,\mathrm{URENTED} \\
& + \underset{(1.64)}{2.970}\,\mathrm{FRENTED} + \underset{(2.94)}{0.2489}\,\mathrm{RSPRF} + \underset{(0.93)}{1.2457}\,\mathrm{PRICE} \\
& \underset{(1.07)}{-6.823}\,\mathrm{DEMC} + \underset{(1.00)}{2.883}\,\mathrm{HOUSING} - \underset{(-7.39)}{0.1194}\,\pi(A^3)\,.
\end{aligned}
$$

$$
\begin{aligned}
* \ \ln\left(\frac{B^3}{P}\right) = {} & -3.1626 - \underset{(-4.24)}{0.5636}\exp(-30\,\mathrm{PHCN}) + \underset{(0.76)}{1.3464}\,\mathrm{LHCN} \\
& - \underset{(-2.68)}{8.8488}\,\mathrm{NHCN} + \underset{(2.43)}{0.7203}\,\mathrm{LRENTED} + \underset{(0.52)}{0.2591}\,\mathrm{URENTED} \\
& + \underset{(0.74)}{0.5595}\,\mathrm{FRENTED} - \underset{(-3.85)}{3.6\times 10^{-9}}\exp(-10\,\mathrm{RSPRF}) \\
& + \underset{(1.71)}{0.7039}\,\mathrm{PRICE} - \underset{(-6.34)}{0.0004}\,\pi(B^3)\,.
\end{aligned}
$$

$$\begin{aligned}
\text{PHCN} = {} & 0.0307 + \underset{(4.97)}{0.4392}\,\text{NET1} + \underset{(7.07)}{0.4513}\,\text{NET2} + \underset{(2.29)}{0.2156}\,\text{NET3} \\
& + \underset{(0.58)}{0.1095}\,\text{LHCN} - \underset{(-6.33)}{0.6190}\,\text{NHCN} - \underset{(-0.24)}{0.0627}\,\text{DEMC} \\
& + \underset{(2.67)}{0.3818}\,\text{NATCH} + \underset{(0.04)}{0.0053}\,\text{PPR} .
\end{aligned}$$

$$\begin{aligned}
\text{LHCN} = {} & -0.0083 - \underset{(-1.40)}{0.1045}\,\text{NET1} - \underset{(-1.28)}{0.0834}\,\text{NET2} + \underset{(0.18)}{0.013}\,\text{NET3} \\
& + \underset{(1.42)}{0.1424}\,\text{PHCN} - \underset{(-2.11)}{0.2067}\,\text{NHCN} + \underset{(2.92)}{0.5109}\,\text{DEMC} \\
& + \underset{(0.50)}{0.0568}\,\text{NATCH} + \underset{(1.29)}{0.1365}\,\text{PPR} + \underset{(2.13)}{0.0906}\,\text{HOUSING} \\
& + \underset{(0.54)}{0.0023}\,\text{LAND} + \underset{(3.71)}{0.0676}\,\text{LRENTED} .
\end{aligned}$$

$$\text{PRICE} = 3.5784 + \underset{(0.28)}{0.0629}\,\text{PHCN} - \underset{(-4.86)}{0.0637}\,\text{LAND} + \underset{(7.16)}{0.1588}\,\text{WKLYE} .$$

Variable definitions

Endogenous

U — male unemployed as proportion of economically active;

PHCN — private-sector house construction 1966–70 as a proportion of 1971 dwelling stock;

LHCN — public-sector house construction (other than in new town or for overspill) as a proportion of 1971 dwelling stock;

PRICE — logged Inland Revenue based price estimates for three-bedroom semidetached house in 1971;

NET1-3 — net migration of economically active males 1966–71 in each of the three migration streams, as a proportion of resident number in 1971;

MECH — male employment change 1966–71, as a proportion of employment in 1971;

WECH — average proportional male employment change 1966–71 by area of workplace in the journey-to-work area of each zone;

$\pi(A^s)\pi(B^s)$ — migration out and in potentials defined as in appendix A.1.

Exogenous

EARNINGS — average male earnings per employed male (full-time or part-time) 1971, £ thousands;

WKLYE — estimated average male earnings standardised for occupational structure;

NATCH — natural growth in male labour supply as a proportion of economically active males, estimated from population in 15–19 and 65–69 age groups;

UNSK	proportion of economically active employed in socio-economic group 11 (that is, unskilled manual);
DEFENCE	armed force employment, measured as a proportion of economically active males in socioeconomic group 16;
AGE65	males aged 65 and over per thousand persons;
NHCN	house construction in new towns and London overspill schemes 1966 - 70 as proportion of 1971 occupied dwelling stock;
DEMC	dwellings removed from stock or closed by demolition or closing order 1966 - 70 as a proportion of those occupied in 1971;
LRENTED	proportion of persons renting from a local authority or new town development corporation;
FRENTED	proportion of persons living in privately rented furnished accommodation;
URENTED	proportion of persons living in privately rented unfurnished accommodation;
HOUSING	proportion of households renting privately unfurnished and lacking exclusive use of one or more amenities;
PPR	number per thousand households living at densities of over one person per room;
RSDNS	persons per area;
LAND	logged measure of land free from constraint for development, per head of resident population;
RSPRF	average area-attractiveness scores of social work trainees, 1977;
MSTRGR	expected rate of change in male employment 1966 - 71 based on 1966 employment structure, and national employment change by Minimum List Heading;
IDC	refusal rate for Industrial Development Certificates as a proportion of sustained applications 1970 - 74.

For further details of variable construction, and details of variable sources, see Gordon and Lamont (1982).

Information Systems for Urban Labour-market Planning and Analysis

L WORRALL
Wrekin Council and University of Liverpool

1 Introduction

Nationally available statistical series in the post Rayner review era in Britain have been extensively criticised (Hoinville and Smith, 1982; Elton, 1983): for example, the Annual Census of Employment is now triennial and is released up to three years in arrears. Most important is the fact that nationally available statistical series do not meet the needs of local authority strategic planning processes and are, in particular, an ineffective medium for urban labour-market research. These deficiencies have stimulated the development of local information systems both in academic institutions and in local government (Healey, 1983; Black, 1985). Many of these systems can be criticised on the same grounds as nationally available statistical series: they are not founded on any generally accepted design principles; they are not synchronised to the pace of change in their host urban or regional systems; they are not capable of identifying emerging problems nor exposing the latent structure of problems; neither are they model based.

In the five main sections of this paper, I discuss some general themes relevant to the design of information systems for urban labour-market planning and analysis, discuss the theoretical basis for a conceptual model of a local labour market, develop such a model, describe the information systems which support the model, and finally I present, primarily for illustrative purposes, some of the research into urban labour-market adjustment and its distributional consequences which the model and information systems have supported.

2 Information systems for urban planning

My purpose is to show that the use of a model-based approach to the design of information systems offers distinct benefits to urban labour-market analysis. Urban labour markets are highly adaptive and open systems which incorporate both market and nonmarket adjustment mechanisms. Intervention should be planned through the medium of model-based information systems in which are replicated the main adjustment mechanisms of the urban labour market. An effective information system should, according to Nijkamp (Nijkamp and Rietveld, 1984, page 4), be "judged by its contribution to solving, organising, or rationalising complex choice and decision problems". Here, the central argument is that urban information systems will lead to more effective policy if they are constructed in the context of a theoretically based model of the urban labour market.

An urban information system can be defined as a body of structured data which can be analysed to improve our understanding of urban structures and processes: the enhanced understanding derived from this analysis should lead to the development of more sensitive and effective policy with which to influence urban change (Worrall, 1986b).

In a recent work, Nijkamp (Nijkamp and Rietveld, 1984, pages 4 and 5) developed criteria with which to evaluate urban and regional information systems:

1. Information systems should provide an "integrative framework for multi-disciplinary work".
2. They should provide a foundation for "operational analysis" to generate effective knowledge of system dynamics.
3. They should act as a "filter for identifying and specifying empirically a precisely demarcated policy or choice problem".
4. "Coherent" information systems "should contain the necessary data on the elements of a socio-economic system, on their properties, their linkages, and their dynamics".
5. Information systems should act as a "vehicle for identifying systematic patterns in a complex, dynamic world".

Nijkamp saw information systems as a "prerequisite for building, testing and using models". But I would argue that a model of the urban labour market is a prerequisite for development of an information system. A model of an urban labour market, based on theory, provides both "a formal accounting framework for data collection" (Scheurwater and Masser, 1981, page 201) and a medium for explaining urban adjustment processes.

An explicit accounting framework offers "a comprehensive and consistent basis for socio-economic research, policy analysis, and planning" (Land and McMillan, 1981, page 242) and ensures consistency in the treatment of stocks in and flows between the various system states. However, accounting frameworks are not theoretically neutral and their design needs to be based on a model, or models, of the system under consideration, in this case the urban labour market. Modelling and accounting are complementary activities. As Land and Juster (1981, page 10) would argue, databases should be built "in the context of certain organising concepts", and "models cannot be grounded in the absence of data bases".

An accounts-based urban information system fulfills three main functions: it provides the basis for the integration of data collection, particularly the development of common definitions, periodicity, and spatial referencing; it facilitates structural analysis of causal relationships which is essential both for policy-development purposes and to improve our understanding of the complex system dynamics of the urban labour market; and it offers a medium for an assessment of the impact of policies through the development of indicators of social and policy performance (Clarke and Wilson, 1986).

Several types of indicator can be routinely derived from an accounts-based information system (see Land and McMillan, 1981). In the labour market these include *state-occupancy indices*, such as the unemployment rate; *state-transition indices*, such as the unemployment inflow rate; *state-movement rates*, such as the redundancy rate; *state-movement ratios*, such as the proportion of involuntary quits among total separations; and *summary indices*, such as average duration of unemployment or measures of employment concentration (Worrall, 1985a). Changes in the levels of indicators can be tested against those expected from theory. Any change which cannot be explained can be used to trigger research to improve our undersanding of the host system. Elsewhere (Worrall, 1986a), an example of the integration of a social indicator system into an urban planning process is described in detail.

The policy orientation of information systems is often badly developed: given a policy objective of improving the distribution of life-chances within an urban system by means of policy based upon redistribution, information systems should be capable of measuring changes in the distribution of welfare between subgroups and the unequal incidence of social problems. An important application of such performance indicators is to measure how unemployment is distributed among individuals and the extent to which the social cost of unemployment is becoming increasingly concentrated among certain groups and the neighbourhoods in which they congregate.

3 The theoretical foundations of an urban labour-market model

An information system needs to be compatible with many different hypotheses about, in this case, labour-market behaviour, which can then be tested within the information provided by the system. However, choices have to be made about the range of data which are to be collected, given finite resource constraints, and about the classification systems to be used—these choices must be informed *both* by particular theoretical perspectives and by the particular policy concerns of the local authority. Thus, whereas neoclassical labour-market theories would give a central importance to wage and price data, and human capital theories concentrate on specific education and training indicators, both of these types of data (which are not readily available for the area) have been excluded from the local information systems.

On the other hand, in the local information systems particular attention is paid to the establishment and individual characteristics emphasised in two other theoretical approaches: segmented labour-market theory and the persona characteristics approach to the analysis of unemployment.

Rietveld (1984, page 163) concluded that a "major feature of the labour market is that it is segmented" because it consists of submarkets which are more or less independent of each other: failure to incorporate the notion of segmentation leads to an "inappropriate understanding of labour market phenomena". Segmented labour-market theory contains the central assumption that the labour market is not a unified market: structurally determined barriers to mobility inhibit movement between enclaves within the labour market. Thus, there exist advantaged and disadvantaged workers who occupy the primary and secondary segments, respectively (Bosanquet and Doeringer, 1973). Jobs in the primary labour market are typified by high wages, stability, and membership of the firm's internal labour market. Secondary jobs are typified by low wages, instability of employment (recurrent unemployment), and poor career prospects. The main elements of the theory are outlined by Loveridge and Mok (1979).

A relationship between the degree of segmentation and the level of unemployment has been identified (Sengenberger, 1981). In recessionary periods two things happen: first, internal labour markets are used increasingly as a recruitment source and groups whom employers regard as unstable or unreliable are "excluded from employment" (Gleave and Sellens, 1984, page 13); second, advantaged workers tighten their attachment to the primary sector (Bosanquet and Doeringer, 1973). In a slack labour market, barriers to mobility become more pronounced and the secondary labour market is used "to provide that degree of flexibility ... required by the system" (Rubery, 1978, page 20). Employees with a low level of fixity with the firm, that is, those in whom the firm has invested least, can be expected to be laid off in a period of demand deficiency (Oi, 1962). The UK labour market has been shown to have become more segmented in the recent past (Meager, 1985): it has become more polarised into 'insiders', who are sheltered by their employers from the vagaries of the external labour market, and 'outsiders' who endure relatively poor conditions of employment (Morris and Sinclair, 1985).

In the employer-employee relationship neither party is indifferent to the identity of the other. The aggregate impact of employers' decisions in a period of fluctuating demand will determine not only the volume of the flows between employment and unemployment but also the *composition* of the flows in either direction. More simply, changes in the volume of the stock of the unemployed are caused by disequilibrium between the gross flows into and out of employment, unemployment, and inactivity: changes in the composition of unemployment are caused by differential flow rates among definable subgroups of the labour force.

An accounting framework for unemployment research must be capable of incorporating these phenomena. Peck (1985, page 2) concluded that "it is a function of the probabilities of becoming unemployed and of remaining unemployed ... that define the set of individuals who are unemployed at any point in time and space". The cause of these differential flow rates lies partly in individuals' positions within the segmented labour market but also involves those personal characteristics of the workers which influence the hiring and firing decisions of employers.

There is a considerable body of literature on the personal characteristics approach to unemployment analysis (Metcalf, 1975; McGregor, 1978; Nickell, 1980; Folmer and van Dijk, 1985; van Dijk and Folmer, 1985). Its basis lies principally in the simple observation that the incidence and structure of unemployment are not random: Daniel (1981) showed that whereas 7% of the working population were unskilled, 40% of the unemployed were unskilled. Not only do certain groups have a higher probability of becoming unemployed, they also have a higher probability of staying unemployed. Folmer and van Dijk (1985) identified "substantial differences" in the duration of unemployment for individuals with different personal characteristics.

The personal characteristics which affect exposure to unemployment can be divided into two groups: those brought into the labour market and those acquired in the labour market. The first group includes age, sex, ethnicity, and education. The second group includes characteristics conferred by employment (such as firm-specific training or a history of employment in a 'good' firm) and those conferred by unemployment or subemployment such as a discontinuous employment history or long duration of unemployment (Norris, 1978a; 1978b). Personal characteristics research has tended to focus on the first set and characteristics have been seen as essentially independent of labour-market position. However, the significance of acquired characteristics is highlighted when individuals are seen in relation to their position in a segmented labour market. As Peck (1985, page 7) notes, a history of work in the secondary labour market is a "principal feature" of the unemployed inflow and long-term unemployment is "a stage through which many workers commonly pass as they slip from the 'primary' to the 'secondary' sector or even into total inactivity as a result of increasing marginalisation from the labour market".

4 A conceptual model of an urban labour market

Urban labour markets are highly adaptive and, in reality, open systems: any model must replicate labour-market adjustment processes, make explicit the flows between labour-market states, and enable an analysis of the determinants of flows to be undertaken. In this instance, the urban labour market is treated as a closed system and, in particular, migration flows across its functional boundaries are omitted.

In the model, attention is focused on three main labour-market states between which flows and subgroup differences in flow propensities are important: the states are employment, unemployment, and inactivity.

Both the volume and composition of flows between labour-market states are important. Differential flow rates impose a measurable structure on the stock of unemployed which, in turn, has implications for the distribution

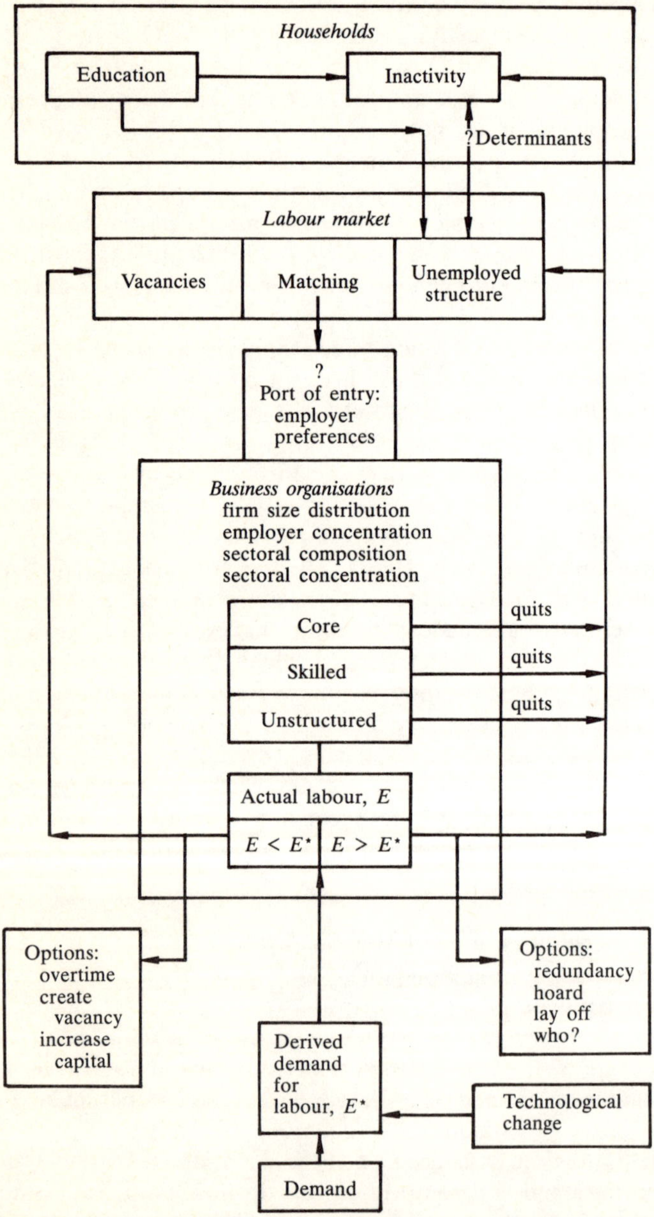

Figure 1. A conceptual model of an urban labour market.

of welfare throughout the urban system. At the macrolevel, changes in the structure of the labour market are the result of the decisions of the many actors within the labour market. To understand labour-market adjustment processes, the options available to decision takers must be identified and their reasons for choosing particular options isolated.

A conceptual model of an urban labour market is shown in figure 1. The model is driven by the demand for those goods and services produced locally. At a point in time an employer will have E amount of labour services available. The existing and expected demand for his product will generate a labour demand of E^*. If $E = E^*$, then the employer will take no action: if $E <> E^*$, then he or she may decide to adjust to E^*. Carmichael (1981) identifed thirty-eight options which employers could use to adjust from E to E^*. If the disequilibrium is expected to be short-lived, or adjustment costs are high, then the employer may decide to hoard labour (if $E > E^*$) or work labour more intensively (if $E < E^*$). If the period of disequilibrium is expected to be of long duration, or adjustment costs are low, then the employer may decide to adjust from E to E^*.

If $E > E^*$, then the employer may discard labour. Given that labour is a heterogenous good, the employer will seek to minimise separation costs by laying off that type of labour which is cheapest to discard and cheapest to replace given an upswing in product demand: employers will discard those in whom they have invested least in the form of training or recruitment costs. If $E < E^*$, then the employer will create a vacancy in the external labour market. Potential employees are ranked into an order of desirability by the employer who filters the applicants using various, often idiosyncratic, criteria which determine who is allowed through the firm's port of entry and who is not. Thus the model incorporates elements both of segmented labour-market theory and of the personal characteristics approach.

The structure of business organisations in a local labour market is also incorporated into the model, as it is assumed to affect the way in which the local labour market adapts (Danson, 1982; Taylor and Thrift, 1983). The dimensions of labour-market structure are the firm-size distribution, sectoral composition, sectoral concentration, and employer concentration (the extent to which one firm or small group of firms dominates employment).

5 Local information systems: a description

A suite of information systems has been developed in Telford, primarily to monitor the growth of the new town. The information systems are unique, certainly within the United Kingdom, and have proved capable of supporting a wide range of urban research. An important aspect of their design is that, when integrated, they provided a comprehensive picture of an urban labour market and thus support the conceptual

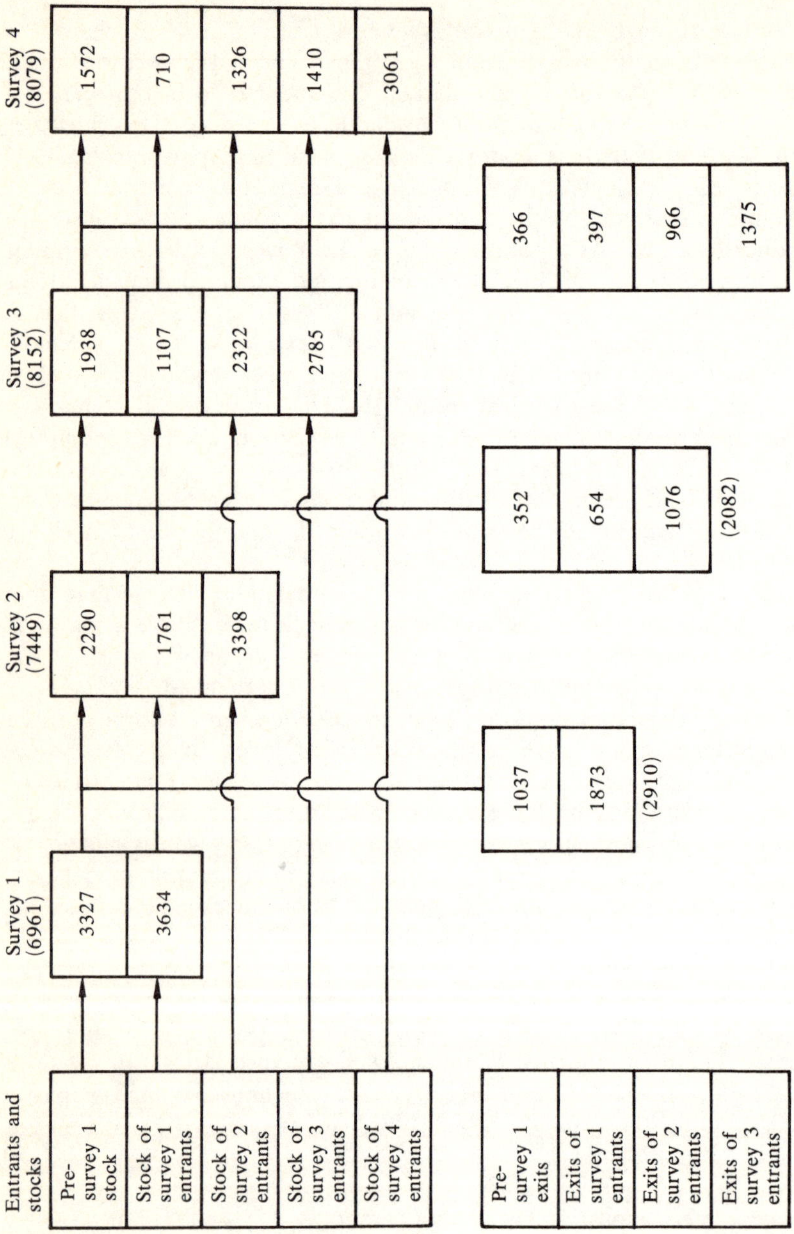

Figure 2. Unemployment accounting framework: adult unemployment from April 1981 to October 1982, Telford.

model of an urban labour market developed above. The accounting-framework approach requires the identification of labour-market states: this is possible in many instances and is a prerequisite to understanding labour-market adjustment mechanisms and explaining different event probabilities for subgroups in the labour market.

5.1 *The population information system*
Population information is derived from an Annual Enhanced Electoral Registration Survey in which each household is supplied with a person-by-person based questionnaire. Four data items are collected for each resident: they are age (single year), sex, employment status, and zone of residence. Household information is derived algorithmically. The availability of both individual and household information is important because individual labour-supply decisions are often made in the context of the household pattern of labour supply.

5.2 *The unemployment information-system*
On a six-monthly basis from April 1981 to October 1982, data on the personal characteristics of each unemployed Telford resident were obtained from Job Centres and Careers Offices. The data collected were age, sex, duration of current spell of unemployment, zone of residence, disability, previous occupation, and previous industry of employment. The individual files were integrated to measure flows into and out of unemployment and this is shown as figure 2.

5.3 *The employment information-system*
Every year a central employment register is updated with the current employment details of each employment-generating establishment in Telford. Employment is collected according to occupation (ten-fold classification), sex, and full-time and part-time employment. Each establishment is spatially referenced using Ordnance Survey coordinates and sectorally coded by Minimum List Heading. The establishment-level database has been aggregated into a firm-level database.

6 Labour-market dynamics: stocks, flows, and determinants
In this section, I shall illustrate, with two examples, the types of policy-relevant analysis which are possible with an urban information system of this type. These examples should indicate the value, first, of working with categories informed by a theoretical model of labour-market behaviour and, second, of linking together variables obtained from different sources.

6.1 *Employment trends and labour-market segmentation*
As indicated in the previous section, employment and unemployment data have been collected for a number of conventional categories of both occupation and industry, with a considerable degree of detail about industry of employment and about the ownership of establishments.

It is neither practical in analytical terms, nor useful for policy purposes, to work with this highly disaggregated information, particularly if interaction effects between occupation, industry, and type of firm are to be expected. On the other hand, there must be considerable doubt as to whether traditional distinctions, between manufacturing and service industries, or between manual and nonmanual occupations, effectively capture variations in employment conditions within contemporary labour markets. Hence it is important to devise secondary classifications of these dimensions which are more closely related to an understanding of labour-market processes, but which retain the capacity to revise these groupings in the light of alternative models.

In the Telford information-system, a segmented labour-market approach has been used to distinguish between three broad types of job: 'core' employment, other 'skilled' employment, and 'unstructured' employment. These categories have been identified using a *combination* of occupation, industry, and firm-size characteristics. For this purpose, the occupational classification has been collapsed into three broad groups: employers, professionals, and managers (OG1); other nonmanual and skilled manual (OG2); and the semiskilled, unskilled, and self-employed (OG3).

The industrial classification has been aggregated to seven broad sectors on the basis of the market position of the activities involved—this is shown in table 1. Within manufacturing, two sectors have been distinguished (from a third residual category) on the basis of the agglomeration economies which are assumed to exist locally; these are the vehicles industry and the metal and engineering industry with their respective satellites. The construction industry is separately distinguished. Within the services sector, following Buck's (1985) schema, activities have been grouped into public, producer, and consumer services. Last, seven size bands of firms within the area have been distinguished, ranging from those with fewer than eight employees to those with more than 256 employees.

Table 1. Industrial sectors: aggregation schema.

Sector	Component Minimum List Headings
Public services (PuS)	601-603, 872, 874, 875, 879, 901, 906
Producer services (PrS)	860-866, 871, 873, 876, 701-709, 810-812, 831, 832
Consumer services (CrS)	881-889, 891-899, 820, 821
Construction (Con)	500
Metal and engineering (M1)	311-323, 331-349, 351-354, 361-369, 390-399
Vehicles (M2)	380-385
Other manufacturing (M3)	411-450, 461-499, 211-240

The way in which the three classifications are combined to assign employment to the core, skilled, and unstructured segments is shown in table 2. In this implementation of the segmental approach, all three manufacturing sectors have been treated identically, so there are in effect five industrial sectors. 'Core' jobs are defined as those of professionals,

Table 2. The assignment of employment to segments.

Sector[a]	Firm size[b]	Occupational groups[c]
The core segment		
M1	⩾256	OG1
M2	⩾256	OG1
M3	⩾256	OG1
Con	⩾256	OG1
PuS	all firms	OG1
CrS	⩾128	OG1
PrS	⩾16	OG1
The skilled segment		
M1	⩾256	OG2
	32-255	OG2+OG1
M2	⩾256	OG2
	32-255	OG2+OG1
M3	⩾256	OG1
	32-255	OG2+OG1
Con	⩾256	OG1
	64-255	OG2+OG1
PuS	all firms	OG2
CrS	⩾128	OG2
	32-127	OG2+OG1
PrS	⩾16	OG2
	8-15	OG2+OG1
The unstructured segment		
M1	all firms	OG3
	<32	OG2+OG1
M2	all firms	OG3
	<32	OG2+OG1
M3	all firms	OG3
	<32	OG2+OG1
Con	all firms	OG3
	<64	OG2+OG1
PuS	all firms	OG3
CrS	all firms	OG3
	<32	OG2+OG1
PrS	all firms	OG3
	<8	OG2+OG1

[a] See table 1.
[b] Number of employees.
[c] OG1—employers, professionals, and managers; OG2—other nonmanual and skilled manual; OG3—semiskilled, unskilled, and self-employed.

employers, and managers in the larger firms, although all public services are treated as large firms, and the size threshold is set much lower for producer services than for other activities. The 'skilled' segment contains other nonmanual or skilled workers in the larger firms plus professionals, etc, from somewhat smaller firms, with the size bands again being applied differentially to each of the industrial sectors. Last the 'unstructured' segment combines the self-employed, the unskilled, and the semiskilled from all firms, with other workers from the smallest firms. In 1982, on this basis, 9% of Telford workers were included in the 'core', 40% in the 'skilled' segment, and 51% in the 'unstructured' segment, with quite similar proportions for males and females.

Theory suggests that different segments of the labour market will exhibit different employment trends, as well as a differing vulnerability to unemployment. Thus, in a period of falling demand, the unstructured segment, or at least the employees within it, should be the first to experience large-scale job loss. This is expected as a result of the more competitive product-market conditions affecting their employing firms which require both rapid adjustment to changing levels of product demand and employment conditions which allow shedding of labour to be accomplished speedily. In those industries which either dominate their product market or are in noncompetitive sectors of the economy, employment conditions are likely to exhibit primary labour-market traits, with a consequential slowing down of the adjustment process.

Table 3, which charts the changing employment in Telford between 1978 and 1982, tends to confirm these expectations. Although total employment declined by 5721, employment in the core segment increased for males and for females. Most of the job loss was amongst employees in the unstructured segment which decreased by 4535 over the period, with most of the decrease occurring between 1979 and 1981. Overall the decline in employment was significantly faster in this segment than among skilled workers, although this was entirely the result of changes in a single year (1980/81). There has been a small offset to the contraction of the unstructured segment through the growth in self-employment, but this trend has been quite unstable.

The unemployed cannot so readily be allocated to segments because of the lack of information on the size of firms of last employer. However, a comparison of unemployment rates across industrial sectors (as shown in table 4), reveals a pattern which is generally consistent with our model. Male unemployment rates in 1982 were particularly high in the highly competitive construction sector, indicative of the external flexibility aspect of a secondary labour market (Rubery, 1978). Conversely, unemployment rates were well below average for males and females in public services—a noncompetitive sector with a high proportion of professional workers.

A simple cross-sectional analysis of stocks will not allow any more sophisticated separation between the effects of employment instability in some labour-market segments and once and for all employment adjustments in others. In this case the relatively high unemployment rates recorded in the M1 and M2 sectors essentially reflect a contraction of what was a 'manorial' labour market with long-standing attachments to a single employer [a discussion of the manorial, guild, unstructured distinction is given by Danson (1982)]. To pursue this type of question further, flows and durations need to be examined in relation to sector of employment. This is possible within the local information system. For a second illustration of the uses of the system we turn to the complementary question of how unemployment experience relates to personal characteristics.

Table 3. Segmental employment trends in Telford 1978–1982.

Segment	1978	1979	1980	1981	1982	Index[a]
Total employment						
Core	3181	3221	3176	3494	3440	108
Skilled	17694	17370	16497	15751	15480	87
Unstructured						
employed	22450	22001	20809	18637	18259	81
self-employed	792	1108	1264	1070	1217	154
Total	44117	43700	41746	38952	38396	87
Male employment						
Core	2148	2222	2218	2226	2196	102
Skilled	11212	10423	10051	9213	8905	79
Unstructured	15064	14657	13811	12041	11554	77
Total	28424	27302	26080	23480	22655	78
Female employment						
Core	1033	999	958	1268	1244	120
Skilled	6482	6947	6446	6538	6575	101
Unstructured	8178	8457	8264	7668	7923	97
Total	15693	16403	15668	15474	15742	101

[a] Index: employment in 1978 = 100.

Table 4. Sectoral unemployment rates (excluding school-leavers) in Telford, October 1982.

Sector	Industrial sector[a]							Total
	M1	M2	M3	Con	PrS	CrS	PuS	
Males	15.6	21.8	20.0	44.9	14.8	21.2	5.0	18.6
Females	9.0	17.0	12.8	13.7	9.0	11.6	2.3	8.2

6.2 *Unemployment duration and personal characteristics*
The information available from the four unemployment surveys in 1981/82 is summarised in terms of an accounting framework in figure 2. These data on stocks and flows can be used to explore the structure of unemployment and the determinants of unemployment duration and off-flows. The objective is to identify differences in unemployment durations and flow propensities for subgroups of the unemployed and to account for these in terms of personal characteristics such as age, skill, disability, previous industry, and area of residence. The analysis refers only to male unemployed and excludes school-leavers.

The four unemployment surveys were analysed separately to identify how the distribution of unemployment durations (in weeks) had evolved through the period. From table 5 it can be seen that the mean duration increased significantly over the period. It now remains to identify the changing pattern of unemployment durations among subgroups of the unemployed.

Four personal characteristics were used in the analysis: they were skill, age, disability, and area of residence. The skill variable was derived by aggregating broad CODOT classes (Classification of Occupations and Directory of Occupational Titles). The 'unskilled' were defined as CODOT class 18 as were those with unknown skill, 'blue collar' was defined as CODOT classes 11-17, and 'white collar' was defined as CODOT classes 1-10. This is a very rough distinction, but it will serve to show that differences do exist in the unemployment durations, and by inference flow probabilities, of broadly defined skill groups.

A dichotomous indicator was used to distinguish between the disabled and able-bodied. A method for aggregating the hundred basic spatial units, which together constitute Telford, into a fourfold classification used to measure relative social stress is described elsewhere (Worrall, 1985b). Single-year age data were aggregated into four groups: 16-24 (labour-market entrants), 25-49 (prime-age males), 50-59 (older participants), 60-64 (preretirement group).

An analysis of variance was carried out using unemployment duration (in weeks) and the four explanatory variables. The results of the analysis for the October 1982 survey are presented in table 6.

The changing effect of the explanatory variables through time was assessed and this is shown in table 7. The effect of residence in an

Table 5. Unemployment durations in Telford, April 1981 to October 1982: key statistics.

	Survey 1	Survey 2	Survey 3	Survey 4
Unemployed	4990	5528	6243	6096
Mean duration (weeks)	43.3	63.9	71.5	80.2

area with high social stress increased steadily through the period and may indicate that employers became increasingly less likely to recruit people from these areas. If this is the case, area externalities like those identified by McGregor in Glasgow may have arisen (McGregor, 1979). The effect of being disabled has remained almost constant and significantly above the average unemployment duration throughout the period. The effect of being unskilled has shown the largest increase. This is consistent with what is expected given segmented labour-market theory and may indicate that a 'bumping down' of skills has taken place: firms are more selective about who they let through their ports of entry in a slack labour market. The effect of being in the 50–59 age group has a major impact on unemployment duration which is not carried into the 60–64 age range because of exit from the register into retirement. This type of analysis can be extended to analyse the relationship between personal characteristics and the flows from unemployment to employment, with a disaggregated version of the accounting framework shown as figure 2. In this case, log-linear methods can be employed to assess the joint impact of personal characteristics on the probability of regaining employment,

Table 6. An analysis of variance in unemployment duration by age, skill, area of residence, and disability in Telford, October 1982.

Source of variation	F	Significance
Main effects	49.3	0.000
Area (Z)	12.1	0.000
Disability (D)	19.1	0.000
Skill (S)	140.0	0.000
Age (A)	14.5	0.000
Two-way interactions	1.8	0.006
$Z.D$	1.3	0.264
$Z.S$	2.2	0.038
$Z.A$	0.7	0.700
$D.S$	1.4	0.235
$D.A$	2.3	0.074
$S.A$	2.4	0.025
Three-way interactions	1.0	0.490
$Z.S.D$	0.2	0.978
$Z.A.D$	0.2	0.993
$Z.A.S$	1.6	0.044
$D.A.S$	0.8	0.524
Four-way interaction	1.1	0.333
$Z.D.S.A$	1.1	0.333
Grand mean	80.15	
Explained sum of squares	6468991	
Residual sum of squares	70574092	
Total sum of squares	77043084	
Multiple R^2	0.07	

and the way in which this may have been changing as local labour-market conditions alter. Preliminary work in this vein suggests that interactions between characteristics serve to compound the disadvantage of certain subgroups of the unemployed. This is an area in which research is continuing.

Table 7. The changing effect of the explanatory variables from April 1981 to October 1982 (unadjusted deviations from grand mean).

Variable	Survey 1	Survey 2	Survey 3	Survey 4
Area				
High stress	2.9	4.2	7.9	10.8
Above average	−1.7	−0.9	−1.3	−1.9
Below average	−0.8	0.4	−3.8	−9.5
Low stress	−3.1	−13.2	−13.0	−9.1
Disability				
Disabled	−4.2	−4.3	−4.6	−4.6
Able-bodied	29.6	32.7	35.1	35.2
Age				
16−24	−12.9	−4.2	−9.6	−13.8
25−49	−1.1	−3.0	0.0	1.0
50−59	19.1	15.2	16.5	19.4
60−64	14.7	5.0	1.4	6.6
Skill				
White-collar	−2.9	−8.7	−16.2	−23.9
Blue-collar	−8.0	−14.9	−13.0	−13.5
Unskilled	17.0	36.4	37.5	41.9

7 Conclusions

The prime purpose of this paper was to show that a model-based approach to the design of information systems offers distinct benefits both to urban labour-market analysis and to policy development. In an era when many local authorities have sought to develop policies to overcome the ever-growing problems of inequality and deprivation caused by labour-market malfunction, the quality of the UK database has deteriorated significantly. In particular, it is incapable of supporting research into, and thus generating effective knowledge about, why distinct groups in the labour market tend to have inflicted upon them more than their fair share of the social costs of labour-market adjustment.

Urban information systems are neither neutral with respect to the theoretical constructs on which they are founded nor the policy arena in which they are used. They must have in-built flexibility so that they can be adapted to incorporate developments in the theories on which they are founded and the changing demands which are imposed upon them by the policy-development processes which they serve.

Although the research exercises described in this paper were included primarily to illustrate the analytical potential of the Telford database, some important conclusions can be drawn which are directly relevant to urban labour-market planning and analysis. First, it was shown that the urban labour market is *not* an internally cohesive and unified market; it has within it enclaves which adapt differently and at differing speeds to exogenous change. Second, it was confirmed that unemployment is not a random phenomenon and that its incidence and duration both vary systematically with a range of personal and situational characteristics. It is important to the development of more sensitive and more effective social policy in local authorities to have the ability to identify the common characteristics of those who fare less well in the economic system and to have the frameworks in which to explain why this should be so.

It is only by understanding the nature of the problem under investigation that effective policy can be developed. Nonspecific labour-market policies will have a selective impact and may not help those whose position in the labour market is the least advantageous. Policy, both at national and at local levels, needs to be tailored to the problems of particular subgroups in the labour market and made specific to individual sectors of the economy.

Acknowledgements. I acknowledge Wrekin Council for supporting my research at Liverpool University and Dr P W J Batey, Dr M Madden, and Ian Gordon for their comments on earlier drafts of this paper. The views contained in this paper do not represent those of the Wrekin Council.

References

Black R, 1985, "Instead of the 1986 Census: the potential contribution of enhanced electoral registers" *Journal of the Royal Statistical Society, Series A* **148** 287-316

Bosanquet N, Doeringer P B, 1973, "Is there a dual labour market in Great Britain?" *Economic Journal* **83** 421-435

Buck N, 1985, "Service industries and local labour markets: towards an anatomy of service job loss", paper presented at the Regional Science Association Conference, Manchester; copy obtainable from Urban and Regional Studies Unit, University of Kent, Canterbury, Kent

Carmichael C L, 1981, "The labour-market behaviour of employers: a framework for analysis and a case study of a local labour market", in *Regional Wage Inflation and Unemployment* Ed. R L Martin (Pion, London) pp 160-187

Clarke G P, Wilson A G, 1986, "Performance indicators within a model-based approach to urban planning" WP-446, School of Geography, University of Leeds, Leeds

Daniel W W, 1981 *The Unemployed Flow* Policy Studies Institute, London

Danson M W, 1982, "The industrial structure and labour market segmentation: urban and regional implications" *Regional Studies* **16** 255-265

Elton C J, 1983, "The impact of the Rayner review of unemployment and employment statistics" *Regional Studies* **17** 143-146

Folmer H, van Dijk J, 1985, "Differences in characteristics between unemployed with different spells of unemployment" paper presented at the Regional Science Association Congress, Budapest; copy obtainable from Faculty of Economics, University of Groningen, Groningen

Gleave D, Sellens R, 1984 *An Investigation into British Labour Market Processes* (Economic and Social Research Council, 160 Gt Portland St, London, SW1)

Healey M (Ed.), 1983 *Urban and Regional Industrial Research: The Changing UK Database* (Geo Books, Norwich)

Hoinville G, Smith T M F, 1982, "The Rayner review of government statistical services" *Journal of the Royal Statistical Society, Series A* **145** 195-207

Land K C, Juster F T, 1981, "Social accounting systems: an overview", in *Social Accounting Systems: Essays on the State of the Art* Eds F T Juster, K C Land (Academic Press, New York) pp 1-21

Land K C, McMillan M M, 1981, "Demographic accounts and the study of social change, with applications to the post-World War II United States", in *Social Accounting Systems: Essays on the State of the Art* Eds F T Juster, K C Land (Academic Press, New York) pp 242-300

Loveridge R, Mok A L, 1979 *Theories of Labour Market Segmentation* (Martinus Nijhoff, The Hague)

McGregor A, 1978, "Unemployment duration and re-employment probability" *Economic Journal* **88** 693-706

McGregor A, 1979, "Area externalities and urban unemployment", in *Urban Development and the Inner City* Ed. C Jones (Croom Helm, Beckenham, Kent) pp 92-112

Meager N, 1985, "Temporary work in Britian: its growth and changing rationales" report 6, Institute of Manpower Studies, University of Sussex, Brighton, Sussex

Metcalf D, 1975, "Urban unemployment in England" *Economic Journal* **85** 578-589

Morris D, Sinclair P, 1985, "The unemployment problem in the 1980s" *Oxford Review of Economic Policy* **1**(2) 1-19

Nickell S J, 1980, "A picture of male unemployment in Britain" *Economic Journal* **90** 776-794

Nijkamp P, Rietveld P, 1984 *Information Systems for Integrated Regional Planning* (North-Holland, Amsterdam)

Norris G M, 1978a, "Unemployment, subemployment and personal characteristics: (A) the inadequacies of the traditional approaches to unemployment" *Sociological Review* **26** 89-105

Norris G M, 1978b, "Unemployment, subemployment and personal characteristics: (B) job separations and work histories: the alternative approach" *Sociological Review* **26** 327-345

Oi W, 1962, "Labor as a quasi-fixed factor" *Journal of Political Economy* **70** 538-555

Peck J A, 1985, "A dynamic approach to the study of unemployment" WP-14, School of Geography, University of Manchester, Manchester

Rietveld P, 1984, "Information systems for regional labour markets", in *Information Systems for Integrated Regional Planning* Eds P Nijkamp, P Rietveld (North-Holland, Amsterdam) pp 163-176

Rubery J, 1978, "Structured labour markets, worker organisation and low pay" *Cambridge Journal of Economics* **2** 17-36

Scheurwater J, Masser I, 1981, "Monitoring spatial planning in the Netherlands: an outline of an information analysis system", in *Strategic Planning in a Dynamic Society* Ed. H Voogd, Delftsche Uitgeversmaatschappij, Delft, pp 193-204

Sengenberger W, 1981, "Labour market segmentation and the business cycle", in *The Dynamics of Labour Market Segmentation* Ed. F Wilkinson (Academic Press, London) pp 243-260

Taylor M, Thrift N J, 1983, "Business organisation, segmentation and location" *Regional Studies* **17** 445-465

van Dijk J, Folmer H, 1985, "Entry of the unemployed into employment: theory, methodology and Dutch experience" *Regional Studies* **19** 243-256

Worrall L, 1985a, "Changing employer concentration in a local labour market: an empirical study of Telford" WP-25, Department of Civic Design, University of Liverpool, Liverpool

Worrall L, 1985b, "Social and economic research in an English new town: local information systems" *Environment and Planning B* **12** 277-286

Worrall L, 1986a, "Information systems for policy planning in a shire district" *BURISA* **72** 8-10

Worrall L, 1986b, "The analysis and management of urban change: the role of local information systems" paper presented at the ESRC Urban and Regional Economics Study Group, Manchester; copy obtainable from the author

Local Labour-market Influences on Early Occupational Attainment

P ELIAS
University of Warwick, Coventry
D BLANCHFLOWER
University of Surrey, Guildford

1 Introduction

In this paper we examine the relationship between the characteristics of local labour markets and their influence upon an important transition in the dynamics of individual economic behaviour—the transition from full-time education to work. Our central concern is with the possible relationship between deficient labour demand in an area, youth unemployment, and the process of early occupational attainment. The study is unique in that it draws upon information collected over a 23-year period from a nationally representative group of young persons, members of the National Child Development Study (NCDS)[1].

The literature on labour-market achievement of young workers is extensive but notably fragmented. Social theories seldom give much consideration to external labour-market influences. Economic studies often pay little or no regard to the socialising influence of parental background. Theories of educational development rarely attempt to relate occupational attainment to the educational process. This study represents an attempt to steer an empirical course through these theoretical channels. It is for this reason that we examine a group of young persons who were aged 23 years in March 1981, the NCDS birth-cohort. Over their lifetimes, a remarkable amount of information has been assembled about this group, from their parents, schools, doctors, hospital records, and from the young persons themselves. It is from the individual records of over twelve and a half thousand members of this study, suitably made anonymous to preserve confidentiality, that this paper draws its information[2].

In our theoretical model we postulate that there are three major processes underlying the early career development of the birth cohort, each of which may interact with local labour markets. We term these processes 'early socialisation', 'education', and 'work experience'. The first process is founded before the birth of the cohort member with the establishment of the economic and social environment into which she or

(1) This paper is based upon some preliminary research findings from a more extensive project financed by the Department of Employment, with assistance from the Manpower Services Commission (Elias and Blanchflower, 1987).

(2) For further information on the various 'sweeps' of the birth cohort, the data collected, tracing procedures, and response rates, see Shepherd (1986).

he will be born. This environment may change as the child grows up—for instance, parents may get better jobs, or lose jobs, or divorce and remarry—but we hypothesise that there are certain aspects of this environment which will 'endow' the respondent with a set of attitudes and values which condition the subsequent educational development of the child and, later still, may influence her or his chances of getting a 'good' job. Given the long-standing social stratification of British society and the evidence of a spatial imbalance between labour demand and labour supply which has changed little over the last fifty years, this process of early socialisation may have a 'generational' link with the characteristics of local labour markets. The second process, 'education', provides a new set of influences which may react with and reinforce the economic socialisation of the child or may serve to counteract the influence of social environment. This process may also be conditioned by the state of local labour markets, but the investigation of such links is beyond the scope of this paper. Last, we assume that the decision to leave school and subsequent work experience, although influenced by early socialisation and education, will be particularly strongly influenced by the balance of labour supply and demand in the local labour market.

We make use of the longitudinal nature of this study to explore some of these links across the generation and to investigate the strength of these relationships. The remainder of this paper is in four sections: in section 2 we discuss the measures of occupational attainment and of work history derived from the NCDS data; section 3 is an outline of the procedure adopted for classifying local labour markets and their relation to occupational experience; in section 4 we discuss the results of multivariate analyses of the direct and indirect influences of local labour-market conditions on occupational attainment.

2 Occupational attainment and work histories

In our view the best indicator of an individual's labour-market prospects at the age of 23 years is the occupation in which they were employed or had most recently been employed. With this information it is posible to make some judgment as to whether or not an individual had made a successful transition from school to work. Following Nickell (1982) and Greenhalgh and Stewart (1982; 1985), we used a scale on which occupations were ranked on the basis of national average earnings in the occupation, in this case derived from the 1981 New Earnings Survey (Department of Employment, 1981), with a separate scaling for males and females. The only practical alternative would have been to use a status ranking such as that defined by Goldthorpe and Hope (1974). However, as Phelps-Brown (1977) and Nickell (1982) have shown, this measure is highly correlated with earnings.

For the statistical analyses, occupational attainment was collapsed to separate four-point scales for males and for females, corresponding to the quartile interval, of the national distribution of earnings, with a small residual category for those who could not be otherwise classified. Those in full-time education were categorised on the basis of the level of qualification for which they were studying.

The work-history data were based on a month-by-month record assembled by interviewers during the 1981 sweep of NCDS[(3)]. These were classified according to the criteria of *job turnover* and the *continuity* of employment experience. *Job turnover* could signal the operation of an efficient labour market, with individuals searching for and obtaining jobs which provide a better match between aspirations and experience. Alternatively, high job turnover interspersed with periods of unemployment could signal deteriorating job prospects and a process of 'bumping-down' the occupational hierarchy. The *continuity* of employment experience (even with different employers) may be viewed by potential employers in a radically different fashion from long spells of unemployment in the work history, with the latter reducing the chances of reemployment considerably. Thus, we required a measure (or measures) of work-history experience which captured information on job turnover and employment continuity, and which could be applied consistently to a sample with varying ages of exit from full-time education.

On the basis of exploratory analyses, six categories of work history were finally distinguished. These included two groups who had been continuously employed, in a single job, or more than one job; educational returners; and three groups with other interruptions to their work history, involving a single spell of unemployment, or out of the labour force, and multiple spells of unemployment, and/or inactivity.

3 Local labour-market characteristics

It is not unreasonable to postulate that the state of the local labour market may have some bearing upon work histories and occupational attainment. Further, local job opportunities may have some moderating influence upon the well-established phenomena of intergenerational mobility (Glass, 1954; Goldthorpe and Llewellyn, 1977) and educational 'streaming' (Ashton, 1973). Although these ideas have intuitive appeal, they pose a variety of definitional and operational problems. What is a 'labour market'? What is meant by the 'state' of such a market?

From an individual perspective, a 'labour market' represents a variety of parameters which define a searchable set of job opportunities. These parameters may relate to geographical locations, job categories, earnings, working hours, and various nonpecuniary attributes of different forms of paid work. The parameters will, in turn, probably be correlated with

(3) Approximately 15% of the month-by-month accounts of work experience were not fully coded in the original data set. A substantial preproject phase was associated with the coding of these data.

factors such as socioeconomic background and education. For example, it is likely that the spatial definition of a labour market which will be of value to a qualified civil engineer will be much broader in spatial terms than that for a building labourer. Although we recognise this problem, we must sidestep the issue, for it poses insurmountable operational difficulties.

The approach we have adopted represents a compromise imposed by the limitations of the data which are available to us. Labour markets are defined in the spatial dimension as travel-to-work areas (TTWAs), geographical areas which derive from de facto commuting patterns observed in the 1971 Census of Population. Labour-market descriptors are unemployment rates and rates of employment change, by sex, for the period 1974–81.

3.1 Methodology

The data available from the sweeps of the National Child Development Survey do not record a geographical locational history for respondents in any detail commensurate with that for which we have work-history information. However, the residential location of each respondent in 1974 (at the time of the third sweep) and 1981 are known for all respondents to the fourth sweep (NCDS4) and have been stored in machine-readable format as postcodes.

For reasons of confidentiality, postcode information was not released by the NCDS User Support Group. However, cooperation between the National On-line Management Information System (NOMIS) at Durham University and the NCDS User Support Group enabled the latter to recode 1974 and 1981 addresses by the 1978 TTWAs.

3.2 A classification of TTWAs

For our present purpose, we wish to derive a broad classification which we can use to describe the evolution of these local labour markets in fairly general terms. For instance, we need to be able to distinguish 'high-growth' areas from 'low-growth' areas and localities with high unemployment from those with relatively low unemployment rates. We derived a fairly simple classification of the 380 TTWAs which were identified in the matching procedure outlined above, on the basis of the prevailing rates of unemployment in these areas in 1974 or 1981, the rate of employment change from 1974 to 1981, and the rate of change of unemployment. The unemployment rate in a TTWA is defined as the number of males (or females) registered as unemployed for benefit purposes, as a proportion of the registered unemployed plus employees in employment. For males, we believe this measure to be a reasonable indicator of the proportion of the work force without work and seeking work. For females, the relationship between the unemployment rate and 'joblessness' is masked by the much lower propensity of women to register as unemployed.

In June 1974, the national male unemployment rate stood at 3.2%. By June 1981 this rate had risen to 13.3%. For females, the corresponding rise was from 0.8% to 7.6%. Table 1 indicates how this rise in unemployment manifested itself over the 380 TTWAs. We note that, in 1974, over half of the TTWAs had an unemployment rate of between 5% and 10%. By 1981, one in six of the TTWAs had a rate lying in the range 15% to 20%.

Table 2 shows the distribution of changes in employment across the TTWAs, from 1974 to 1981. In this table we note the remarkable contrast between the changes in employment for men and women. Although not shown in this table, we noted that in over 10% of TTWAs male employment declined by more than 20%.

On its own, the information presented in tables 1 and 2 gives little indication of the changing labour markets facing members of the birth-cohort study. However, it does indicate the significant temporal and spatial variations in employment conditions which existed in Great Britain in the period in which members of the birth cohort made the transition from school to work. Of more interest, though, is the actual change in local labour-market conditions experienced by the study members. Table 3 classifies NCDS respondents in terms of employment change from 1974 to 1981 for the TTWA in which they lived in 1974 and the TTWA in which they lived in 1981. Two points are evident

Table 1. Travel-to-work areas by unemployment rate groups, 1974 and 1981, June each year.

Unemployment rate group[a]	June 1974	June 1981
<5%	39.5	2.1
⩾5% but <10%	53.2	2.1
⩾10% but <15%	7.1	42.9
⩾15% but <20%	0.3	16.1
⩾20%		1.3
Base (= 100%)	380	380

[a] Combined males and females

Table 2. Travel-to-work areas by male and female employment change, 1974–81.

Employment change, 1974–81	Male	Female	Total
< −5%	50.8	21.6	37.1
⩾ −5% but <5%	30.8	30.5	36.6
⩾5%	18.4	47.9	26.3
Base (= 100%)	380	380	380

from a comparison of this table with table 2. First, the distribution of respondents by TTWAs is such that the proportion of respondents who experienced a significant reduction in the level of employment in their local TTWA is higher than the proportion of TTWAs showing a significant decline in employment. This arises because of the residential concentration of respondents in urban areas and the subsequently greater 'weighting' attached to the more rapid decline in employment in such areas. Second, we note the major difference in employment change by gender. Almost one in three female respondents lived in TTWAs in which female employment had grown by more than 5%, whereas fewer than one in twelve of male respondents lived in TTWAs in which male employment had grown by 5%.

Table 3. NCDS4 respondents classified by employment change, 1974–81, by 1974 and 1981 travel-to-work areas (TTWAs), and by gender.

Employment change	Males (%)		Females (%)	
	1974 TTWA	1981 TTWA	1974 TTWA	1981 TTWA
< −5%	67.4	67.2	25.7	24.2
⩾ −5% but < 5%	24.0	24.4	44.4	46.1
⩾ 5%	8.6	8.4	29.9	29.7
Base (= 100%)	6153	6153	6164	6164

3.3 Geographical mobility and employment decline

A complicating feature of table 3 is the need to identify both the 1974 and the 1981 TTWAs. Obviously, many respondents will have moved between TTWAs in this period. We cannot identify all respondents who moved between TTWAs between 1974 and 1981, simply because some may have moved back to their 1974 TTWA by 1981. Nor can we identify multiple moves between TTWAs. We can distinguish between respondents who lived in a different TTWA in 1981 from that in which

Table 4. NCDS4 respondents classified by employment change (1974–81) in 1981 travel-to-work area by whether or not 1974 TTWA is same as 1981 TTWA and by gender.

Employment change 1974–81 in 1981 TTWA	Comparison of 1974 and 1981 TTWA of respondent			
	males		females	
	'mover'	'stayer'	'mover'	stayer'
< −5%	61.0	68.8	18.6	26.2
⩾ −5% but < 5%	28.2	23.5	46.5	46.0
⩾ 5%	10.9	7.8	34.9	27.8
Base (= 100%)	1268	4885	1672	4492

they were recorded in 1974. This group we call 'movers' as opposed to 'stayers', but we must bear in mind the correct interpretation of this variable.

Table 4 decomposes the information presented in table 3 into the two categories, 'movers' and 'stayers'. We note that 21% of male respondents and 27% of female respondents were in a different TTWA in 1981 from that in which they were recorded in 1974. Both for males and for females, fewer of the 'movers' are located in TTWAs in 1981 which recorded a 5% fall in employment from 1974 to 1981 than is the case for 'stayers'. In other words, 'movers' have, on balance, moved away from areas of extreme employment decline to areas with more favourable rates of employment change in the period 1974 to 1981.

3.4 Local labour markets and work histories

Table 5 focuses upon those respondents within the birth-cohort study for whom an occupational attainment score in the range 1–4 was derived (see section 2) and for whom a postcode sector/TTWA code match was derived in the linking of NCDS records to NOMIS data. In the derivation of the attainment scale we were unable to classify 316 males and 502 females. In the postcode sector/TTWA linking, we 'lost' 107 males and 97 females. This represents an overall loss of 8% of the available sample.

For males, we note from the first, second, and third rows of table 5(a) that TTWAs with high rates of employment decline over the period 1974–81 are associated with a higher proportion of work-history patterns which contain multiple spells of unemployment or periods 'out of the labour force'. Conversely, the proportion of male respondents who were continuously employed, but had held more than one job since leaving school is lower in the areas experiencing high rates of employment decline. For all other work-history patterns, the proportion of respondents who display such a pattern is not related to the state of the local labour market. For females, the relationship between employment change and work-history patterns is not so clear. The contrasts are more evident, for females as well as males, in table 5(b) which repeats these distributions, with the 1981 TTWA unemployment rate instead of employment change as the indicator of the state of the local labour market. This suggests that those persons who change jobs put themselves 'at risk' of becoming unemployed in those labour markets which have relatively poor employment prospects.

We have noted, then, a relationship betwen two of the six work-history patterns and local labour-market conditions. We conclude this section by investigating the possibility of a link between local labour markets and occupational attainment. To do this we relate the change in employment over the period 1974–81, and the 1981 rate of unemployment in the respondent's 1981 TTWA, to the occupational attainment scale. Table 6(a) shows these distributions for 1981 TTWAs for employment change. Table 6(b) shows the corresponding information for TTWAs classified in terms of their 1981 unemployment rate. We note that the rate of change of employment in the 1981 TTWA does not appear to correlate with the occupational attainment of NCDS4 respondents. However, there is a very clear association between the rate of unemployment in the TTWA and the occupational attainment scale, both for males and for females.

Table 5. Gender-specific employment change (1974–81) and unemployment rate categories in respondent's 1981 travel-to-work area (TTWA) by work-history type.

	Work-history type[a]						Base[b] (= 100%)
	1	2	3	4	5	6	
(a) Employment change, 1974–81 in 1981 TTWA							
Males							
< −5%	22.4	25.8	7.3	14.2	2.8	25.4	3927
⩾ −5% but < 5%	20.9	32.0	8.0	13.0	3.5	20.7	1423
⩾ 5%	22.9	34.6	7.3	13.4	1.2	18.0	494
Total	22.1	28.0	7.5	13.9	2.8	23.7	5844
Females							
< −5%	18.6	17.7	5.5	10.9	12.0	34.3	1355
⩾ −5% but < 5%	17.5	23.1	6.4	8.6	12.3	30.4	2639
⩾ 5%	16.6	21.2	7.1	8.3	12.2	33.3	1677
Total	17.5	21.2	6.4	9.1	12.2	32.2	5671
(b) Unemployment rate in June 1981 in 1981 TTWA							
Males							
< 10%	21.6	31.7	8.7	12.2	3.5	19.7	1780
⩾ 10% but < 16%	22.4	29.0	7.1	14.8	2.5	22.5	2576
⩾ 16%	22.2	22.0	6.7	14.3	2.6	30.6	1488
Total	22.1	28.0	7.5	13.9	2.8	23.7	5844
Females							
< 6%	16.3	24.7	8.7	7.9	12.3	27.9	1917
⩾ 6% but < 11%	17.9	21.1	5.6	9.8	13.2	31.4	2633
⩾ 11%	18.6	15.7	4.4	9.3	9.5	41.4	1121
Total	17.5	21.2	6.4	9.1	12.2	32.2	5671

[a] The work-history types are 1 continously employed in one job, 2 continuously employed in more than one job, 3 educational returners, 4 one spell of unemployment, 5 one spell out of the labour force, 6 multiple spells of unemployment or out of the labour force. Percentages do not sum to 100 across the rows because of 118 males and 80 females for whom no work history pattern could be derived (principally continuing students).

[b] The base for this table consists of persons for whom a postcode sector/TTWA match could be derived and for whom an occupational attainment scale score was developed.

Table 6. Occupational attainment by 1974–81 change in employment and 1981 unemployment rate categories in 1981 travel-to-work area (TTWA) by gender.

	Occupational attainment scale				Base (= 100%)
	1	2	3	4	
(a) Change in employment 1974–81 for 1981 TTWA					
Males					
< −5%	13	34	41	13	3927
⩾ −5% and < 5%	13	34	41	12	1423
⩾ 5%	11	35	41	14	494
Females					
< −5%	17	20	44	19	1355
⩾ −5 and < 5%	22	24	39	16	2634
⩾ 5%	17	22	42	19	1677
(b) 1981 unemployment rate group in 1981 TTWA					
Males					
< 10%	16	35	39	10	1780
⩾ 10% and < 16%	11	35	41	13	2576
⩾ 16%	10	31	44	14	1488
Females					
< 6%	26	25	27	12	1917
⩾ 6% and < 11%	17	23	42	19	2633
⩾ 11%	13	18	45	24	1121

4 Occupational attainment, social background, work histories, and local labour markets

We have shown in the previous section that in labour markets with high unemployment, persons who engage in job changing are more likely to have a personal experience of unemployment in their work histories. This phenomenon is not observed if we classify labour markets in terms of employment growth or decline. We noted also that a much higher proportion of young men and women are in potentially higher-paying jobs in areas of low unemployment than in areas of high unemployment. Again, no simple relationship between occupational attainment and spatial differences in employment change could be detected.

An obvious explanation of these findings would relate to the geography of Britain's class structure. Areas of high unemployment are more likely to be the metropolitan labour markets of the major cities. Through the operation of the housing market, we know that such areas have a higher proportion of residents in semiskilled and unskilled manual occupations. The process we termed 'early socialisation', perhaps moderated by the influence of education, would lead us to expect that a higher proportion of the children of parents in such occupational groups would leave school at the minimum school-leaving age, change jobs more frequently, experience unemployment between such changes, and have jobs at age 23 years with lower than average earnings. In other words, the relationships observed in table 6 could derive solely from the process of childhood socialisation coupled with the operation of housing markets. Without further information on the social background of the study members, we would be unable to pursue this hypothesis further. However, we are in the fortunate position of having information on the social class category of the respondent's father at the time of birth of the respondent. Also, we have information on the study members' scores on standard educational achievement tests of English and mathematics at age 11 years. Thus, we can investigate the interactions between these variables to determine the relative importance of the processes that we postulate will influence occupational attainment.

Figure 1(a) represents the theoretical model we used to investigate the relationship between local labour markets and occupational attainment. In this diagram we have indicated with bold arrows those relationships which we assumed to be dominant. Clearly, the principal influences we postulated in this model are through childhood socialisation to educational attainment, then through the subsequent experience of work to a position in the distribution of occupations. We have assumed also that parental 'socialising' influences can have a further and direct impact upon work history (for example, by persuading children to enter unstable versus stable forms of employment) and upon occupational attainment. The second relationship might exist through children from professional or middle-class families having different career aspirations or work motivation than children with a working-class background. Local labour-market influences are assumed to impact upon work histories and directly upon the position of each respondent in the occupational distribution at age 23 years.

Figure 1(b) redraws these relationships using information derived from a multivariate analysis of occupational attainment. Some simplifications have been made, particularly so for women, for whom the situation is complicated by early childbearing. Nonetheless, this diagram portrays the major influences between these processes which we have detected. The most significant feature of this diagram is its relative lack of complexity. We hypothesised that the observed relationship between local area unemployment rates, work histories, and occupational attainment could derive from the spatial distribution of social class categories, with areas of high unemployment containing a higher proportion of nonprofessional and less skilled workers which, in turn, leads to a lower level of occupational attainment among their children. This does not appear to be the case. Social background (measured as parental occupation) has a strong and direct influence on educational attainment only, not on the work history or upon occupational attainment of the study member at age 23 years. Not surprisingly, educational

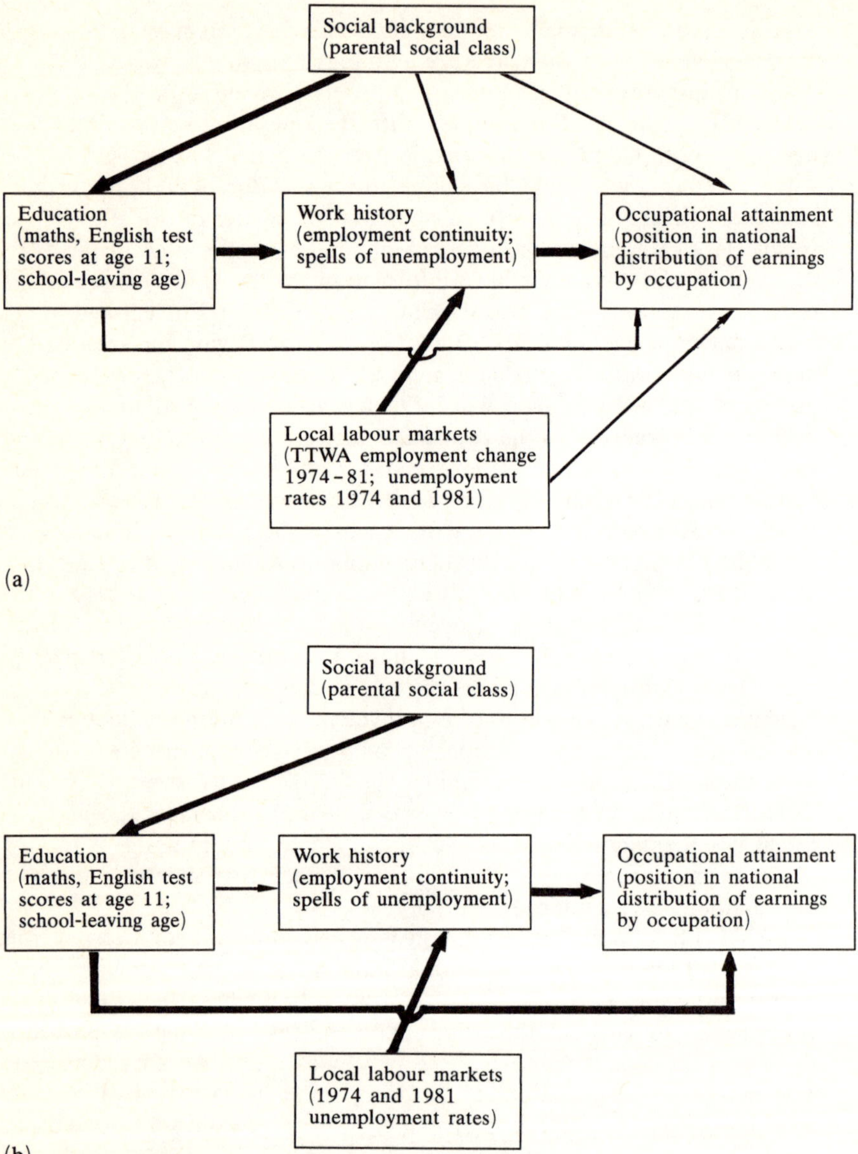

⟶ (thick arrow) indicates that the theoretical or empirical relationship is of major significance

→ (thin arrow) indicates a theoretical or empirical influence additional to that shown as of major significance

Figure 1. Occupational attainment, work histories, education, socialisation, and local labour markets: (a) the theoretical model, (b) the empirical relationships. (The items in parentheses are the operational variables used in the multivariate analyses, TTWA is travel-to-work area.)

attainment and occupational attainment are highly correlated, but personal work histories intervene to modify this relationship. Local unemployment, measured in terms of 1981 TTWA unemployment rates, does have a powerful link with the individual's work history which is, in turn, correlated with occupational attainment.

We also investigated the relationship between social background, educational attainment, local area unemployment, and our crude measure of geographical mobility. In terms of the social background variables, the respondent's father's school-leaving age was found to be significant, but not social class. Male or female respondents whose father left school at the minimum school-leaving age were about 8% or 9% *less* likely to be in a different TTWA in 1981 from that in which they resided in 1974.

Below average scores for reading or maths at age 11 are also correlated with a lower likelihood of having moved. In terms of a local labour-market influence, we initially found, using 1974 unemployment rates, that the influence was only significant for females, although its direction accorded with our expectations. The higher the rate of unemployment in the respondent's 1974 TTWA in 1974, the greater the likelihood that the respondent was a 'mover'. We repeated the regression, this time using the 1981 rate of unemployment in the respondent's 1981 TTWA and found that, both for males and for females, there was a strong and significant negative relationship. These findings confirm the 'push-pull' influence of local labour markets, indicating that the 'pull' effect of job opportunities elsewhere is more marked than the 'push' effect of reduced job opportunities in the respondent's local labour market in 1974.

A number of issues are raised by these findings. First, we need to pursue further why it is the local area *unemployment rate* which characterises the employment and occupational opportunities of young people and not the *rate of employment growth or decline*. In this respect we are mindful of the need to consider the role of local changes in population and labour-force participation rates in linking changes in employment with unemployment. An area may be characterised as one of employment growth, but this might result from a significant increase in the participation of married women working part-time, or from a major influx of new workers, leading to little change in the employment opportunities facing young persons.

Further work needs to be done on the link between educational attainment at age 11 years and occupational attainment at age 23 years. We have not investigated spatial differences in the relationship, which could reflect spatial variations in the provision of education. This is an important topic given the current debate about local control of educational expenditure and the introduction of a national curriculum.

Finally, we are puzzled as to why local labour-market influences upon occupational attainment are concentrated within two particular work-history patterns. Contrary to our expectations, persons who took one job did better than persons who had more than one job. It seems that young people who change jobs 'expose' themselves to a risk of unemployment, particularly where unemployment is high. If this is the case, the role of careers guidance becomes an important factor in occupational attainment. Any mistakes a young person makes, in his or her choice of job, are costly to rectify, especially in areas of high unemployment.

Acknowledgements. We wish to express our thanks to staff at the National Children's Bureau, particularly to Peter Shepherd (now at the NCDS User Support Group, City University) for much help with the diary coding project and for assistance with our enquiries. Others who have helped us with comments and advice include Barbara Ballard, Mark Stewart, Joan Payne, Vince Keddie, Linda Ammon, Peter Helm, William Smith, Francis Butler, Ken Fogelman, and members of the research division, Norwegian Central Statistical Bureau.

We are especially grateful to Bob Wellburn (formerly at City University) and Bob Nelson at Durham University for organising the linkage between travel-to-work areas and NCDS residential locations in 1974 and 1981, and for providing information from the NOMIS database.

Finally we would like to thank Eric Roughley and Marcia Taylor at the Data Archive, University of Essex, who met all our requests for data and documentation with their usual efficiency and to Ian Gordon for editorial assistance. Christine Jones and Tim Clarke at the Institute for Employment Research have provided us with first-rate clerical assistance.

This project was financed by the Department of Employment (Social Science Branch) with additional assistance from the Manpower Services Commission. We remain responsible for errors and it must be stressed that the views presented here are not necessarily those of the DE or the MSC.

References

Ashton D N, 1973, "The transition from school to work: notes on the development of different frames of reference among young male workers" *Sociological Review* **21** 107–125

Department of Employment, 1981, "New Earnings Survey 1981, Part D", Department of Employment, Caxton House, Tothill St, London SW1

Elias P, Blanchflower D, 1987, "Who gets the good jobs? Parental background, education, work history and location as factors in early career formation", Institute for Employment Research, University of Warwick, Coventry

Glass D (Ed.), 1954 *Social Mobility in Britain* (Routledge and Kegan Paul, Andover, Hants)

Goldthorpe J, Hope K, 1972 *The Social Grading of Occupations: A New Approach and Scale* (Clarendon Press, Oxford)

Goldthorpe J H, Llewellyn C, 1977, "Class mobility in modern Britain: three theses examined" *Sociology* **11** 257–288

Greenhalgh C, Stewart M, 1982, "The effects and determinants of training", Warwick Economic Research Papers 213, Department of Economics, University of Warwick, Coventry

Greenhalgh C, Stewart M, 1985, "The occupational status and mobility of British men and women" *Oxford Economic Papers* **37** 40-71
Nickell S, 1982, "The determinants of occupational success in Britain" *Review of Economic Studies* 43-53
Phelps-Brown H, 1977 *The Inequality of Pay* (Oxford University Press, Oxford)
Shepherd P, 1986, "The National Child Development Study: an introduction to the origins of the study and the methods of data collection" WP1, NCDS User Support Group, Social Statistics Research Unit, City University, London

Informal Economy and the Labour Market: Relations with the Economic Order

J G LAMBOOY, P H RENOOY
University of Amsterdam

1 Introduction

In recent studies the development of informal activities has been represented both as an attack on the current economic order (Heertje, 1984), and as an expression of economically rational behaviour (Sandmo, 1983; Stuart, 1984). An overheated government machine, high marginal taxes, the increasing complexities of social institutions, and other factors are cited as indicators of the end of centralisation, government control, and the welfare state. The Reagan administration's version of supply-side economics has furthered the slogan that "Government is bad; market is good" (Ostrom, 1986). All this has modified our evaluation of the informal economy. It was usual to look to it as a source of moral decay, or the misallocation of resources. Increasingly, however, it is being seen as a source of jobs and as a symptom of disequilibria created by excessive regulation, or as the result of new opportunities for 'homework' created by technological development, in the form of electrical tools, computers, etc.

It is not easy to assess the development and the importance of the informal economy. Conclusions depend partly on the definitions used and on the perspectives chosen. If one looks at the phenomenon as a distortion of social relations, on the one hand, or as a possible last resort of unemployed persons on the other, the results of the analyses are liable to differ. The same goes for measurement. The informal economy can be measured in money terms, in relation to the output of goods and services, or as a labour-related phenomenon; each method may yield a quite different answer.

In this paper, the labour market is the central issue, but it will be dealt with in connection with the economic order. Labour-market developments are intricately interwoven with the whole of society and may be seen as basic indicators for economic developments. The informal labour market can thus be an interesting source of knowledge about societal development. The reverse also applies, however. Existing studies of the size of the informal labour market offer only a weak basis for international comparisons, and have even less to say about possible regional variations. To improve our understanding of the regional role of the informal economy we need to understand how it fits into the overall economic and social order.

In the next section of this paper, we start with definitions of the informal economy, and the activities within it. In section 3 we then focus on the informal labour market and the evidence which existing national and international studies offer on its role and on methods of assessing its significance. The applicability of such methods at the regional level is considered in section 4, which concludes with a series of hypotheses about other aspects of the economic order affecting the role of the informal sector in particular regions.

2 Definitions

The literature about the informal economy is very diffuse where definitions are concerned. Notions such as 'black', 'grey', 'off-the-books', 'underground', 'hidden', 'unofficial', and 'parallel' already show that the early researchers were quite often motivated by a more or less moral indignation. A uniform definition is lacking, because *the* informal economy, as a separate 'sector' or as a group of discernible activities, does not exist. All activities can be found in the formal as well as in the informal economy. No distinction can be found as to the kind of *activities*; attention has to focus on the *institutional structure* in which the activities occur. And here we come to the need to connect the informal economy with the changing economic order.

By 'institutional structure' we mean the configuration of the set of rules and values which are important for the coordination, regulation, and cooperation of economic agents. The rules and values are expressed in institutional arrangements. Governments, or—in case of self-regulation—private groups and organisations, can enforce behaviour in accordance with the prescriptions or within a limited range of options. Taxes, price restrictions, quality control, the determination of minimal working and housing conditions, and other instruments are used by governments for a variety of goals. Depending on the perceived effects on 'the order', dissident behaviour will be punished, be classified as a crime, or simply as socially 'not done'.

Informal activities are mostly associated with an absence of governmental control or supervision. It is possible to explain this lack of control in relation to four related sources of 'disorder':

(1) new technologies: for example, electrical tools, home appliances, etc;

(2) institutional rigidity: that is, the discrepancies between formal rules and 'real world' conditions;

(3) moral decay: if one views the world and the development of values from the 'solidarity' standpoint, many informal activities are considered to be 'egoistic', because taxes are evaded;

(4) rational reaction of the market: if the viewpoint of the 'overorganised economy' is chosen, then the informal economy may be seen as a rational instrument to improve the allocation of resources.

Despite the general relevance of these factors, it cannot be denied that some kinds of activities fit better into either the formal or the informal economy. Activities related to repair and maintenance, catering, and other person-related activities, such as health care, care for the elderly, and low-knowledge activities with relatively high wage costs, are dominant in the informal economy.

Neither the kind of activities, nor the kind of transactions or income as such, can be used as a unique criterion to identify the informal sector, but they all may be useful for further analysis.

2.1 The elements

A number of authors consider *activities* to be the main elements of the phenomenon they are seeking to describe. Thus Macafee (1982, page 147) describes his 'hidden economy' as "economic activity, generating factor incomes, which cannot be estimated from the regular statistic sources used to compile the income measure of GDP". Feige (1981) and Gershuny (1979) also use activities as the basis for their descriptions. A related concept, which is regularly used for definition, is *work*. De Grazia (1983, page 9) even uses the term 'professional work' in his description: "professional work on the fringes of, or outside the statutory rules, aimed at making profit, on a non-temporary basis". A last author to be mentioned is Skolka (1984b), who describes the 'hidden economy' as consisting of 'concealed activities', leading to the production of legal as well as illegal goods and services.

A second element which we find in attempts to define the informal economy is the *transaction*. Rose (1983, page 5), for instance, describes his 'unofficial economy' as follows: "transactions not reported or recorded by government (cash only)". Also, approaches meant to measure the informal economy, such as those of Gutmann (1984) or Feige (1979), take transactions as their point of departure. However, when a description is based on transactions, an identifiable section of activities within the informal economy is ruled out, namely all those activities or all that work which do not lead to transactions. Activities in the 'do-it-yourself' sphere, production for own consumption, or—as Toffler (1980) calls it—"prosuming", form an important group in this respect. More generally, however, the selection of transactions as the subject of description means that nothing can be said about the nature of the work preceding the transaction. Formal transactions may be preceded by informal work, and vice versa. Such a problem arises, for instance, in the definition used by Rose.

Yet another group of authors take *income* as the basis for their description. This group are primarily economists who are interested in the extent of the informal economy. An important representative of this group is Tanzi (1982, page 103), who describes the 'underground economy' as "income that is not reported to the tax authorities".

Following from this, yet another type of description can be distinguished, namely one based on flows of goods, services, and incomes. This definition can be found in the work of, among others, Heertje et al (1982).

They describe the 'unofficial circuit' as "that section of flows of goods, services, and money, which has not (yet) appeared in the National Accounts" (page 4, compare also Broesterhuizen, 1983). Comparable with the definition of Heertje et al, but less explicit, is Frey and Weck-Hanneman's (1984, page 3) description, of the 'hidden economy' as "that part of the economy which escapes the purview of our present social measurement apparatus".

2.2 The criteria

Although there is little agreement on the elements of the informal economy there also appears to be no great degree of conformity in the criteria used for classification. In a large number of descriptions, the statistical distinction "registered (or not) in the official statistics" can be found. In most cases, 'official statistics' is used to refer to the national accounts (Heertje et al, 1982; Tanzi, 1982). Although such a distinction seems plausible at first glance, it inevitably raises objections. In the first place it provides no insight into the nature of the work or the activities which precede the transaction or payment which should have been registered. Second, as Broesterhuizen (1983) makes clear in the case of the Netherlands, an important part of nonregistered transactions are still included in the national accounts, by means of estimates. If this description is used, then the concept of the informal economy is made strongly dependent on the statistical conventions used by particular government agencies.

Another problem arising through use of this distinction, is that of implementation. Which transactions and/or activities should be registered? We may distinguish eight possible alternative methods (Begeer and Van Tuinen, 1984, page 41) which include the following information:

(1) only primary production;
(2) only the production of material products;
(3) only production for the market;
(4) all activities leading to a monetary remuneration;
(5) all activities leading to a monetary remuneration plus some other well-defined activities;
(6) all activities which produce commodities that have an equivalent in the formal economy;
(7) all activities which can be done by a third party in such a way that they would lead to an equivalent result;
(8) all activities on which time has to be spent.

The description used by the British Inland Revenue (cited from O'Higgins, 1982, page 2) should also be mentioned. This involves the motivation of the worker to distinguish between the formal and the 'black' economy, that is, "economic activities generating incomes which are concealed from the revenue collecting authorities with the intention of evading tax".

Whereas the above descriptions tend to stress a statistical distinction, other authors emphasise institutional aspects as the classification criteria. The definition used by De Grazia is an example of this and the Dutch Inter-Departmental Steering Group on Abuse and Misuse (ISMO, 1985, page 261) defines 'black' work as "work carried out without (full) compliance with the relevant obligations under fiscal and social security legislation".

Del Boca and Forte (1982) recognise that most informal activities conflict with most existing legislation and regulations, but they nevertheless do not see this as 'the' distinguishing characteristic of informal activities. These authors say that activities similar to those in the regular economy take place in the informal economy; the distinguishing characteristic of informal activities, however, is the lack of formal transactions. It is also for that reason that they speak of the 'parallel economy'.

Lozano (1983) makes yet another distinction. After a discussion of various classification criteria, he contends that the essence of the informal economy is the absence of routine government regulations.

2.3 A more complex description

As can be seen from the above, it is not a simple matter to arrive at a universal description of 'the informal economy'. To achieve greater clarity, various authors have made further subdivisions of the informal economy. At the Dutch Central Bureau of Statistics (CBS), a matrix has been designed in which the fiscal and statistical distinctions could be compared, to arrive at the classification of productive activities shown in table 1. This matrix provides a workable division for the achievement of specific aims, such as a measurement of the sensitivity of national accounts calculations in estimating fraud. However, if we wish to gain a closer understanding of what may analytically be defined as the 'informal

Table 1. Classification of productive activities (source: Blokland, 1982; Broesterhuizen, 1983). The items listed are examples only.

Category	Fiscal or legal distinction (official)[a] within NA	Statistical distinction (nonofficial)[a]	
		within NA	outside NA
1 'white'	fully registered production	statistical undercover age of legal activities, for example, street musicians	do-it-yourself and domestic work
2 'black' but lawful	supply of products without a bill	dabbling in the building sector	clandestine subletting of rooms
3 'black' and illegal	shoplifting	trade in narcotics	blackmail

[a] NA National Accounts.

economy', the matrix offers too few results. Clarity about the elements of the phenomenon, as well as its distinguishing characteristics, is still lacking.

The same problem arises with regard to Gershuny's (1979) much quoted division of the informal sector into three subsectors:
(1) the *household economy*, which is defined as activities with no financial payment, which provide useful goods and services for members of the household;
(2) the *communal economy*, defined as those activities which are carried out voluntarily and without financial payment, for society as a whole or for members of the community other than those of the household;
(3) the *underground economy*, by which is meant activities which also take place in the formal economy or which are often performed by the same people, but which remain hidden from the authorities, because of their illegality or to evade taxes and other regulations, or because they involve theft.

Within this 'underground economy', Gershuny distinguishes a further three groups:
(a) activities which are always linked with formal employment and which leave a trail as costs in production in the national accounts;
(b) activities which are less closely linked to the formal economy; production which is supplied to the formal sector, but which does not form a part of it (for example, home workers, sweatshops);
(c) manufacture of finished products and services, directly to the consumer.

This far-reaching treatment of the informal economy agrees to a great extent with the CBS-classification. Thus Gershuny's underground economy falls entirely within the CBS 'black' activities and the domestic and communal sectors fall within the categories (1) to (3). Rose (1983) also makes a global distinction between a 'domestic economy' and an 'unofficial economy'.

The above typologies can be made even more precise by applying Mingione's (1983) distinction between informal work as primary employment in which over 40 hours must be worked in order to obtain sufficient means, and informal work as supplementary employment, in which insufficient income is obtained for the purpose of maintenance.

These distinctions provide a reasonable insight into the concept of the informal economy. Gershuny's description in particular has a number of strong points, including the specification of the underground economy and the relations between the formal and the informal economies. Yet, his description leaves us with a number of unclear points. The question of whether work or activities should be listed under the underground economy, is linked to the nature of the transactions which result from these activities. These transactions as such do not belong to the formal economy. However, which characteristics should be shown by the work, so that it falls outside the formal economy, is not made explicit.

The lack of clarity over what exactly should be understood by the 'informal economy', has led some authors to leave out a descripion (Isachsen and Strøm, 1982), or to adopt unacceptable simplifications, as for instance Smith (1983, page 1), who describes his 'irregular economy' as "some or all of the economic activities of entrepreneurs that are missed, or probably missed, by the national income accounts. Sometimes distinctions are made between legal and illegal activities ... ."

The existence of a variety of descriptions is confusing. It makes it difficult to compare results of research and a nonstandardised apparatus of concepts does not allow us to formulate concrete questions for further study. In the next paragraph we will try to produce a more general description of the informal economy.

2.4 Towards a general description

If we wish to make the description of the informal economy more specific we should first distinguish those elements, which (together) make up the 'informal economy'. We will do so on the basis of a simple cyclical plan, which can be described as follows: subjects undertake *activities* (work), which may or may not lead to *transactions*, from which *payments* may or may not result, which produce *income*, which again may be used in various ways (see figure 1).

Activities, transactions, and income can all form elements of the informal economy. However, they may be independent of each other; that is, informal activities can lead to formal payments (for example, working for a lump labour subcontractor leads to a formal product; a 'black' barkeeper sells a 'white' beer), or vice versa, or, of course, the entire cycle may take place outside the formal sphere. Thus, each of the elements may have an informal character, and for the sake of analytical clarity, we should describe this separately for each element.

By '*informal activities*' we mean activities aimed at producing a positive effect on income (both for the person executing the activities, and for the person receiving the results, for example, the goods or the service), for which the terms of legislation and regulations (planning

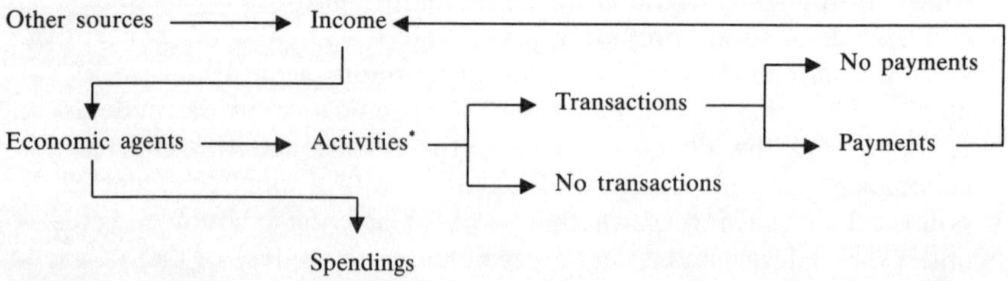

Figure 1. Cyclical plan of the informal economy.

requirements, social security legislation, collective labour agreements, and the like) applicable to the activities are not being met. Here deduction of taxes and contributions are deliberately ignored, in view of the fact that they have nothing to do with the work as such, but only play a role in the payment for the work.

The above description will cover the activities of the do-it-yourselfer and those of, for instance, the employee of a lump labour subcontractor. The 'black' work, carried out by a small independent entrepreneur during normal working hours, however, will not be covered. This concerns the fiscal aspects of payments and incomes.

Virtually no statements can be made on whether *transactions* as such are formal or informal. That is determined by the institutional framework. *Payments* may or may not follow upon transactions. If payments do not take place, we find ourselves in the sphere of Gershuny's household or communal economy, in which the nature of the activities forms the characteristic element. If payments are made after formal or informal work, or for the purchase of goods, then we speak of informal payments when relevant commitments in respect of fiscal or social security legislation are not met. This could include both payments for goods or services in which value added tax requirements are not met, and payments for work for which no social security contributions are paid.

The income, which results partly from the payments and partly from other sources, can also be characterised as informal. This will be the case when this income is not reported to the inland revenue, social security authorities, or other organisations which have a statutory right to the information. A similar situation may arise with regard to income obtained from *savings* or from *capital*. If these are kept outside the interaction between citizen and (semi)governmental institutions, they may be referred to as informal savings or informal capital.

The above descriptions are based on activities which, as such, are justifiable or, as Gershuny (1985) puts it, which lead to commodities which can also be produced in the formal economy. In that way, he distinguishes activities, such as drugs distribution, which are generally illegal, from the production of legally unexceptionable commodities in circumstances which contravene tax or other relevant regulations, which become contextually illegal. The second type we include in the informal economy, whereas the first are part of what we will call the 'underground economy'.

Thus we arrive at a combination of elements, which together form the informal economy. The characteristic of this informal economy which distinguishes it from the formal sector is the *lack of governmental control of rules*.

The description of the informal economy which we have put forward here is a broad one. It contains a wide variety of activities, from work for a lump labour subcontractor to domestic work. Therefore it is necessary to devise a further specification of the parts of the informal economy.

In general, we can distinguish two major parts of the informal economy. A first group which may be identified contains transactions which, by the labour or the payments involved, can be characterised as informal. These transactions also ought to be included in the national accounts. We will call this part of the informal economy the *'black' sector*.

A second group to be identified contains activities and transactions that are not followed by payments in money. Domestic labour and do-it-yourself activities, for example, belong to this group. Following Gershuny, we will refer to this group as the *'domestic and communal' sector*. (For a survey of this sector in France, see Gaudin and Schiray, 1982.) To what extent the output of these activities should be included in the national accounts, depends on the statistical conventions used.

2.5 A further division

Within the two main groups we have just described—the 'black' and the 'domestic and communal' sectors—a further subdivision is possible and, for the sake of clarity, necessary. We follow Gershuny (1979) in distinguishing three types of informal activities within the black sector:

(1) Linked informal activities: these are informal activities which take place within a formal framework (for example, firms). They are executed either by the employer or by the employee, and the income involved accrues to the firm and not to the individual. The best known example is the category of 'off the books' activities.

(2) Semi-autonomous informal activities: informal production of goods or services for the formal economy. Examples are the lump labour subcontractor and parts of homework and sweatshops.

(3) Autonomous informal activities: informal production of final goods and services directly for the consumer.

It is also possible to make a further subdivision within the domestic and communal sector. We distinguish two groups, based on whether or not activities are followed by transactions. When no transactions follow, we are dealing with do-it-yourself, 'prosuming', domestic labour, subsistence, and such like. When transactions do follow, without money being involved, we speak of barter, specific types of volunteer labour, and reciprocal work. In the classification presented in figure 2 we have followed and have tried to integrate internationally frequently used descriptions (Gershuny, Skolka, Lozano), since such a mutual comparison will be beneficial.

Summarising, we have the following descriptions:

Informal activities: those activities generating a positive income effect on either the executing or the receiving party, in which the terms of legislation and registration are not met.

Informal payments: those payments for which relevant commitments in respect of fiscal or social security legislation are not met.
Informal transactions: transactions in which informal payments, informal activities, or both, are involved.
Informal income: income which is not reported to or recorded by the inland revenue authorities, social security authorities, or other organisations which have statutory rights to the information (the same goes for informal capital or informal savings).

The whole of informal activities, payments, transactions, and income form the *informal economy*. A general characteristic of this informal economy is the lack of government control or regulation and the motivation of the participants to obtain a positive income effect. Within the informal economy, a division can be made between a '*black*' sector, comprising informal transactions aimed at enlarging the income of the executing or receiving party, and a '*domestic and communal*' sector, comprising informal activities or transactions where no payments are involved and which are intended to save on expenditures. As will be clear from the above description, it is not difficult to think of examples of informal activities. Almost any activity that can be found in the formal economy can also be done in an informal way. Of course, there are certain activities that are easier to carry out informally. Especially when small amounts of investments and a low level of training are sufficient, as with small maintenance jobs in and around the house, within the hotel and restaurants sector, and other person-oriented services, such as barbers, washing activities, and paramedical activities, or in parts of the clothing industry, one will frequently find informal activities.

Time spent

Productive labour	Paid
	Unpaid
Other uses of time	Recreation; biologically necessary activities

Type of economy

Formal economy		
Informal economy	Black sector	Linked informal activities, semi-autonomous informal, and autonomous informal activities
	Domestic and communal sector	Do-it-yourself, self-service and 'prosuming'; domestic labour
		Barter, reciprocal work, forms of volunteer labour*

* Volunteer labour which does not meet the description of informal activities is excluded, for example, distributing flowers in a hospital.

Figure 2. Classification of the economy.

3 The informal labour market: an international comparison

For some indications of how the importance of the informal economy may vary between areas, and the bases on which this can be assessed, we turn first to international comparisons, on which more work has been undertaken than at the interregional level, partly because of the availability of a richer set of statistical sources. Efforts to compare the informal economy in several countries are hampered by at least three serious problems. The first is that of inconsistent definitions of the informal economy. This means that we are hardly ever discussing the same phenomenon in comparing the informal economy in different countries. A second problem is time. For a good comparison, we need comparable studies, which are held in the same year, or over the same period of years. A third problem that we are confronted with is that, over time, in different countries different methods are used to measure the informal economy. Even when methods are consistently applied, different methods lead to varying conclusions about the relative importance of informal activities in particular countries.

We shall discuss first a number of national studies which use direct survey methods to quantify the scale of informal activity. These relate particularly to involvement in the 'black labour market', with a much more limited treatment of the domestic and communal sectors, on which information is very scarce. Second, we shall consider some of the attempts which have been made at international comparisons using indirect methods, again focusing more on those relating to the 'black labour market', in part because these offer more scope for transfer to the regional level than those relating to 'black money market' variables (compare Heertje, 1984; Tanzi, 1982).

3.1 National studies of 'black' labour

The most direct way in which information on the informal economy may be obtained is to undertake a large-scale representative sample survey of the population. As yet, little research of this nature has been carried out. The most important reason for this, apart from technical and organisational problems, appears to be the fear of obtaining incorrect answers: "respondents have a direct interest in reticence on sensitive details" (Feige, 1981, page 982). The importance which should be attached to the results of such research, depends to a large extent on the nature of the study, in which the method of questioning and the degree of anonymity play particularly important parts. Researches of this nature have been carried out in Belgium (Pestieau, 1984), Norway (Isachsen and Strøm, 1983) and the Netherlands (Van Eck and Kazemier, 1985).

In the Belgian research, a stratified random sample of people in the Liège area was used to seek information on the 'black' sector. The results showed that 47% of the population over 14 years of age had income from the 'black' sector, and 36% of the population over 14 years of age had paid for unregistered services. Since 18% were both demanders and suppliers of unrecorded activities, a total of 65% of the population over 14 years of age was involved in 'black' sector activities. The hours devoted to the 'black labour market' averaged 9.4 hours weekly. Pestieau (1984) reported that suppliers of 'black labour' were especially to be found among manual workers, unemployed or unoccupied persons, low-income and uneducated groups, and younger people. The demand for unregistered services reached its peak among middle-aged groups, especially those with a higher income or occupational status.

These findings do not coincide with the results of a Dutch survey of unregistered income from labour, undertaken by Van Eck and Kazemier of the Central Bureau of Statistics. Their results, based on a sample test on the total Dutch population during 1982/83, showed that women, elderly people, the less educated, and the unemployed were greatly underrepresented in the market for 'black sector labour'. Again, contrary to the Belgian findings, the highest supply of 'black labour' was found in the category with higher education and higher incomes (over US$1800 per month). Overall, the sample showed that around 12% of the population over 16 years of age had incomes from 'black labour'. The average income amounted to Dfl 2250 per year (about US$1000). About Dfl 3 billion were involved in total, or around 1% of gross national product (GNP). Unfortunately, the Dutch research does not contain information on the demand for 'black labour'.

The third study which we will discuss here was carried out by Isachsen and Strøm in Norway, in 1980. Overall, they found that 40% of the population over 15 years of age participated in the market for 'black labour' (20% as suppliers of 'black labour'; 29% as demanders, of whom 9% were both suppliers and demanders). Further findings of the Norwegian survey were that demand for 'black labour' services increased with the number of years of education, and reached its maximum for males between 25 and 54 years of age; for females the maximum was reached between 25 and 39 years of age, and at 55 years and over. The supply of 'black labour services' first increased, and then decreased, with the number of years of education. In money terms, the size of the 'black' sector in Norway amounted to 2.3% of GNP of 1979.

Unfortunately, very few efforts have been made to produce estimates of the other part of the informal economy: the household and communal sector. On a qualitative level, Toffler (1980, page 272) reports that: "German and Dutch do-it-yourselfers tend to treat their projects very soberly, set high standards and equip themselves carefully. Italians, by contrast, are just beginning to discover the DIY-movement, many older husbands insisting that it is degrading to do the work themselves". Pahl (1984) has conducted extensive research on the domestic economy on the Isle of Sheppey in England. This research is unique so far and his estimates cannot be compared with any studies done elsewhere.

In another English study, however, Rose (1983) estimates the division of total working time between three spheres, namely the official economy, the unofficial economy, and the domestic economy. These parts of the economy coincide with what we have called the formal economy, the 'black' sector, and the 'household and communal' sector. Table 2 presents the distribution of working hours over the 'three economies', showing that less than half of working time was spent in the official economy.

A similar distribution was found by Renooy (1984), when households in Amsterdam were asked to report on the way in which they procured several kinds of services. In this case respondents were asked whether use was made of the formal sector, or whether activities were carried out by the respondents themselves. Again, table 2 shows the results of this enquiry.

In an explanation of the size of the informal economy, it may be important to consider certain demographic factors as well. Vinay (1985) and Pahl (1984), for instance, have drawn attention to the 'life cycle' of families. Young families and old ones may differ in income, in needs, and in opportunities, and may react accordingly.

3.2 Indirect approaches to international comparison

Owing to the lack of comparable information on the informal economy from such direct sources, international comparisons have had to rely on indirect indicators. In particular, there have been a number of attempts to measure the 'black money' side of the phenomenon, by using discrepancies between elements in the national accounts or monetary data. The results have been quite inconsistent, however, both with each other and with alternative estimates based on variations in formal participation rates among males of working age. Moreover, since these data are not generally available in reliable form at the urban or regional level, there is little to be learned as to what might be accomplished there.

Table 2. Comparison of results of two studies into division of labour between sectors of the economy.

Economy	Percentage of	
	hours per week [a]	activities [b]
Official	46	43.3
Unofficial	3	9.5
Domestic	51	47.2

[a] Percentage of working hours per week in 1975 (source: Rose, 1983).

[b] Percentage of activities in enquiry, 1984 (source: Renooy, 1984).

Another weakness of these methods is that little or no consideration has been given to the motives and institutional conditions which lead people to take part in the informal economy. These factors, however, do play a central part in a method recently adopted by Frey and Weck-Hanneman (1984) and related to the 'public choice' theory, in which the nature of institutions is explained by the 'egoistic' behaviour of individuals. The informal economy partly exists as a 'natural response' to inefficient, but popular, public institutions (Heertje, 1984). Their method is also based on the idea that the informal economy is an unobserved variable. It is not only influenced by certain causes (determinants), but itself influences other variables, which must be observed as indicators of the existence of an informal economy. Thus, the approach is an indirect one.

As determinants, the authors use the real and the perceived tax burden, the burden of regulation, tax immorality, the rate of unemployment, and per-capita disposable income. As indicators, on the other hand, they use the male participation rate, the hours worked, and the growth of real GNP. Once the determinants and the indicators have been established, the relative extent and the development of the informal economy (that is, the 'black' sector) can also be established, with the aid of the LISREL (Linear Interdependent Structural Relationship) computer program. Table 3 shows the resulting estimates of the size of the informal economy as a percentage of GNP for a number of countries, with Sweden and Norway as bases.

The advantage of this method is that it simultaneously incorporates several causes and effects in the analysis. Weaknesses remain in the establishment and measurement of the relevant determinants, as well as the correct way of estimating the effects.

In looking at the figures for the different countries, however, one should always bear in mind that, even if the figure is accurate, great differences may occur within each country. The 'black' sector, for instance, can differ between the city and the countryside or between regions, for reasons which are not recognised in the international comparisons. In the next section we will discuss these differences and the impact of the informal economy on regional development.

Table 3. Size of the 'black money sector' in 1978 as percentage of gross national product for fourteen countries of the Organization of Economic Cooperation and Development, calculated with the unobserved variable method (source: Frey and Weck-Hanneman, 1984).

Sweden	13.2 (base)	West Germany	8.3
Belgium	11.5	United States of America	8.2
Italy	10.5	United Kingdom	8.1
The Netherlands	9.2	Ireland	7.0
Norway	9.2 (base)	Spain	6.0
France	8.7	Switzerland	4.5
Canada	8.6	Japan	3.9

4 A regional approach

The informal economy can be investigated on different scales. In our review of international research, national and household levels have been stressed. Until now, the local and the regional contexts have not received much attention in general studies, with the exception of publications about so-called 'local initiatives', 'local associations', and other related topics. These kinds of studies are, however, not directed specifically at the informal economy as we have defined it, but rather at questions concerned with organising the unemployed to establish formal enterprises through subsidies and temporary aid.

The regional scale of analysis of the informal economy is as yet more or less virgin territory. An established body of theory is lacking and data from fieldwork or other direct sources are scarce. Our discussion is based essentially on one published article (Button, 1984) and on our own fieldwork comparing six locations in the Netherlands (Mevissen and Renooy, 1986). Yet analyses of the differences between regions, more than case studies of particular regions, have considerable potential in leading us to the decisive explanatory factors in relation to the scale of informal activity.

One approach to such interregional comparison draws directly on the international studies discussed in the last section. Button (1984) attempts to develop a so-called 'soft model', based on nonparametric methodology and aimed at examining spatial differences in an area where direct measurement is difficult. After a process of selecting relevant variables and the development of weights to be attached to these variables, Button produces an ordering of regions that (possibly) reflects the pressures for *growth* in the informal economy. His basic model takes the form:

$$\Delta I = \alpha_1 \Delta X_1 + \alpha_2 \Delta X_2 + \dots + \alpha_n \Delta X_n \,,$$

in which ΔI is a change in the scale of the informal economy as a function of changes in a set of explanatory variables X_i, α_n are parameters reflecting the weights (influences) exerted by the right-hand variables.

The selection of weights and variables is a subjective process, because empirical studies are lacking. Button assumes that interregional differences in the level and duration of unemployment are most important. "While unemployment can provide a potential source of labour for the hidden economy, it is likely that initially the unemployed seek to return to jobs in the formal sector, before turning to the hidden economy" (page 387). The next hypothesis is that "the demand for the output of the irregular sector is likely to be inversely related to income growth". Although several other variables are mentioned, Button emphasises unemployment and low income as the main explanatory variables.

Button refers to Frey and Weck-Hanneman (1984) for his choice of variables, but these authors attach more significance to institutional variables such as government regulation and taxes, than Button. He defends his choice by arguing that "regional variations in tax burden are considerably less than those between countries" (page 388). He is right, of course, but this should have led him to interregional differences other than the ones used by Frey and Weck-Hanneman. As it is, his analysis is far from complete, although the method is most promising. The main weakness, however, is that he does not start from an explicit analysis of real interregional differences, other than the (un)employment variables. In our own fieldwork (Mevissen and Renooy, 1986) we have not been able to find a clear relationship between informal activity and either the level or the duration of unemployment. What we did find was that it was the best educated part of the unemployed who benefitted most from the opportunities of the informal sector.

There are many other factors which need to be incorporated in a regional perspective: for instance, the existence of specific regional products and the local and regional economic structure, or even something which might be called 'regional cultural atmosphere'. Furthermore, we know that ethnic minorities are relatively overrepresented in the urban informal economy. Their sociocultural relations quite often are the basis for new economic networks or 'parallel markets'.

In our investigation in Amsterdam, as well as in several other Dutch areas, we found social relations to be decisive in the informal market. People who know each other are the basis for informal market relations. In nonregulated markets, knowledge and trust are important. Regulations are not only impediments for economic dynamism; they also channel market relations. Regulations may have negative effects, but one positive effect certainly is more security. The informal market by contrast involves highly insecure situations, particularly in those parts where the real 'black' criminal activities happen.

Our conclusion is that, when one looks at interregional differences, it is not only the level of income, or the level of unemployment, that is important for the explanation of the informal economy. This part of the economy is strongly linked with many characteristics of daily life, economic structure, and the institutional and social environment. The same may be argued for the labour side: the typical characteristics of workers, their skills and knowledge, will also make a difference, as would domination of the region by manufacturing industry or the services sector, or whether a strongly differentiated structure exists, with small enterprises and a handicraft tradition.

All of these characteristics have to be taken into account when we consider the scale and character of the informal economy. The conceptual framework for such analyses needs to include five important groups of factors:

(1) market relations, transactions, incomes and prices,

(2) the 'human capital' factor,

(3) the local and regional production structure,
(4) the local and regional physical structure,
(5) institutions and attitudes.

From Button's perspective, regions which have been affected by high levels of long-term unemployment would be the best candidates for growth of the informal economy. In our opinion, however, those regions with large urban agglomerations, many minority groups, a differentiated economy, and many old buildings, would be better candidates for a high rate of participation in the informal economy. Thus, even the distribution of the informal economy may be skewed against the weak regions—even more so if one looks at the money side of the 'black' economy.

This argument, however, needs some further elaboration, because of the possibility that parts of the informal economy may be growing more rapidly in the weaker regions. In the case of agricultural production, the peripheral regions may well have an increasing share in the informal economy, because many unemployed may be able to do some gardening. But it is hardly conceivable to think of other opportunities for these regions, whereas the large urban regions in the core of the country offer a great variety of opportunities. It is important to look not only at the need to earn more money, or to reduce the costs of living, but also at the 'structural opportunities' which are available. Although unemployment may be important, certain 'agglomeration advantages' may also be relevant with regard to the opportunities for the informal economy. We have to add, however, that rural regions quite often still possess a traditional social structure in which patterns of mutual aid are strong. This social environment may be regarded as a fertile seedbed for associations and communal activities (Gaudin and Schiray, 1982).

Rose (1983) has provided us with another consideration, namely the structure of the regional economy and, more specifically, its sectoral composition. In his study he shows that certain sectors of the economy are more 'vulnerable' than others to informal activity. Construction, the textiles industry, and several services are presumed to have a higher level of 'irregular activities'. If this is correct, then this line of reasoning also would lead to an interregional distribution of the informal economy, differing from that suggested by unemployment rates alone. It is important in any case to remember the heterogeneity of the informal sector. The 'deep black' parts of it, related to criminal activities such as drugs and prostitution, are clearly distributed over space in an uneven way, and most probably are concentrated in the large heterogeneous agglomerations. Irregular selling of garden produce, and informal activities related to house repair, however, are probably spread more evenly, whereas 'white-collar black' activities should be concentrated in the spatial core of the economy.

5 Conclusion

Because of the scarcity of data and of theoretical work, firm conclusions about the regional distribution of informal activity cannot yet be offered. However the arguments in this paper lead to a number of substantial hypotheses.

(1) The informal economy is quite heterogeneous, involving a range of elements which we have identified. If regions and locations differ in socioeconomic structure, the configuration of activities in the informal economy is likely to differ also.

(2) Traditional mutual aid structures offer superior opportunities both for communal activities and for the domestic economy. Urban regions possess more opportunities for anonymity and have more market channels and networks in which the informal economy can flourish. The criminal parts of the 'black' economy are possibly more centralised than the other parts. A major part of the informal economy may thus occur in the larger heterogeneous urban regions.

(3) A further factor is the strong influx to many large cities of ethnic minority groups with a strong orientation both toward mutual aid networks and toward other informal activities.

(4) Unemployment and low income are not the most decisive factors in an explanation of interregional differences in the informal sector. They constitute only a part of a configuration of many factors, including ethnicity, skill levels, and social attitudes, all of which are relevant to the development of informal activities of various kinds.

The study of regional characteristics and interregional differences in the informal economy is as yet in its infancy. In our opinion, it is extremely important to promote more regional and interregional studies of the various constituent categories of the informal economy. Such studies could be very helpful in understanding this part of our society. They may also possibly help towards constructing organisational innovations in the approaches for attacking unemployment. Bekemans (1983) suggests that government or organisations for 'local initiatives' should promote the legalisation of informal activities, in order to stimulate formal employment. This is in itself a good proposition, but most probably impossible to realise, because of the cost-benefit ratio of 'black' versus 'regular' activities. Taxes, regulations, and social security arrangements may be such a heavy burden on marginal activities, that these would disappear together with formalisation. Many fear that the informal economy will continue to increase even if economic growth is resumed. Much is so uncertain in our society, that it would be dangerous to be dogmatic about the future of this sector. But one thing is certain: we have to know much more about the regional dimensions of the informal economy.

References

Begeer W, Van Tuinen H K, 1984, "Statistische operationalisering van het begrip informele economie" in *De Informele Economie Vereniging voor Staathuishoudkunde* Dutch Economic Association (Stenfert Kroese, Leiden) pp 37–58

Bekemans L, 1983, "Local employment initiatives" EEC-Series, Department of Economics, University of Limburg, Maastricht

Blokland J, 1982, "Het officieuze circuit: een nadere begripsbepaling" *Statistisch Magazine* **2** 4–9

Broesterhuizen G A A M, 1983, "The unobserved economy and the national accounts in the Netherlands: a sensitivity analysis", in *The Economics of the Shadow Economy* Eds W Gaertner, A Wenig (Springer, Heidelberg) pp 105–127

Button K J, 1984, "Regional variations in the irregular economy: a study of possible trends" *Regional Studies* **18** 385–392

De Grazia R, 1983 *Le Travail Clandestin: Situations dans les Pays Industrialisés à Économie de Marché* (ILO, Genève)

Del Boca D, Forte F, 1982, "Recent empirical surveys and theoretical interpretations of the parallel economy", in *The Underground Economy in the United States and Abroad* Ed. V Tanzi (Lexington Books, Lexington, MA) pp 181–199

Feige E L, 1979, "How big is the irregular economy?", in *Challenge* **22**(5) 5–14

Feige E L, 1981, "Onzichtbare sector en macro-economie", in *Economisch Statistische Berichten* 7 October, pp 980–984

Frey B S, Weck-Hanneman H, 1984, "The hidden economy as an 'unobserved' variable" *European Economic Review* number 26, pp 33–53

Gaudin J, Schiray M, 1982, "L'économie cachée en France: état du débat et bilan des travaux", Brussels, October; copy obtainable from FAST, Directorate-General for Science, Research and Development of the Commission of the European Communities, Rome

Gershuny J I, 1979, "The informal economy, its role in post-industrial society" *Futures* February issue, pp 3–16

Gershuny J I, 1985, "Prospects and policies for the informal economy", in *Informele Economie: Perspectieven en Gevaren* Eds R C Van Geuns, J W M Mevissen, P H Renooy (SMO, Leiden) pp 17–36

Gutmann P M, 1984, "The subterranean economy", in *The Economics of the Shadow Economy* Eds W Gaertner, A Wenig (Springer, Heidelberg) pp 2–19

Heertje A, 1984, "Informele economie: van analyse tot beleid", in *Vereniging voor Staathuishoudkunde* (Stenfert Kroese, Leiden) pp 1–36

Heertje A, Allen M, Cohen H, 1982 *The Black Economy* (Pan Books, London)

ISMO, 1985 *Hoofdlijnen van het rapport van het ISMO* Interdepartementale Stuurgroep Misbruik en Oneigenlijk gebruik, Den Haag

Isachsen A J, Strøm S, 1982, "The hidden economy in Norway, with special emphasis on the hidden labour market" paper presented at an International Conference on the Unobserved Economy, Netherlands Institute for Advanced Studies, Wassenaar

Lozano B, 1983, "Informal sector workers: walking out the system's front door?" *International Journal of Urban and Regional Research* **7** 340–362

Macafee K, 1982, "A glimpse of the hidden economy in the national accounts of the UK", in *The Underground Economy in the United States and Abroad* Ed. V Tanzi (Lexington Books, Lexington, MA) pp 147–163

Mevissen J W M, Renooy P H, 1986, "De informele economie gelokaliseerd" Ministerie van Sociale Zaken en Werkgelegenheid, Den Haag

Mingione E, 1983, "Informalization, restructuring, and the survival strategies of the working class" *International Journal of Urban and Regional Research* **7** 311–339

O'Higgins M, 1982, "Assessing the underground economy in the United Kingdom" paper presented at an International Conference on the Unobserved Economy, Netherlands Institute for Advanced Studies, Wassenaar

Ostrom E, 1986, "An agenda for the study of institutions" *Public Choice* **48** 3-25

Pahl R E, 1984 *Divisions of Labour* (Basil Blackwell, Oxford)

Pestieau P, 1984, "Belgium's irregular economy" Paper Colloque IV, Économie Parallèle, Department of Economics, Free University of Brussels, Brussels

Renooy P H, 1984, "De schemerzone; 'werkplaats' tussen vrije tijd en arbeid" Ministerie van Sociale Zaken en Werkgelegenheid, Den Haag

Rose R, 1983, "Getting by in three economies: the resources of the official, unofficial and domestic economy" Centre for the Study of Public Policy, University of Strathclyde, Glasgow

Sandmo A, 1983, "Progressive taxation, redistribution, and labor supply" *Scandinavian Journal of Economics* **85** 311-323

Skolka J, 1984a, "Hidden economy: a few facts" paper presented at a seminar on the unofficial economy, Trento, Italy; copy obtainable from Austrian Institute for Economic Research, Vienna

Skolka J, 1984b, "The parallel economy in Austria", in *The Economics of the Shadow Economy* Eds W Gaertner, A Wenig (Springer, Heidelberg) pp 60-76

Smith J D, 1983, "Market motives in the informal economy", in *The Economics of the Shadow Economy* Eds W Gaertner, A Wenig (Springer, Heidelberg) pp 161-178

Stuart C, 1984, "Welfare costs per dollar of additional tax revenue in the US" *American Economic Review* **74** 352-362

Tanzi V, 1982, "A second (and more skeptical) look at the underground economy in the United States", in *The Underground Economy in the United States and Abroad* Ed. V Tanzi (Lexington Books, Lexington, MA) pp 103-119

Toffler A, 1980 *The Third Wave* (Bantam Books, New York)

Van Eck R, Kazemier B, 1985, "Zwarte inkomsten uit arbeid; resultaten van in 1983 gehouden experimentele enquêtes" *CBS Statistische Katernen* number 3, Central Bureau of Statistics, The Hague

Vinay P, 1985, "Family life cycle and the informal economy in Central Italy" *International Journal of Urban and Regional Research* **9** 82-99

Subject Index

Author Index

Previous volumes in the series

Volume 13

Section 1 Regional Science and Health Care Planning: A Review

Health Services Planning: Searching for Solutions in Well-defined Places *M Dear*

Modelling for Health Services Planning: An Outline and an Example *M Clarke, A G Wilson*

Section 2 Primary Medical Care

Health Care in London: Planning Issues and the Contribution of Local Morbidity Surveys *S E Curtis, K J Woods*

The Use of Primary Medical Facilities: The Complex Case of Measles Vaccinations in the USA and the UK *A M Kirby*

Section 3 Resource Allocation and Hospital Location: Theory and Practice

Models of Resource Policy of Regional Health Authorities *R G Bevan, A H Spencer*

Health Services Planning: Observations on the Relationship between Theory and Practice *T Rathwell*

Hospital Planning and New Town Development: Examples from North East England *J Mohan*

Elderly Severely Mentally Infirm (ESMI) Units in Lancashire: An Assessment of Resource Allocation over Space *J R Beaumont, A Sixsmith*

Resource Allocation in Multilevel Spatial Health Care Systems *L D Mayhew, G Leonardi*

Patient Travel and the Use of Hospitals in Massachusetts: An Application of RAMOS *E J Rising, R S Segall, L D Mayhew*

Volume 14

Introduction *D E Pitfield*

Towards Behavioural Models of Spatial Choice: Some Recent Developments *W C Halperin, N Gale*

Dynamic Choice of Alternatives, Innovation Diffusion, and Ecological Dynamics of the Volterra-Lotka Model *M Sonis*

Diagnostics and Resistant Fits in Logit Choice Models *N Wrigley, R Dunn*

Towards an Approach to Forecasting Attendance at Unique Events Using a Discrete Choice Model and Experimental Design Data *D A Hensher, J J Louviere*

Discrete Choice Models versus Decompositional Multiattribute Preference Models: A Comparative Analysis of Model Performance in the Context of Spatial Shopping-behaviour *H J P Timmermans*

Cost Saving Methods in Travel Demand Forecasting *A Daly*

Comparative Evaluation of Intercity Demand Models *Y J Stephanedes, V Kumar*

Elasticity Parameters of Disaggregate Models of Freight Modal Choice *B Benabi*

Perspectives of Disaggregate Choice Models on the Housing Market *W van Lierop, P Nijkamp*

Comparing Discrete Choice Models: Some Housing Market Examples *P A Longley*

Microlevel Econometric Analysis of Retail Closure *S R Lerman, T-K Liu*

Volume 15

Volume 16